A PRACTICAL ISLAMIC PARENTING GUIDE

Muslim Teens
Today's Worry, Tomorrow's Hope

Drs. Ekram & Mohamed Rida Beshir

amana publications

First Edition
(1422AH/2001AC)

Second Edition
(1423AH/2003AC)

Third Printing
(1427AH/2007AC)

Fourth Printing
(1435AH/2014AC)

Copyright © 1422AH/2001AC
amana publications
10710 Tucker Street
Beltsville, Maryland 20705-2223 USA
Tel: (301) 595-5777
Fax: (301) 595-5888 / Fax: (240) 250-3000
E-mail: amana@amana-corp.com
Website: www.amana-publications.com

Library of Congress Cataloging-in-Publication Data

Beshir, Ekram.
    Muslim teens : today's worry, tomorrow's hope : a practical Islamic parenting guide /
Ekram & Mohamed Rida Beshir.
        p. cm.
    Includes bibliographical references.
    ISBN 1-59008-004-1
    1. Child rearing--Religious aspects--Islam. 2. Parenting--Religious aspects--Islam. 3.
Muslim youth--North America--Conduct of life. I. Beshir, Mohamed Rida. II. Title.

HQ769.3 .B472 2001
297.5'77--dc21   2001045793

Printed in the United States of America by
International Graphics
Beltsville, Maryland

Contents

Acknowledgments   v

Foreword   vii

Preface   viii

Introduction   ix

1. Know Your Teen and his Environment   1

2. North American Teenage Culture   13

3. Road Map   37

4. A Strong Confident Personality for Your Teen
    – Why and How to Reach it   51

5. From Knowledge to Conviction   65

6. Basic Concepts
    – How to Instill Them in Your Teen   105

7. Case Studies   149

8. Anatomy of Case Studies   163

9. Tools You Need and Ideas You Can Use   193

10. Positive Teen Experiences   221

References   257

Acknowledgments

We would like to express our sincere gratitude to our daughter *Noha* for the endless hours she spent in front of the computer, the tireless dedication she showed in editing this book, and the gracious patience that she conducted herself with through the entire experience. May Allah keep her always patient and dedicated to the Islamic way of life and reward her with the best rewards.

We would also like to express our sincere gratitude to all our children, *Amirah*, *Hoda*, *Noha*, and *Sumaiya*, for all their help with this book. Their assistance in formulating the case studies and practical examples is much appreciated. We would like to thank them for sharing their personal experiences as a result of their realization of the importance of illustrating concepts with practical, real-life examples, which took the book from a theoretical standpoint to a hands-on, step-by-step, personal guide for Muslim parents.

We recognize that the time spent writing this book was precious time that we could have spent with our children; however, because of our children's maturity, they themselves encouraged us to embark on this project for the benefit of Muslims everywhere. May Allah reward them and all the dedicated Muslim boys and girls who struggle in the path of truth.

Drs. Ekram and Mohamed Beshir

Foreword

There has been considerable growth of the Muslim community in North America in the last few decades. Alongside with this growth there has been, generally speaking, a deepening commitment to Islam as a way of living.

One central concern of Muslims in North America and in other similar environments relates to parenting and other family-related matters. This concern seems to have been enhanced by a number of factors including the following:

A large influx of students from various Muslim countries who came to study in North America, especially during the 1960's and 1970's. Due to the turmoil in several countries and for other reasons, many decided to apply for immigration and eventually settled and became citizens of the USA and Canada. When married, if they were not married before, also when their children began to grow up, the issues of family life and parenting became more pressing. Greater concern has been expressed relating to teenagers in particular. This concern was accentuated by the fact that the vast majority of Muslim children were and still are educated in public schools. A phenomenal expansion of Islamic schools may explain a response to this concern. The fact remains, however, that most Muslim children and youth have no access to these schools.

The increase of the number of immigrants from Muslim countries as well as refugees from "hot spots" in the Muslim world, including Somalia, Bosnia, Kosovo and in the aftermath of the "Gulf War". Many such families were already settled for decades in their countries, and they came with their families, including teenagers who had to adapt to life in a different culture. There have been problems in the process, leading to increasing attention to parenting, not only from the Islamic viewpoint, but also in consideration of the legal and social framework of their new homes.

Many Muslims who immigrated many decades prior to the new influx seem to have been assimilated in the North American society, in differing degrees. Many were "discovered" or began to discover more vividly their roots and were encouraged by the recent immigrants. With deepening commitments, they began to share the same concern about parenting

In the midst of these major changes, there was hardly any systematic program to address family problem, including parenting. Drs. Ekram and Rida Beshir are indeed pioneers in this endeavor. Through their books, lectures and workshops they made a major contribution to this central issue. Their work has been very well received by all. The present book is but one welcome addition to the well being of the Muslim community. May Allah [*Subhanahu Wata`aala*] continue to reward and bless them, their families and all the *Ummah*.

Jamal Badawi
Professor of Management also Religious Studies
Saint Mary's University, Halifax, NS, Canada

viii

Preface

To our beloved children: *Amirah*, *Hoda*, *Noha*, and *Sumaiya*, because of whom we hope Allah will have mercy on us and admit us into paradise.

Teen years, we are told by society, are the time for school dances, house parties, and road trips, the time for underage drinking, for dating, for casinos and gambling, the time for exploring and discovering, discovering beer, discovering drugs, discovering the opposite sex, the time for finding yourself; teen years, we are told, are the time of your life.

Teen years are the paradoxical highlight of life in the western world. They are the time in which one is bombarded with knowledge and freed from responsibility. Teens have the privileges of an adult and the responsibilities of a child; teens rebel by conforming; they stand out by melting into their group of friends.

Being a teen means wanting independence but not having the wisdom it requires; it means having energy and conviction and needing a cause to which to devote them.

For those of you who, by the will of Allah, wish to instill knowledge and wisdom into their independent teens, to give their teens the Islamic cause into which they can pour their energy and conviction, those who wish to raise teens who can raise the *Ummah*, this book is for you.

Introduction

I n his article, "Countering Violence", in the Chairman's Corner of US Airways *Attache* magazine of July 1999, Mr. Stephen M. Wolf says,

> "In her insightful book, "Mayhem, a study of the impact of violence in the media on society", Dr. Sissela Bok, quotes a frightening statistics from research done in the early 1990s that estimated by the time a child left elementary school he or she would have watched 8,000 murders and more than 100,000 acts of violence on television, in the movies and video games.

In a chilling anecdote, she quotes one mother who, with her husband, had kept all violent programming out of their family TV viewing and refused to purchase the popular video games. Soon she began to notice that her 7 year old son's friends would not come to the house. The reason, according to one youngster: "There is no killing there."

It is equally clear that the events in Littleton and Conyers were very real, and it seems inescapable that there is today a pervasive and unacceptable level of vicarious violence in the lives of your young. For the vulnerable individual, how many times can you see someone die in a video game or on a screen before the mind tells you that somehow that this is an accepted aspect of life. These screen images inculcate a pervasive fear that "enemies" will do violence to you if you don't do violence to them first."

According to CNN's *Headline news* of March 8th, 2001 statistics, 39 kids have died in school shootings since the Columbine shooting. This statistics came after the Santana high school shooting in Santee, California north of San Diego. In the CNN news commentary, they highlight the fact that, after Columbine, every politician had a plan, now nobody is even talking about it, which indicates a fear of normalization for such violent actions in our schools.

Dear brothers and sisters in Islam as well as brothers and sisters in humanity, this is not the only prevailing negative aspect of the environment our children are facing in North America. The problem of violence grows substantially when children move to adolescent years. In addition to violence, numerous other challenges present themselves in the lives of our teens: drugs, premarital sex, alcohol, and disrespect towards authority figures to name a few.

There is no doubt that all parents have to be concerned with this fact, especially those who care about the well-being of their teens and those who understand that children are a trust from Allah and we will be asked about the way we brought them up. In our case as parents of teens, we certainly and seriously care about their well-being. We also hope that on the day of Judgment, we will be able to humbly respond to Allah's question in a positive way and with His grace say:" We did our best to fulfill the trust."

In addition to this and since we published our first book, "Meeting the challenge of parenting in the west, an Islamic perspective", various communities have been inviting us to conduct parenting workshops. We have learned a lot from these workshops and gained tremendous experience related to teens' problems through discussing and interacting with parents. If we, after all these years, had to come up with the most important issue and concern parents have in North America, with no hesitation, we would say that it is raising teens in a western culture. Parents are concerned with how to take good care of their children to ensure that they are non-troubled teens and contributing individuals to society and humanity in general. That is what triggered us to write this book. We hope our contribution in this area will help parents all over the world and particularly in North America to achieve the tough task at hand. We hope that through this book, they can do it in a systematic and tested way based on guidance from *Qur'an* and the teachings of Prophet Muhammad peace be upon him (PBUH) as well as ample practical experience and plenty of real life examples.

Since Islam encourages dealing with everything based on knowledge, the first two chapters of this book are targeting the area of understanding the nature of teenage years and the environment teenagers live in. As such, section one summarizes the characteristics of adolescent years. It covers physical, psychological, spiritual and emotional changes, which take place during the adolescent stages. The second chapter covers the environment our teens are living in, this is to say the North American environment. It brings to the attention of parents the nature of this environment as well as the North American teenage culture and shows very clearly how different it is from our Islamic values. It goes on to list some of the challenges facing our Muslim teens in this society and provides some shocking statistics related to the subject, with the hope that parents will realize the seriousness of the issue and be careful in the way they handle it.

To protect your teen from the effects of this environment, in chapter three, we try to present the skeleton for the solution, where we give a broad outline of what can be done. We draw a road map for parents to follow. This road map has six major components which we feel are the most important elements a parent needs to achieve the task at hand: an early start, being an approachable friend for your children, a clear and common vision of tarbiya between both parents, the active participation of both parents in the process, the use of proper methods to ensure a teen's strong personality, and elevating your teen's level from a state of knowing Islam to a state where he is fully convinced that it is the only way of life to live and follow.

Due to the importance of the fifth and sixth components, we have dedicated one chapter to each of them in order to discuss them in further detail. As such, chapter four deals with the importance of training our Muslim teens to grow up with a strong and confident personality. It discusses why this component is critical and provides some tips as to how to achieve it successfully. The tips are complemented with basic principles from *Qur'an* and *Sunnah* to help you achieve this task. Chapter five is fully dedicated to helping you elevating the level of your teen from a state of knowledge to one of conviction. It elaborates on the importance of this component of the road map, lays down the conditions and environment you, as a parent, should set up to help your teen achieve this state of conviction, and illustrates some practical methods you should use in this endeavor. Again, this is complemented by more basic principles from *Qur'an* and *Sunnah* to help you achieve this task.

It is essential that parents invest the precious years of childhood, where their approval matters most to their children, in instilling important Islamic concepts into the children's personality. As such, chapter six addresses this subject. It lists each important concept, describes the Islamic source of the concept, explains the importance of the concept in a teenager's life, and suggests practical ways to instill the concept in the heart and mind of your teen.

Chapter seven discusses common cases and typical problems that are usually faced by parents. Many case studies are described for various teens' ages and genders. The readers are asked to analyze these case studies and answer certain questions, thus helping them to apply the principles they have learned.

Chapter eight deals with the same case studies presented in chapter seven, but with explanations and more details. For each case, we explain the cause of the problem, the symptoms for the problem, and a detailed analysis suggesting proper solutions.

Chapter nine provides simple tools to help parents help and support their teens in the face of the intimidating environment they live in. It also provides tools to help parents reduce the amount of peer pressure their teens are facing. These tools are particularly useful for teens attending the public school system. They include samples of letters that parents should send to school administration prior to various Islamic celebrations or events such as the beginning of *Ramadan, Eid-ul Fitr, Eid-ul Adha,* etc.

Finally, in chapter ten, we present the reader with a variety of positive teen experiences. These are real life experiences lived by our teens. The teens relate these experiences in their own writing. We feel that it is very important to the reader to realize that, if we as parents try our best to use the proper Islamic ways of *tarbiya* with our children, the good results, with the help of Allah SWT, are guaranteed.

A Note about the Writing

Through out the book, instead of using he/she and his/her referencing, we will alternate between feminine and masculine to make the text more readable. This is not meant to reflect in any way that the topic being discussed is strictly for males or females, but applies to teens of both genders.

Italicized fonts refer to Arabic names or common Arabic terminology used by Muslims.

For our non-Muslim readers, the use of (Q j, V i) denotes that this reference is the ith verse from the jth chapter in the *Qur'an*. For example, (Q 2, V 7) denotes the 7th verse in the 2nd chapter of the *Qur'an*.

There are six major books referring to the collections of sayings (*hadeeth*) of the prophet PBUH: these books are: *Bukhari, Muslim, Abu Dawoud, An-Nisa'ee, At-Termithy, and Ibn Majah*. After a hadeeth, the names in brackets refer to which book the *hadeeth* was taken from. When the expression"agreed upon" appears in the brackets, it means that this *hadeeth* is reported by both *Bukhari* and *Muslim*

When the abbreviation PBUH is used, usually after the name of Prophet Muhammad, it stands for peace and blessings be upon him.

1. Know Your Teen

To be able to deal with any subject we have to understand the subject under discussion and learn everything we can about it. Islam encourages knowledge in everything to the extent that the first verse revealed in *Qur'an* talks about the most important tool of acquiring knowledge, which is reading:

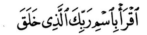

"Read in the name of your Lord and Cherisher, Who created." (Q 96, V1)

As such, it is essential for every parent to understand the nature of teenage years as well as the physiological and psychological change teens go through during their development in these years. This knowledge will help parents to see things in the right perspective and understand how to handle various situations and conflicts that could arise in their dealings with their teens. The environment they grow in also affects teens. The culture of their peers also constitutes a certain level of pressure and often impacts the way they behave. These are important factors that parents have to clearly understand and be fully aware of to ensure that they deal with their teens properly in this society. As such, the first two chapters of the book will try to provide basic information on these topics. We will start the journey into the teens' personality with a look at the profile of an adolescent. Then we will continue to discuss the various stages of adolescence and the changes associated with each stage at the physical, psychological, social and intellectual levels in this opening chapter. The predominant teen culture in North America is then described in chapter two.

Profile of an Adolescent

In her valuable book, *Safeguarding your teens from the DRAGONS of life*, Bettie B. Youngs defines the adolescent as a person who...

- Is leaving behind the stage of childhood and working through the stages of adolescence.
- When scared or frightened, slips back into the security of the previous stage.
- Is undergoing rapid and intense of physiological and psychological changes.
- Wants to be independent, but does not have the backlog of personal experience to function independently in the society to which he belongs.
- Needs to express personal needs and have these needs taken seriously.
- Has not yet formed a cohesive value system that would support her in what to "live for," so this tremendously important anchor of security is not yet within reach.
- Is locked into financial and emotional dependence on the family.
- Is trying to make decisions of lasting importance --- career exploration, life values, relationships.
- Vividly notices when there is a discrepancy between the rules and values espoused by adults and adult behavior.
- Has limited understanding as to what highs and lows of emotions mean.
- Has limited understanding as how to cope successfully with the ups and downs of mood swings.
- Has strong need for adult mentoring and guidance.
- Is constructing a sense of selfhood.
- Feels lonely and alone when parents are physically and emotionally absent.
- Needs parent to show love, acceptance and attention.
- Needs guidance and direction.
- Learns mostly by exploration and trial and error.
- Needs skills to cope with stress and crises at hand.
- Needs adults to model healthy adult behavior.
- In the absence of effective adaptive coping skills becomes debilitated by the ravages of stress.

– When the family unit fails to provide an environment that is nurturing and supportive, turns to peers for the fulfillment of these needs.
– Is a high risk for incidence of poor health, alcohol and drug abuse, sexual abuse, family violence, sexual promiscuity, alienation and suicidal tendencies.
– Is by law a minor.

Stages of Adolescent

Most psychologists divide adolescence into three stages. These are: the early stage from 12-15 years old, the middle stage from 15-18 years old, and the later stage from 18-20 years old.

In the early stage teens are concerned about their body image and it is not strange to hear them making comments indicating that they hate themselves. In this stage peer pressure may be the most important aspect in the teen's life. They like to go around in groups and don't like to be alone. They like very much to conform to their peers, feel accepted and not get left out. Sometimes they are very impulsive and don't use common sense. The expert's advice to parents in this stage is to protect and discipline, be calm, and never enter into power struggle or confrontation with your teen.

In the middle stage, teens can move from one extreme to another. They want to feel more independent and often put too much emphasis on themselves. Also, at this stage, they are not good at managing their time. Parenting in this stage should stress on preparing teens to take responsibilities and providing focus for their teens to organize their lives.

As for the later stage, adolescents become more flexible and reasonable. They become better with their siblings, and peer pressure is not a big factor in their behavior anymore. They also become better planners and get more organized. In this stage, teens start challenging any inconsistency in parenting style. Now, they are in an equal relationship with parents. As such parents, should act as consultants who affirm and validate the choices of their teens and benefit them with their experiences.

The above three stages closely align with the inherited saying that one should play with his child for the first seven years and discipline him for the second seven years, then befriend him for the third seven years.

Changes and developments during Adolescent

During the adolescent years, many developmental changes take place at various levels covering a range of aspects of the teen's life. These changes and developments manifest themselves at the intellectual level, physical, social, moral and ethical levels.

For the early adolescent stage, at the intellectual level, teens learn best under two conditions: (1) when the activity is experiential (active/doing) rather than passive (listening or reading); and (2) when they can interact with same-sex peers during the learning experience. At the later part of the early adolescent stage, the 14-and 15-year-old child is a curious learner, but considers academic goals secondary to personal social concerns. They also show strong willingness to learn things they consider to be useful, that is, related to real-life problems.

At the physical level, teens at this stage gain more weight, height, heart size, lung capacity and muscular strength. This stage of puberty produces some of the most dramatic sexual changes in teen's life: the growth of pubic hair, development of breasts, etc. At this stage girls are more likely to focus on the physical changes that accompany sexual maturation; while boys are more likely to feel anxious about receding chins, cowlicks, dimples and changes in tone of voice. Teens at this stage also experience fluctuations in basal metabolism that can cause extreme restlessness and listlessness. In the later part of this stage, internal and external physical maturation occures at an amazing rate. The key hormones are working to move this child from preadolescence to full scale puberty. It is a time of enormus physical development in height, weight, lung capacity, heart size and muscular strength. For the teens, coping with the growing pains is traumatic and they are often tired and hungry.

The child's bone growth is still exceeding muscle development, resulting in poor coordination and awkwardness (especially for boys).

The 14-and 15-year old child desires to experience sex, but is largely unable to grasp the meaning of intimacy. Hormones moving the body toward sexual maturity are in motion, causing the child to feel sexual as well.

At the psychological level, moods will fluctuate frequently because of the acceleration of hormones in the body related to sexual development. Inconsistent mood swings, tantrums, and crying occur spontaneously and often for the most trivial reasons. The teens move quickly between feeling jovial and being "down in the dumps." At this stage they are often introspective, easily offended and sensitive to criticism. At the later part of this stage, they are even more easily offended and very sensitive to critisism of personal shortcomings. They also exaggerates simple occurrences and believe that their personal problems, experiences and feelings are very unique, as if nobody else has ever experienced them. Also at this stage, the child attempts to search actively for his identity. During his serious search for a stable sense of self, "Who am I?", he turns to others for a sense of self and is vulnerable to their comments. It is important at this stage that adults should show sensitivity towards him; especially parents and teachers.

At the social level, a teen depends on positive relationships with the same sex, and experience grave anxiety and disorientation when peer group ties are broken. She is easily confused and frightened by settings that are large and impersonal, such as a new school. She is easily provoked. Humour, tears, agression and shyness can all be experienced in matter of moments. She needs frequent affirmations from parents and peers about intrinsic worth.

Boys pair up with boys and girls also cling together in search of reinforcement of their own role.

At the later part of this stage, the 14-and 15-year-old child experiences traumatic conflicts due to conflicting loyalities to peer groups and family. This child may be rebellious toward parents but is still strongly dependent on parental values. He wants to make his own choices. This child also refers to peers as sources for standards and models of behaviour. Media heroes and heroines are important in shaping both behaviour and fashion.

In addition to being fiercely loyal to peer group values, a14-15 year-old child is also sometimes cruel or insensititive to those outside the peer group.

For the Middle adolescent stage, at the intellectual level, personal-social concerns dominate the thoughts of an adolescent. Learning about his world takes priority over school. At this stage, learning is best motivated when it is considered to be useful. He prefers active over passive learning experiences; and favors interaction with peers during learning activities. He is generally considered intellectually at risk because decisions have the potential to affect major academic values with life long consequences; yet it seems so difficult to get his attention or awareness in participating in these decisions and goals.

At the physical level, Mood swinging is quite common because of hormonal changes. Learning about oneself as a sexual being is a big task at this stage (femininity for girls and masculinity for boys). It is indeed a time of identity crises and an age of frustration. In general this age group has poorer physical health, lowered level of endurance, strength and flexibility and is heavier and more unhealthy than the previous stage. A teen at this stage is physically at risk, as most reported suicides among adolescents occur at this stage.

At the psychological level, at this stage, a teen is really desperate to get an answer for some very important questions such as: who am I?, why am I here?, what is life all about?, etc. As she tries to figure out just who she is and what is going on, it is not uncommon that she experiences a wide range of feelings such as being confused, embarrassed, guility, awkward, inferior, ugly and scared. She easily swings from childish and petulant behaviours to being sedate or acting rational or irrational, all in the class of an hour; from intellectual to giddy, back and forth.

Also at this stage, teens see their parents as hopelessly old fashioned and naïve. They are looking for independence. Some teens in this age group actually do leave home or threaten to. This act is done out of frustration and is seen by teens as a way to coerce parents into providing them with more rope to be independent, to gain a bigger share of self-power in making more decisions on their own.

At the social level, teens need their friends but their relationship with them is not strong; it can very easily turn into a contest of who can outdo whom. They are looking for total independence, yet are rarely capable of it. They believe that their parents are a road block stifling their own life. Although they don't really want to leave their parents, because of this belief, they may try to leave home, just to prove their point.

At the moral and ethical level, they ask indepth questions about the meaning of life and expect to have absolute answers. They are usually turned off by what they see as trivial adult responses. They are trying to complete developing their moral and ethical values. The absence of moral guidance at this stage may put them at risk. Adults should try to understand their needs and deal with them as budding adults rather than as children.

As for the Later adolescent stage, it is the stage where the adolescent is trying to establish a sense of total independence, a desire to go from being dependent on others to being dependent on himself. At this stage the young person is faced with major issues to deal with. One of the most important of these issues is determining vocation, and answering questions like "What am I going to do for work?", "Can I take care of myself?", "What kind of life style will I have?" Answering these questions helps the self-esteem of the individual and gives meaning to his life. It helps to experience positive feelings of strength, power and competence. Establishing values is another very important task at this age and the goal is to sort out personal values, deciding which ones to keep and which ones to discard. This is the way a teen can develop integrity at this age and parents' help and gentle guidance are of great help at this stage. A third important task at this stage is establishing self-reliance. The need is to be oneself looking at life through one's own lens and not through a role such as student, athlete, son or daughter and so on. Accomplishing this task develops self-trust and confidence. Having a clear set of values and principles is of great help to the young person in achieving this task. At this stage, an 18 year old is ready to go to the outer world, to leave high school and join college or university. With this, all school friends become scattered at different colleges all over the North American continent and she experiences a great sense of loss. As such the need to establish new friends becomes essential for the teen at this age. It is a hard and frightened time for her.

At the intellectual level, this stage does not bring any major break-through development, the adolescent has already learned to reason, analyze and question attitudes, assumptions and values and she can transfer skills from one setting to another. This is a stage of using her skills, not necessarily gaining new ones. Again, active learning experiences and interaction with peers during these activities are preferred by the adolescent over passive ones.

At the physical level, usually boys grow more at this stage compared to girls. They both-especially girls- experience fluctuations in basal metabolism that can cause extreme restlessness at times and equally extreme listlessness at other times.

At the psychological level, the 18-year-old continues to search for answers to various questions related to his beliefs and what he is going to do with his life. He is psychologically at risk of experiencing feelings of alienation and loss of both adult and peer relationships.

At the social level, the 18-year-old experiences conflicts due to losing friends and knowing they must go (because of graduation from high school). He also misses his parents, knowing that he will soon be leaving them. He is less rebellious towards parents but still strongly dependent. The unknown future that lies ahead causes him to be a little bit confused and frightened.

At the moral level, the 18-year-old confronts hard moral and ethical questions, and now must act on moral and ethical choices and behaviors. Although she is reflective, analytical and introspective about thoughts and feelings, she greatly needs guidance from parents to stay on the right track as far as her value system is concerned.

In summary, the following are a few very important features and characteristics about the adolescent stage that all parents should know very well and should remember to help them in dealing with their teens:

- Adolescents are going through tremendous physical, psychological, and emotional changes.
- Due to these changes, teenagers themselves are in a state of almost continuous struggle from within trying to understand what is happening.
- These changes cause them to be moody and very sensitive.
- The need to be accepted by their peers and fitting in with their age group is of utmost importance to them.
- The majority of them enjoy active learning experiences and enjoy participating in projects related more to life situations.
- This is the stage where they soul search and have a great number of questions related to finding the meaning of life. Their goal is to understand the purpose of creation and clearly see where they fit into the bigger scheme of things.
- Although they may not ask for it, deep inside they are always looking for the support of their parents. However, they wanted this support offered at the right time and in a proper and gentle way that is not embarassing to them.

Searching for an Identity

If we could summarize the main issue teenagers are trying to deal with, it would be their search for an identity. The teen notices the changes that are taking place in his body. He realizes that he doesn't even have any control over them and he feels awkward. His body is undergoing a drastic process that he can't seem to keep up with. Certain questions start going through his mind. He wonders about what's happening to him and who he really is.

Soon, he also notices that his friends and classmates are changing and beginning to look different. Some of them are even acting different. He asks himself, "where do I fit in to all of this? What's my place? Who are my real friends and do they still like me?"

More than anything, a teen wants to be part of the group; he wants to be liked by those around him; he wants to fit in, even if that means copying those around him.

The teenage years are a transition stage from childhood to adulthood. It is crucially important that parents understand it as a transition period for their children so that they can deal properly with it. A person at this stage is no longer a child but not yet an adult. She has a little bit of both elements in her. She wants to feel independent and self-sufficient. She wants to be able to go places without her parents, do things without getting permission, and choose her own friends.

Because the teen is so driven by the need to fit into a peer group, she might want to dress like her friends and follow the fashion trends. There is also a yearning to be part of the popular group at school: to look, talk, and act like them; to use the kind of language they use, even if it's inappropriate or rude; to watch the same movies and TV shows they watch; to listen to the same music they listen to; to go to their "hang-outs", and so on.

Feeling rejection from his peer group is such a painful thought for the teen that he is willing to do anything to avoid it. He strongly feels that anything he does to be part of the crowd is well worth the sacrifice.

A teen could try to express his independence by rebelling against some rules by his style of clothing, not tidying up his room, smoking, skipping classes and so on. Parents are advised to handle these situations with absolute wisdom. Parents need to realize that this is a stage of growing up and to be considerate with their teens when dealing with these issues. They should always allow opportunities for the teen to express his views and listen to him when he does. They should also discuss the situation and agree about a course of action where both the parents and the teen might compromise, as long as it does not break the basic rules of Islam, violate decency and modesty, or risk the teen's safety. For example, seeing their son wear a cap backwards or dress in really baggy clothes may be irritating to the parents but is something that should be overlooked, as it is a stage that he is going through. However, the parents should follow up on him frequently and be actively involved in his life so that this stage does not lead to more serious problems. On the other hand, things such as skipping school, smoking, and wearing tight or and indecent clothes should not be overlooked.

Continuous confrontation and conflicts without reaching an agreement might risk the good relationship between the teen and his parents and he might start doing things behind their back. This is why parents need to take the gradual approach when the issues do not concern safety, modesty, or basic Islamic rules. Here is a real-life example by our daughter *Hoda* that illustrates the application of this technique.

"I committed myself to wear the *hijab* before I was even ten years old. Alhamdulillah, I prayed and fasted and never compromised my *hijab*, but the most thing that I stood out in was my style of dressing. I liked a certain look that was called "the skater style." Skaters wore big T-shirts, really baggy pants, sneakers, and caps. So I got myself a couple of big, casual, long-sleeved shirts and wore them underneath my big T-shirts. I got myself a few long belts so that my pants, which I could fit into twice, would stay on my waist, I wore a baseball cap over my head scarf (*hijab*). I wore 3 or 4 rings on my fingers on each hand and sometimes I painted my nails bright colors like blue and green. That was my style between grade six until about grade ten. By the time I was in grade eleven, I was letting the skater style go and starting to dress in a more appropriate manner. I wore flairs, reasonably loose slacks, or skirts with loose, long button-up shirts or sweaters and didn't paint my nails anymore. Finally, I took the decision to wear only skirts and no pants as my mother was urging me to do.

This clothing rebellion was a stage and it passed Alhamdulillah. When I look back at my middle and high school experience, I can see that it was a very delicate time in my life. I wanted to feel independent and free to express my individuality. My parents understood that need and they dealt with me with great wisdom. They didn't fight with me regarding tidying my room or wearing my clothes in a way that would give me the traditional, perfect-Muslim look. They guided me firmly but also with understanding. There were always the bottom line rules that I couldn't cross, so there were some clothes that I wanted to wear badly but was not allowed to and other clothes which I am sure they would rather I did not wear, but allowed me to wear for a bigger purpose. They had a clear plan in mind wherein I would pass through these different stages that I needed to go through with their guidance so that I would eventually end up where I am today. During those stages, my parents were very involved and followed up on me closely so that they could change the direction I was taking whenever they needed to.

My parents were very aware of what was going on in my life and they used every incident as a means for discussion and every discussion as a way to show me the wisdom, the beauty, and the importance of Islam and Islamic rules. When we debated rules and what I could and could not do, the topic of discussion was never about what they thought. It was about what Allah SWT told us, and that way, we were all one team that was working together to find the best solution instead of me against them and each one trying to beat the other. There were times, of course, when they stood their ground despite my disappointment; the rule was not going to change, but they were there for me to discuss my feelings and my reasoning with them. There were things that I knew all along were just a temporary stage, like wearing pants. From the beginning, I was informed that this was not the proper *hijab*, that it was just a training period and I knew that I needed to get myself ready to start wearing loose, covering skirts in order to fully complete the requirements for *hijab*. Then, there were, of course, the times that I needed that extra little push to go from stage to stage and *Alhamdulillah*, they gave it to me at just the right time.

What I mean to say is that my parents didn't passively accept my stages and say, "It's just a stage. She'll grow out of it." No, they took an active role in helping me move from one stage to the next without making me feel like I was just following orders. This enabled me to come out of these stages a confident *Muslimah* with conviction in the path that I chose. For this, I am thankful to Allah first, and to my parents."

Parents should try to always remember the qualities and characteristics of the teenage transition period. This will help them in keeping an open channel of communication with their teens as well as selecting the right methods of training and help they can provide to them. It will also help parents anticipate certain questions and prepare the proper answers for their teens in a way that can easily be understood by those young men and women.

Now you have enough basic knowledge about the nature of the adolescent stage and the changes every teen goes through. What you need to know next is the nature of the environment and the culture your teen is living in: the North American teens' culture. You as parents have to understand this culture. You have to know what it calls for to understand how it might influence your teen so you can prepare yourself to help your teen safely maneuover her way while interacting with this culture. This is the subject of our next chapter, "Understanding teen culture in North America."

Summary

In this chapter, we presented a detailed account of the stages of adolescence (early adolescence, middle adolescence and late adolescence) and the changes and developments that take place during these critical years. The changes cover the physical, psychological, social and intellectual aspects of the teen's life. These changes represent great challenges for the teen and usually leave him confused unless he is gently guided by his parents. Adolescence is the transition period between childhood and adulthood. It is a time when every teen searches hard for his identity.

2. North American Teenage Culture

I n this chapter, we will try to take a look at North American teenage culture, especially the negative aspects of this culture, which go against the Islamic values, you as parent are trying to instill in your teen. Some of these aspects include the promotion of an individualistic and materialistic attitude toward life, the great emphasis placed on physical appearance and lack of spirituality, and lack of respect for authority or elders, etc. Every Muslim parent needs to recognize that not actively participating in your teen's lifestyle is not an option. If you as a parent don't instill certain Islamic values in your teen's personality, this society will mold him to the dominant culture, which in most cases may completely contradict your values as a Muslim. After discussing general North American values and contrasting them with the Islamic values, the chapter ends with a list of challenges our Muslim teens are facing as well as shocking statistics to shake Muslim parents into an awareness of the dangerous environment their teens are living in.

Negative aspects

Here are just some of the negative aspects of North American society that bombard our Muslim teens everyday. Some of these aspects were written about by two of our daughters, *Hoda* and *Noha*.

Individuality

One of the basic concepts that runs western society is individuality. While Islam looks at what is in the best interest of the group (shura), teens in the west are taught that the most important thing is what they want or need, with little regard to others This can be seen in the huge rate of divorce that exists in this culture. Instead of looking out for the best interest of the family or group, a person may choose to get divorced because she is bored with the relationship, instead of struggling to fix it. This starts a general attitude of competition instead of cooperation. It prompts people to feel that it's "you against me" and so there is little importance placed on helping others. Teens are taught that if they are good at something, they should make sure they are better than everyone else instead of helping somebody else also improve. One main effect is inconsideration and a lack of respect for others, including those in authority, such as teachers and parents.

Fulfilling desires

A great deal of importance is placed on desires, often raising them to the same level as basic needs. To want something is a good enough reason to do it, and so many people make stupid decisions without seriously considering their consequences. This means that a teen might shoplift because he wants a CD at the music store and he is two dollars short. It means that a teen might start smoking because she wants to fit in with the people around her who smoke, or that she might get drunk at a party because she doesn't want to look lame for refusing a drink. In some groups, a certain status accompanies the more daring kids, so you're cooler if you drink more, smoke more, swear more, steal more, do more drugs, are rude to more teachers, or get suspended more often. People are encouraged to act on their urges, to ignore their inhibitions, and to be as "wild" as possible. Those who don't get involved in the fun stuff are "losers" or "chickens".

Enjoyment and fun

The teenage years are seen as the time to party, make mistakes, and have "all the fun you can have before you have to grow up and act your age". They are seen as the time to experiment with different lifestyles, including drugs and drinking, and see where one fits in. It is practically unheard of to learn from somebody else's mistakes, and even more unheard of to stay at home on a Friday night instead of going out to a party. Anyone who stays home has no life, or no friends, or both. The majority of my friends see every movie in the theater the same week it comes out. They go out for dinner or to the mall, or just to hang out downtown, to pass their time. Many people will give me funny looks if I say I have work to do and I can't go. The teenage years are seen as the years you spend entertaining yourself. In some crowds, there isn't even room for schoolwork.

Physical indulgence and following fashion

This is one of the biggest problems teens face today and are bombarded with from every angle. An enormous emphasis is placed on physical and sexual indulgence. To not have a boyfriend or girlfriend is seen as extremely unusual. If a teen is able to avoid that, it is still virtually impossible to avoid conversations about the opposite sex and the topic of dating in general. Comedy, movies, music, newspapers, books, TV shows: all of these are constantly discussing the issue of sexual activity, promoting it, or even showing it as it happens. Another huge challenge to overcome is fashion. In the west, fashion is practically a religion, and especially for girls, it becomes very difficult to dress differently and follow *hijab*. Aside from discrimination, many girls are also singled out on account of not wearing the right kind of jeans, or not wearing jeans at all. The fashion usually contributes to the physical indulgence, with most of the clothes being tight and revealing. This problem causes many girls to feel insecure and many others to become slaves to fashion as well.

This life only (short term)

One of the most destructive and opposite concepts in Western cultures is the focus on short-term gratification. This is a major cause for all of the other destructive concepts already discussed. This concept almost completely does away with a focus on consequences and so people have no limits. They basically follow whatever path will lead them to their most immediate desire, giving little thought to the future and none to the hereafter. This is what makes it easy for people to cheat or lie without feeling guilty. If they feel that they do not have to answer to any serious authority in the long run, that they are not actually accountable for what they do, then they will do anything. Once this basic concept of accountability for one's actions is changed, the rest follows easily.

High school culture

Here is a descriptive piece about high school culture, as prepared by our daughter *Hoda*:

"Let me try to paint you a picture of the high school culture that I experienced. In grade nine, all the kids are thrown into a new environment with completely new people. Everyone is trying to get to know everyone else and if the grade nines can get to know people in the older grades then that's a bonus. The easiest way to get to know people is by smoking, so a lot of non-smokers become smokers in grade nine. People from all the different grade levels hang out at the smoking section before school, at lunch, and after school where they borrow cigarettes and lighters from each other and make small talk while they smoke.

Another way to get to know people in grade nine was that when someone announced that they were cutting science class today, then two or three other people would join that person. Together these people would skip class and go down to a store, a park, or just walk around the neighborhood while they got acquainted.

All through high school there were many social events that would be the topic of discussion at school for a week before they took place and a week after they happened. At my school, these events were mostly the dances. Dances were always going on; there was the first dance of the year, the Halloween Dance, the Christmas Dance, (which they might call by a different name so that it has no religious affiliation and does not exclude any religious minority groups,) the Valentine's Day Dance, the Spring Dance, and, of course, the Last Chance Dance (which was the last dance of the year). There were also the special dances like the Electric Circus Dance or the Video Dance, where the school would rent a bunch of expensive and complicated equipment that could produce cool special effects with a certain theme.

As you can imagine, the dances were not only the topic of discussion but also of activities. Girls went shopping for their outfits together, borrowed each other's clothes, and did each other's hair. Students threw parties before the dance started, then came together from the party to the dance and then went to more house parties after the dance. These parties could be co-ed slumber parties where boys and girls drink and sleep over in the same living room. The next week at school, talk swirled around about who was the most drunk even before they got to the dance, who was able to sneak by the teachers drunk, who got caught, and who danced with whom.

All through high school, at different times for different groups, people tried out drinking and drugs and that became the focus of their social life for a while. Students got fake identifications and went to the cheap bars so they could drink underage, or they went to someone's house whose parents either were out or didn't mind that stuff and they drank and did drugs there.

By the last year of high school, smoking and drugs were not cool anymore. Many students tried to quit, but they couldn't. Everyone had tried it and had their excitement and now people had either quit or were trying to quit but having a hard time because of the dependency factor. There were still a few groups who did drugs regularly, but not everybody was racing to be included. Smoking had died down a little but not nearly as much as drugs. Many girls who had smoked proudly before now did so out of necessity and wished that they could quit. They had started smoking for social purposes and now they felt that the habit was unhealthy and a waste of money. Many girls I know tried to quit smoking, but I only remember two that were successful by the end of high school.

Drinking didn't die down at all. Now that everyone was of legal age, they could go to the classy bars and 'drink like adults.' The grad trip to Cancun during the Spring Break was all about swimming, tanning, and drinking. The fundraisers for our end of the year graduation party was all through events to pubs and even the skiing trips were organized by the student graduation committee included drinking. Even those teens who had been too ethical to make fake IDs and drink underage felt that there was nothing wrong with drinking once they were of legal age. In fact, to celebrate their 18th birthday, even the most reasonable and mature students would drive to Hull (a city very nearby, about ten minutes away from Ottawa) where the legal age for drinking and gambling is 18. In Hull, they would spend the night in the Casino, gambling and drinking with all their friends. The next year, when they turned 19, they'd reach the milestone of being of legal drinking age in Ottawa, (the city that we live in,) so, again, the celebration would be held at a classy Ottawa bar or pub. Since society accepts drinking as normal and mature, I found that it didn't decrease, as my friends grew older; in fact, if anything, it increased.

Another focus throughout high school was, of course, boys. The girls who dated told about their dating expeditions and asked everybody's advice on who to date and what to say to 'him' and those who didn't date talked about who they liked, whether it was a boy at school or a guy on T.V.

My high school was not the exception; it was not a low standard school that was known for its drugs and booze and rebel students. In fact, my high school was in an upper middle class neighborhood, and it's students came from respected families. It was known for it's high academic standards and it's graduates had high grades and high acceptance rates into well-known and respected universities. Despite all of this, the high school environment was just as I described it. Alhamdulillah, I did not fall into any of these evils during my time in high school. I conducted myself politely and focused on my studies and never used foul language or bad manners. Of course it was not easy and I had my share of pain struggling through it."

Contrary to the above conditions, Islam promotes positive virtues and values related to relationships. For example, Islam does not promote the spirit of individuality, rather, it emphasize teamwork, family ties, and values. The child- parent relationship is one of respect, mercy and kindness. This is very well emphasized in many places throughout the *Qur'an* and the teachings of Prophet Muhammad PBUH. We read in Surah Israa' in *Qur'an*,

وَقَضَىٰ رَبُّكَ أَلَّا تَعْبُدُوٓاْ إِلَّآ إِيَّاهُ وَبِٱلْوَٰلِدَيْنِ إِحْسَٰنًاۚ إِمَّا يَبْلُغَنَّ عِندَكَ ٱلْكِبَرَ أَحَدُهُمَآ أَوْ كِلَاهُمَا فَلَا تَقُل لَّهُمَآ أُفٍّ وَلَا تَنْهَرْهُمَا وَقُل لَّهُمَا قَوْلًا كَرِيمًا ﴿٢٣﴾ وَٱخْفِضْ لَهُمَا جَنَاحَ ٱلذُّلِّ مِنَ ٱلرَّحْمَةِ وَقُل رَّبِّ ٱرْحَمْهُمَا كَمَا رَبَّيَانِي صَغِيرًا ﴿٢٤﴾

"Your Lord has decreed that you worship none but him and that you be kind to parents. Whether one or both of them attain old age in your life say not to them a word of contempt, nor repel them, but address them in terms of honor. And out of kindness lower to them the wing of humility, and say: My Lord, bestow on them the mercy even as they cherished me in childhood." (Q 17, V 23,24)

In the same Surah, *Qur'an* tells us

وَءَاتِ ذَا ٱلْقُرْبَىٰ حَقَّهُۥ وَٱلْمِسْكِينَ وَٱبْنَ ٱلسَّبِيلِ وَلَا تُبَذِّرْ تَبْذِيرًا ٢٦

"And render the kindred their due rights, as (also) to those in want, and to the wayfarer; but squander not your wealth in the manner of spendthrift." (Q 17, V 26)

In Surah Al Nisa' *Qur'an* tells us

۞ وَٱعْبُدُوا۟ ٱللَّهَ وَلَا تُشْرِكُوا۟ بِهِۦ شَيْـًٔا وَبِٱلْوَٰلِدَيْنِ إِحْسَٰنًا وَبِذِى ٱلْقُرْبَىٰ وَٱلْيَتَٰمَىٰ وَٱلْمَسَٰكِينِ وَٱلْجَارِ ذِى ٱلْقُرْبَىٰ وَٱلْجَارِ ٱلْجُنُبِ وَٱلصَّاحِبِ بِٱلْجَنۢبِ وَٱبْنِ ٱلسَّبِيلِ وَمَا مَلَكَتْ أَيْمَٰنُكُمْ إِنَّ ٱللَّهَ لَا يُحِبُّ مَن كَانَ مُخْتَالًا فَخُورًا ٣٦

"And serve Allah and join not partners with Him; and do good to parents, kinsfolk, orphans, those in need, neighbors who are near, neighbors who are strangers, etc..." (Q 4, V36)

In Surah Luqman, Allah tells us

وَوَصَّيْنَا ٱلْإِنسَٰنَ بِوَٰلِدَيْهِ حَمَلَتْهُ أُمُّهُۥ وَهْنًا عَلَىٰ وَهْنٍ وَ فِصَٰلُهُۥ فِى عَامَيْنِ أَنِ ٱشْكُرْ لِى وَلِوَٰلِدَيْكَ إِلَىَّ ٱلْمَصِيرُ ١٤ وَإِن جَٰهَدَاكَ عَلَىٰٓ أَن تُشْرِكَ بِى مَا لَيْسَ لَكَ بِهِۦ عِلْمٌ فَلَا تُطِعْهُمَا وَصَاحِبْهُمَا فِى ٱلدُّنْيَا مَعْرُوفًا وَٱتَّبِعْ سَبِيلَ مَنْ أَنَابَ إِلَىَّ ثُمَّ إِلَىَّ مَرْجِعُكُمْ فَأُنَبِّئُكُم بِمَا كُنتُمْ تَعْمَلُونَ ١٥

"And we have enjoined on man to be good to his parents: in travail upon travail did his mother bear him, and in two years was his weaning: Show gratitude to Me and to your parents: to Me is the final goal. But if they strive to make you join in worship with Me things of which you have no knowledge, obey them not; yet bear them company in this life with justice and consideration and follow the way of those who turn to Me. In the end the return to you all is to Me and I'll tell you the truth of all that you did." (Q 31, V 14,15)

In Surah Al Ahqaf, *Qur'an* says

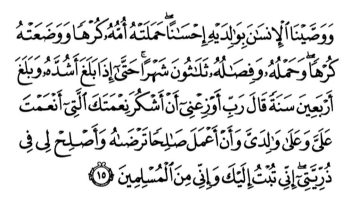

"We have enjoined on man kindness to his parents. In pain did his mother bear him and in pain did she give him birth. The carrying of the child to his weaning is a period of thirty months. At length, when he reaches the age of full strength and attains forty years, he says, " Oh my Lord! Grant me that I may be grateful for your favor which you have bestowed on me, and both my parents, and that I may work righteousness such as you may approve; and be gracious to me in my off springs. Truly have I turned to you and truly have I bowed to you in Islam." (Q 46,V 15)

The teachings of our beloved prophet (peace and blessings of Allah be upon him) are full of advice towards being good to our parents in particular and our kin and fellow Muslims in general. Here are some of these teachings:

— It is reported on the authority of *Abu Hurairah* (Allah be pleased with him) that the Messenger of Allah, PBUH, said, "May he be disgraced; may he be disgraced; may he be disgraced; he who finds his parents one or both approaching old age and does not enter paradise by rendering services to them." (Muslim)

— It is reported on the authority of Abdullah Ibn Mas'ud (Allah be pleased with him) that I asked the Messenger of Allah, PBUH, which of the deeds takes one nearer to Paradise? He said: Prayer at its proper time. I said: what next, Messenger of Allah? He replied: kindness to parents. I said: what next? He replied: Jihad in the course of Allah (agreed upon).

— It is reported on the authority of *Abu Hurairah* (Allah be pleased with him) that the Messenger of Allah, PBUH, said," He who believes in Allah and the last day does not harm his neighbor, and he who believes in Allah and the last day shows hospitality to his guest, and he who believes in Allah and the last day speaks good or remains silent" (agreed upon).

— It is reported on the authority of *Abu Hurairah* (Allah be pleased with him) that a person came to the Messenger of Allah, PBUH, and said: who among people is most deserving of a fine treatment from my hand? The prophet PBUH said: Your mother. He again asked: Then who? He said again: It is your mother (who deserves best treatment). He again asked: Then who? He said again: It is your mother. He again asked: Then who? Thereupon he said: Then it is your father, then your nearest relatives" (agreed upon).

— It is reported on the authority of *Anas* (Allah be pleased with him) that the Messenger of Allah, PBUH, said: He who desires that he be granted more provision and his lease of life be prolonged, should treat his kith and kin well" (agreed upon).

— It is reported on the authority of *Aisha* (Allah be pleased with her) that the Messenger of Allah, PBUH, said: The ties of relationship are suspending from the throne and says: He who keeps good relations with it, Allah will keep connection with him, but whosoever severs relation with it, Allah will severe connection with him" (agreed upon).

It is very clear from all the above verses and teachings of our prophet PBUH that Islam encourages good and strong family relationships at all levels.

Contrary to fulfilling desires, Islam calls for carrying duties and self-control.

Contrary to enjoyment and fun, we find Islam encourages self-elevation and avoiding causing harm to others. If you remember the recommended *dua'a* of the Prophet PBUH when you leave your home in the morning you understand how important it is to set your child in the right mode and prepare her to have the right attitude during her day. Rather than saying to your child before leaving home in the morning "Go, have fun", you send her out with this beautiful *dua'a*:

"Oh Allah, I seek refuge in you not to misguide anybody or to be misguided; not to humiliate anybody or to be humiliated; not to oppress anybody or to be oppressed; and not mistreat anybody or to be mistreated." Such is a wonderful *dua'a*. When your teenager remembers, understands and repeats this *dua'a* everyday when leaving home in the morning, he will always behave in a responsible way towards himself and others. He will understand that he is created on this earth for a noble role to play and honorable objectives to achieve, not just to have fun whenever he can and to fulfill any desires he feels. He will think of the consequences of his actions and the effect of the fulfillment of such desires to his life as well as to others' life.

Also, on the contrary to the North American teen culture of physical indulgence and emphasis on fashion and body shape, Islam promotes modesty and spiritual nourishment. Islam always promotes a balanced way of life. The *Qur'an* tells us in Surah Baqarah,

$$ وَكَذَٰلِكَ جَعَلْنَٰكُمْ أُمَّةً وَسَطًا ۝ $$

"And thus We have made you a justly balanced *Ummah*." (Q 2, V 143).

Prophet Muhammad PBUH approved the advice of Salman to the great companion Abu Aldardaa' saying, "Your body has a right over you, your family has a right over you, your visitors have a right over you, etc., so give each one his/her due rights." So, in addition to taking care of our body and fulfilling our physical needs of food, drinks and lawful sexual relations in the proper and moderate proportion, Islam also prescribes ways to attain high spirituality and lead a balanced life. Among these ways are regular obligatory prayers as well as extra prayers, night prayers, supplications and *dua'a*, fasting during the month of *Ramadan* and voluntary fasting. Physical indulgence turns the human being into an animal-like person whose sole purpose in life will be to consume. The *Qur'an* condemns this type of attitude, which is adopted by those who reject faith. In *Surah Muhammad,* Allah says,

إِنَّ ٱللَّهَ يُدْخِلُ ٱلَّذِينَ ءَامَنُوا۟ وَعَمِلُوا۟ ٱلصَّٰلِحَٰتِ جَنَّٰتٍ تَجْرِى مِن تَحْتِهَا ٱلْأَنْهَٰرُ وَٱلَّذِينَ كَفَرُوا۟ يَتَمَتَّعُونَ وَيَأْكُلُونَ كَمَا تَأْكُلُ ٱلْأَنْعَٰمُ وَٱلنَّارُ مَثْوًى لَّهُمْ ﴿١٢﴾

"And those who reject Allah, will enjoy this world and eat
as cattle eat; and the fire will be their abode." (Q 47, V 12)

Finally, we find that contrary to the short-term approach that most teenage culture promotes in North America, "the what is in it for me now", Islam promotes a more comprehensive and long-term approach to the question of life. As we have seen, in the North American teen culture, the emphasis is on me and now. But in Islam, life stretches across various stages, this earthly life, the life of *Barzakh,* and the eternal life in the hereafter. While a Muslim is working hard in this life, she is not looking forward to fast immediate gains. She is always looking for the reward in the hereafter. As such, it is easier for a Muslim to do good deeds, even if she can't see the immediate benefits for these deeds in this life because she is always hoping for a greater reward from Allah in the hereafter. *Qur'an* instructs us to direct our resources in seeking the goodness of this life as well as the hereafter. In *Surah Al-Qasas,* Allah says,

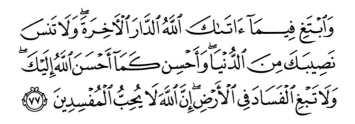

"But seek with the (wealth) which Allah has bestowed on
you, the home of the hereafter and don't forget your portion
in this world. And do good as Allah has done good to you
and seek not mischief in the land for Allah does not love
those who do mischief." (Q 28, V 77)

Due to the differences and contradictions in North American culture
and Islamic belief, Muslim teens are faced with a tremendous amount
of pressure and numerous challenges on a day-to-day basis. Here, in her
own words, are some of these challenges as presented by our daughter
Sumaiya:

Stress

Most people say that when entering high school you begin to feel lot of
stress. You are in a new school, you are the youngest, and you don't know
many people. For me, however, that was not at all the case. I mean, sure
it feels a little strange and it's going to take sometime to get used to, but
for me, I think I felt the most stress when I was entering grade 8. Now,
this was also very strange, because I knew everybody in my class well,
I was with all my friends, and I knew the teachers and the building like
the back of my hand. Yet from the first day of the school, I came home
crying hard and this ended up being a recurring pattern that went on for
several months. The routine was set, I would go to school everyday
feeling miserable and as soon as I would step foot into my house at
the end of the day, the tears would begin rolling down. No one could
understand why: I had many friends, my grades were great, and I had an
amazing teacher, but to me the reason was very clear: my friends were all
changing.

Now, popularity was their ultimate goal in life. Schoolwork and good
grades were no longer their number one priority, and I was completely
confused because, just two months ago in grade 7, these same people had
been good. My friends had also decided to expand their vocabulary a
little and swear.

I guess that to many people, this problem I faced in grade 8 would be
nowhere near a dilemma, but for me, I knew that the solution couldn't
simply be to act like them. This was not just because I'm very religious
and it would go against everything I was ever taught, but because

it didn't look or feel right. It didn't look or feel natural; it was so obviously superficial.

So for a few months, I experienced major loss of appetite and some weight loss. I would also experience some pretty bad headaches that came from crying too much and the symptoms of stress were clear. However, now that I look back on those depressing days, I realize that I have actually triumphed, because if I had given in to save myself some stress, I may have become a shallow stereotypical teen: a fashion slave who's biggest fear is whether or not she'll be popular, someone who will do anything to be socially accepted and look like the girl on the cover of the teen magazine.

Alcohol

Alcohol is a horrible thing. It takes away your mind and leaves you with a crazy body that does whatever it wants. Some people drink alcohol just to be cool and meet the social standard. Others drink it because it takes them on a little trip away from their problems. Unfortunately they wake up next morning to find their problems eagerly awaiting them.

Personally, I'll never, ever take even a sip of alcohol in my life. I would never even sit with someone drinking it. Both of these things are absolutely forbidden in my religion.

With a substance like alcohol, which is extremely addictive, you have to stop the problem before it even starts. Once it starts, it is harder to stop, and from then on it gets worse. Alcohol is a depressant, so, physically, it makes you slow down and feel relaxed. It also makes you make stupid decisions that you will most likely regret. Alcohol may make you "up there" socially (nobody wants to be drinking milk at a party when everyone else is drinking beer), but is it really worth it? Is it worth the gross taste and painful aftermath? Is it worth calling your best friend a bad name that will probably stick with him forever? Is it worth the risk of one day, maybe drinking a little too much and while driving home, hitting an innocent young child? Of course, you won't get charged with anything since you were drunk and you didn't know what you were doing.

The young child's family mourns for months. Alcohol's effects are cruel and ever lasting. It tears families apart; it abuses young children. Why can't people drink cranberry juice or root beer? Why is alcohol so special? That is a question that I have yet to find an answer for.

Drinking and Driving

They say you shouldn't drink and drive
But it's okay to drink
One, two, three beers are okay
As long as you can still think
"Drink responsibly" they tell you
"Know when to draw the line"
Because we all know impaired driving
Is an awfully dangerous crime
I know a girl who was paralyzed
Due to this despicable drink
She watched her mother burn to death
Because someone didn't think
She lives her life in a wheelchair now
Unable to feel her waist
While he who chose to drink and drive
Can jump hurdles in a race
The criminal got two years in jail
But was a "good boy" so left at six months
It seems to me that the criminal
Is really having fun
Can this be called justice?
Was justice really served?
Can we be sure that no one else
Will drink and drive in this world
"Drink responsibly" I'm sorry to say
Really makes no sense
It's called an oxymoron
Because it contradicts itself
Doctor's, scientists, they've all proved
What the consumption of alcohol does
We all know that this disgusting drink
Makes your brain turn to fuzz
So how are you expected
To make a rational decision
When you can't even take a step
Without causing a collision

I'm sorry to burst this big bubble
And be the one to break the news
But drinking and driving will never stop
Until we first put an end to the booze.

Negative Peer Pressure from Fellow Muslims

Good Muslim teenagers are always searching for a good crowd to hang out with, be they Muslims or non-Muslims. Of course it's always more comforting to hang out with fellow Muslims because you figure they will have the same values, morals, restrictions and goals as yourself — or so you think. Unfortunately, that is often not the case. I, personally, know that many times, when with my Muslim friends, I'm shocked to hear the subjects they discuss, (boys, bad movies,) and the language they use (swearing). Parents have to be aware that even other Muslim children can be a negative influence on their teenagers.

I remember one year (I believe I was turning 14) I had a big birthday party where I invited about 10 Muslim friends over for a sleepover. Now, if I was inviting my non-Muslim friends over, I'd make sure to remind them that they shouldn't swear around me or talk about boys or other such things. However, with my Muslim friends I didn't think it was necessary to review all these rules because they were Muslim like me. I assumed that I wouldn't have any problems with people swearing or talking about inappropriate topics because I had only invited Muslims to my party.

Boy was I shocked: some of the girls swore regularly and weren't even ashamed about it, and when they swore, I was the only one that ever told them to stop out of 10 other Muslims. I was actually quite upset because, though I always tell my non-Muslim friends not to swear around me, I didn't think I had to tell my Muslim friends too. That day I came to the realization that peer pressure to do bad things can take place within a Muslim group as well. You shouldn't feel that whatever you do when you're with your Muslim friends is okay just because you're with Muslims. As well, don't be afraid to correct your Muslim friends and remind them that it's wrong to swear and talk about certain things. We expect that, because they're Muslim, they already know all this and there's nothing we can do about it, but that's not the truth. Even if they really do already know it's wrong to swear and talk about boys, it's our responsibility as their sisters in Islam to remind them and pressure them to stop, just as they once pressured us to start.

Another example concerning Negative Peer Pressure from other Muslims:

It was the first day of school and I was entering grade 10 that year. After we had gotten our schedules and went all to our classes, the Students Council asked that we attend a BBQ at lunchtime for all the students and teachers in order to get better acquainted with each other. I was standing in line with a non-Muslim friend named Anna when a Muslim friend, *Aisha*, approached me. She was new to the school this year, and I looked forward to having a fellow Muslim with me since our school wasn't exactly full of Muslims. She came and stood in line with Anna and I for about ten minutes.

Anna and I are pretty good friends, and since this was our second year in high school together, she already knew that she couldn't swear around me and tried extremely hard not too. She was actually very successful and controlled herself wonderfully around me. Well, anyway, all three of us were standing around talking when *Aisha*, not Anna, suddenly swore. I turned in shock and glanced at her sideways, thinking that maybe the word slipped out accidentally. But as our conversation continued, *Aisha* continued to swear, and not just rarely, she actually swore quite often. I kept reminding her to stop again and again, but it seemed as if she had no control over her tongue at all. Every time *Aisha* swore, Anna looked over at me. I felt very embarrassed; because here was a Muslim teenager, in *hijab* and all, swearing every fourth word while Anna, my non-Muslim friend watching the whole thing, was trying her hardest not to say a single swear word in order not to offend me. Anna must have been confused as to why I always asked her not to swear around me when *Aisha*, a Muslim just like me, swore so often.

This is just one example of a Muslim friend influencing you negatively. The important thing to remember is that when you pick your friends you should pick them for their character and not just because they call themselves "Muslim." Pick a Muslim, who really is a Muslim.

Feelings of annoyance and frustration and struggling to hold on to your beliefs and principles are often normal in this society. Teenagers see and go through many things on a daily basis that force them to question themselves and their values. They are constantly bombarded with subliminal messages telling them to conform to society and promising phony ways to be "happy." If the teen has grounded beliefs and a strong family to provide support, acceptance, and reassurance, though the pain and frustration will still be there, he will not succumb to society's way or answer to society's call. Here is a poem, which is actually more of a release of frustration, expressing a teen's annoyance after a trying day at school. It is obvious that though she is annoyed, she still feels a strong sense of belief, which helps her to get over the difficulties she is facing. She may consider her challenges minor because she understands the bigger picture and her role in life.

Good grades aren't everything
Neither are looks
If people don't like you, hey, Allah loves you
If you feel like you're worth nothing,
You're wrong
You are a Muslim
And that's a reason enough to live
Not just live but live proud
Do you think the pretty are happy?
Do you think the popular are happy?
Do you think the intelligent are happy?
They don't know the meaning of life
They feel a constant void, a gap, an emptiness.
They will eventually search madly to find an answer
An answer that you were born knowing
Life changes, people change, you think it's not fair
And you're right, it's not
But life is not fair, it's a test
Tests don't always come in the form of enormous
Moral dilemmas, catastrophes that you watch on the news
Quite often, they're so small you overlook them
Or silently wonder why they happened to you
A bad mark is a test
A bad teacher is a test
Having no friends is a test
Complaining won't solve anything
Praying will
You are a Muslim
Your ultimate goal is to worship Allah

Serve Allah, Please Allah
Not to please your friends, your teachers, your society
Will they defend you in the hereafter?
Will they even know your name in the hereafter?
Will they even know your name in 10 years?
Let's keep our goal in mind
Stay focused and work towards it.

Keeping your children Muslim in America

Here is a story that was published in the Soundvision newsletter of October 2nd, 2000. We reprint it here in its entirety to illustrate the tremendous challenges facing young Muslims in this continent as well as to emphasize the fact that it takes knowledge, wisdom, continuous effort and, before all, the help of Allah to protect our teens from going astray in North American society.

"*Fatima*" was a young, practicing *Muslimah*.

At 13, she was part of a family that tried to apply Islam in all aspects of life. They were role models for their local Muslim community. They were one of the very few Muslim families who did not even have a television set in their home.

Fatima talked about Islam enthusiastically, got good grades, and respected her parents. While she did do some home schooling, much of her time was spent in public school where she made sure to pray on time, wore her *Hijab* with pride and was active in encouraging others to do the same. But then things changed: she began smoking, her *Hijab* came off. Then, on her 18th birthday, she ran away from home and eloped with a boyfriend she had been seeing for some time. *Fatima*'s story is not new. Nor is it uncommon.

What went wrong? How could someone from a family that had tried so hard to maintain an Islamic environment, struggled to raise kids who were practicing Muslims, take a turn on the wrong path?

No human being is an island. What happens to our neighbor, our children's classmates and our coworkers can very likely happen to us whether it's the soaring divorce rate, family miscommunication, domestic violence or the loss of religious values. In other words, society's problems are not the problems of "those people out there". They are our problems, and if we ignore them they will come creeping up to us at one point.

The secret to keeping your kids practicing Muslims

Parents who practice Islam, an Islamic home environment, limited exposure to media with un-Islamic messages: these are some of the ingredients Muslims often promote for ensuring their children are raised as good Muslims.

But these alone are not the solution. Such an approach works for a number of Muslim kids, but not for all. *Fatima*'s example above should make that very clear.

It takes more work than all of that: it takes making the society around you better.

Caring is the first step

Making the West, this powerful entity that has dominated Muslims' lives for over 300 years in the military, political and cultural spheres, obedient to God, is an awesome, and some would say virtually impossible task.

How can we make the West or America an Islamic place? It's by caring about the future not just of our own kids, but by caring about the future of others.

From "these *Kafirs*" to "my people"

How many of us have caught ourselves saying it, whether to our kids or to our friends or under our breath: "these *Kafirs*" and their corruption; "these *Kafirs* (unbelievers)" and their mentality; "these Kafir children" and their perverse, immoral ways? If you have, you're not alone. This attitude though, was not the one adopted by Allah's Prophets. In the *Qur'an*, the Prophets would say "*Qawmi*" (my people). They preached and persuaded and endured persecution to bring the guidance of God to their people. They did all of these things because they cared about their people. They cared that these people, their people, were headed on the road to Hell and misery in this world and the next.

They did everything in their power to preach and persuade their people to accept the Truth so they would be saved. They were motivated by a mission, by a sense of responsibility, and a feeling of deep concern for those around them.

They refused to isolate themselves and their followers. They kept inviting and calling. Most importantly, they kept caring. They realized that this was a cause worth fighting for because they cared about humanity: men, women, poor, rich, believers, and nonbelievers.

<u>Lessons for us</u>

Inviting others to the Creator is not a responsibility for just Prophets or those claiming to belong to groups that specialize in this task.

It is our responsibility.

We cannot present our message if we have contempt and disgust for those around us.

How can we expect our children to be saved from smoking if we don't care about our neighbor's child, whose parent is a chain smoker while she is getting sick because of it in front of our eyes?

How can we say we want our children to go to safe schools if we refuse to work with other parents, Muslim and non-Muslim, to ensure that not just our kids, but all kids at the school are safe?

<u>America: the good life, but with a price</u>

Most Muslims who come to the West come to seek educational, employment and economic opportunities. They come seeking the good life they could not find back home.

But this good life comes at a cost: the struggle to maintain Islam in an environment in many ways diametrically opposed to Islamic values.

A very small number choose to go back. Some decide to fight it out by struggling to curb the negative influences, like *Fatima*'s parents. But many simply give up and allow themselves to be washed away in the wave of assimilation.

Parents in the last two groups may look back and lament over how they lost their children. Some of them may think they did all they could: shelter their children, teach them right and wrong, provide a good home environment, etc.

But these parents forget one thing. They forget that in this land of opportunity in which they sought wealth and prosperity, there was opportunity for something else too: to invite others to the Truth of Islam: to care about the things other parents cared about; to form a common agenda which could not only have saved their children and helped them to keep their Islam intact, but which would have also given back to the community they had chosen to make their home; to care as the Prophets cared about not just their own families, but the families and the children of all, not just the converted few.

Shocking Statistics

–   More 12- to 17-year-olds named drugs as the biggest problem they face (more than social pressures, violence, crime or any other issue) or the fourth straight year.

–   By age 13, half of US teens say they can buy marijuana and 43 percent of them say they can buy acid, cocaine or heroin.
Marijuana use among teenagers has been increasing. Adolescents ages 12 to 17 who use marijuana weekly are nine times more likely than nonusers to experiment with other illegal drugs and alcohol, six times more likely to run away from home, five times more likely to steal, nearly four times more likely to engage in violence, and three times more likely to have thoughts about committing suicide.

–   Alcohol is the most frequently used substance among adolescents. In 1997, 11 million children and adolescents were drinkers and more than 40 percent of them were binge drinkers (that is, they had five or more drinks on one or more occasions in the past month). Research indicates that the earlier an individual begins to use alcohol, the greater the chances of developing a serious substance abuse problem.

–   Smoking has increased dramatically among young people. Between 1988 and 1996, the rate of adolescents first trying cigarettes increased by 30 percent and those smoking daily increased by 50 percent for adolescents between the ages of 12 to 17.

–   Teen substance abuse cuts across all socioeconomic, racial, and ethnic lines.

–   Young people give five main reasons for using alcohol, tobacco and illegal drugs: to feel grown-up, to fit in and belong, to relax and feel good, to take risks and rebel, and to satisfy curiosity.

–   In the next 24 hours in USA alone: 1 439 teens will attempt suicide, 2 795 teenage girls will become pregnant, 15 006 teens will use drugs for the first time, and 3 506 teens will run away.

–   It is estimated that the average time spent by fathers with their children is 3 minutes per day

–   In 1996, 4 643 children and teenagers were killed with guns – 2 866 murdered, 1 309 by suicide, and 468 in accidental shootings. That means 13 deaths by a gun every day.

- In 1998, 37.8% of grade 8 students, 49.3% of grade 10 students, and 56.1% of grade 12 students tried at least one drug. In the same year, 22.2% of grade 8 students, 39.6% of grade 10 students, and 49.1% of grade 12 students tried Marijuana or Hashish.
- In the last three decades:
  a. The percentage of families headed by a single parent has more than tripled.
  b. The divorce rate has more than doubled.
  c. Scholastic Aptitude Test scores among all students have dropped 73 points.
- One fourth of all adolescents contract a sexually transmitted disease before they graduate from high school.
- In 1940, the top disciplinary problems, according to public school teachers, were talking out of turn, chewing gum, making noise, running in the halls, cutting in line, dress code infraction and littering. By 1990, the top disciplinary problems had developed into drug abuse, alcohol abuse, pregnancy, suicide, rape, robbery and assault.
- Between 1940 and 1990, the percentage of families that have one parent at home with children during the day dropped from 66 percent to 16 percent.
- On average, every child spends 1 500 hours per year watching television and only 900 hours in the school.
- The average numbers of TVs per North American home is 2.24.
- 50% of these TVs are in children's bedrooms.
- Three out of four adults say it is much harder for parents to do their job in today's world.
- Between 1970 and 1997, child abuse has increased 365%, teen suicide increased 64%, and births to unmarried teen mothers increased 91%.

The conditions we have described to you above are only a sample of what happens with teens in this society. The real situation can be much worse at times, to the extent that we do not feel comfortable reporting it in our book because Islam encourages us to observe modesty in all aspects of our lives. Though some members of the general society are concerned, most either don't know or don't care enough to do anything about it. We urge parents to keep themselves aware of the ever-worsening situation by checking the following website regularly and keeping an open eye for other sources of information: www.dateline.msnbc.com.

Here is an e-mail that we received recently which stresses the negative condition of this society. It is very well written, and extremely true:

A Columbine High School student wrote: The paradox of our time in history is that we have taller buildings, but shorter tempers; wider freeways, but narrower viewpoints; we spend more, but enjoy it less.

We have bigger houses and smaller families; more conveniences, but less time; we have more degrees, but less sense; more knowledge, but less judgment; more experts, but less solutions; more medicine, but less wellness.

We have multiplied our possessions, but reduced our values. We talk too much, love too seldom, and hate too often.

We've learned how to make a living, but not a life; we've added years to life, not life to years.

We've been all the way to the moon and back, but have trouble crossing the street to meet the new neighbor; We've conquered outer space, but not inner space; we've cleaned up the air, but polluted the soul; we've split the atom, but not our prejudice. We have higher incomes, but lower morals; we've become long on quantity, but short on quality.

These are the times of tall men, and short character; steep profits, and shallow relationships. These are the times of world peace, but domestic warfare; more leisure, but less fun; more kinds of food, but less nutrition.

These are days of two incomes, but more divorce; of fancier houses, but broken homes. It is a time when there is much in the show window and nothing in the stockroom; a time when technology can bring this letter to you, and a time when you can choose either to forward this message and make a difference... or just hit delete.

Dear Muslim parents who live in the west, our Muslim teens living in North America are not immune to the influences of this culture. Whether we like it or not, this is the culture that our teens are living in. As such, they may end up adopting the same culture unless their parents provide them with the proper concepts and training required to live as Muslims in this society. This is not what you want for your teen. If you want your teen to resist being engulfed by this culture, you have to make sure that he possesses certain qualities to protect him from the devastating impact North American culture can have on his personality and values.

In the next few chapters, we will try to present you with a road map to help you learn how to handle this situation. We will also try to present certain important concepts and qualities you need to instill and ingrain in your teens to be able to resist the temptations of this culture and live as strong Muslims in the North American Society.

Summary

In this chapter, we discussed the negative aspects of the North American pop teen culture, which include individuality, fulfilling desires, physical indulgence, following fashions, and short sightedness We also provided some practical examples of the negative aspects of the high school culture. These negative aspects were then contrasted with the good virtues that Islam teaches. To illustrate the effect of these contradictions, we provided a list of challenges that Muslim teens are faced with including alcohol and peer pressure from non-Muslims as well as fellow Muslims. Shocking statistics regarding drugs, sex, alcohol, substance abuse, and teen pregnancy were presented to raise parents' awareness about the reality of the dangers of their teen's culture and surroundings.

3. Road Map

In this short section we will try to draw a road map to clarify the main factors you should consider in the process of *tarbiya* to ensure successful results with the help of Allah. There are six main factors to consider. These are the following:

- The early start,
- Being an approachable friend to your teen
- A clear and common vision of tarbiya between both parents,
- Active participation of both parents in the process of *tarbiya*,
- A strong, confident personality for your teen, why and how to reach it,
- The elevation of your teen's level from Islamic knowledge to Islamic conviction.

Let us now talk about these factors in detail:

Start Early

This is a very important element in *Tarbiya* since the child is naturally seeking the acceptance of his parents in the early stage of his life. There are two main stages that children go through when it comes to seeking approval. In the first stage, which extends from birth to almost around ten years old, a parent's approval and acceptance is the most important thing in a child's life. It is what every child is seeking at this age. The younger the child, the more important the approval of his parents to him. That explains the close attachment of children to their parents during this period of their life. They love their parents' company and they love to be around them most of the time; they love to be noticed and observed by their parents, and they accept their parents' instruction and guidance without much resistance.

As the child grows older, the importance of parents' approval to him decreases and the importance of peers' approval increases. By the time the child is ten, the second stage, where the importance of peers' approval maximizes and importance of parents' approval almost diminishes, begins. The child wants to dress and talk like his peers because he is seeking their approval and acceptance. As such, if parents have neglected the early stage of their children's life and haven't used it to properly instill good concepts and train their child to do the right thing, the child will grow to the next stage without strong beliefs and without good moral fibers. If parents truly spend time and effort in the early stage of the child's life, this will protect the child in the second stage, acting as a shield against peer pressure to accept the wrong values, and to follow the crowd. The child will be able to resist most temptations and deviations because he has already formed a strong personality and is supported by a good value system. The child will be able to distinguish between what is right and what is wrong. He will be able to make the right decisions and right choices when he is faced with certain situations.

The investment parents make in the early stage of their child's life will act as a strong immune system to protect her from the attacks of a great number of social germs and microbes. These germs and microbes are surrounding your teen from every angle. These are the ills of teen culture in the North American society we talked about in the previous chapter.

It is quite unfortunate that a great number of parents don't spend enough time with their children during the first stage in building their strong personality and in having a strong channel of communication established between them and their children. The reason may be that those parents have not realized the importance of investing time and energy in their children in the early stage of their life. They also don't realize the dire and potentially devastating consequences of not investing effort during this stage. As such, they leave their child subject to pressures in the second stage with a weak immune system that is open to all the attacks of the North American social ills. On the other hand, some parents may spend all their time with their child making sure that she is memorizing lots of *Qur'an* without helping her understand what she memorizes or linking her to Allah and the love of Allah and His messenger. Memorization alone is not enough to make the child loyal to Islam and to build the strong personality that can resist the temptation of the North American teen culture.

Ahmad Shawqi, the most distinguished Egyptian poet of the twentieth century in the Arab world, emphasized this concept in one of his poems.

بين الحديقة والنهر   وجمال ألوان الزهر

والطير يشدو بالغنا   ء العذب في شتى الصور

سارت "مها" مسرورة   مع والدِ حانٍ أبر

فرأت هناك نخلة   معوجة بين الشجر

فتناولت حبلاً وقالت   يا أبي هيا انتظر

حتى نُقوّمَ عودها   لتكون أجمل في النظر

فأجاب والدها لقد   كَبَرَت وطال بها العُمُر

ومن العسير صلاحها   فـات الآوان ولا مفر

قد ينفعُ الاصلاح والتهذ   يب في عهد الصغر

والنشء ان أهملته   طفلاً تعثَّرَ في الكبر

Here is a modest attempt to translate it into English:

> While I was walking with dad in the park
> The sun was smiling, bright as a spark
> The trees were beautiful, birds were singing
> The shadows were light, not a shade of dark
>
> There were wonderful trees, big and small
> Beautiful trees, short and tall
> Colorful, amazing, Allah's creatures
> Subhan Allah, it touched my soul
>
> Among the trees, I saw one that was bent
> "Wait dad", I said, rushing over in a sprint
> With long, strong rope, I tied the tree
> Pull, pull to straighten it up, that was what I meant

Dad watched surprisingly, looking for a while
He tapped my shoulder, with a big, wide smile
He said: sweet heart, this tree is grown old
It can't be corrected by you, little crocodile

Things when grown old are hard to change
The habit has hardened, the fuse is short-range
You have to start early to correct any flaws
A late start is always doomed. Not strange!

The same with kids, you have to start early
They value what they learn, they value things dearly
What they learn young stays with them forever
If neglected when little, their future is curly

Dear parents, please start early. From the birth of your child, start to link him to Allah and instill the right Islamic concepts and values in him in order to protect him from the ills of the North American teen culture and make sure he can resist following mainstream popular culture for fear of not being accepted.

Be an Approachable Friend

Let's take a few moments to reflect on your teen's situation. We saw, from chapter one, how the teen is struggling through all the changes he is experiencing in every area of his life: physical, emotional, and social. We saw that his search for his own identity is preoccupying him and affecting everything he feels and does.

Throughout this struggle the teen is being bombarded with negative messages from this society. What's worse, these messages are considered completely natural and an imminent part of every "normal" teen's life.

He will go to school and hear about the movie everyone just went to see, or the party everyone was at on Saturday night. He'll hear about "Paul and his gorgeous new girlfriend." She'll hear about "Melissa and her boyfriend from college."

Even the conservative kids who weren't at the wild party over the weekend can stay out with their friends until one a.m. Even the kids who don't get drunk each week still have a beer with dinner every now and then. It's a rarity to find kids who get along with their parents, but when he does, he's shocked to discover that they go to R-rated movies and watch disgusting shows together.

Posters advertising the upcoming Halloween dance in the school gym surround her in the hallways. Over lunch, her friends ask each other what they should wear as costumes. She is asked more than once why she isn't coming.

After the dance, everyone is talking about who danced with whom and the daring outfit Kelly was wearing. People laugh as they remember Sean and his friends coming to the dance completely drunk and getting kicked out by the vice-principal. He overhears one of his friends saying, "I wish I had the guts to do that, by my parents would kill me."

Walk through any high school hallway and you'll hear everyone swearing, and nobody is shocked by it or even notices. They don't have to be angry or frustrated; it's just a normal part of their vocabulary. In some groups, swearwords are used as complements or nicknames. Teachers don't bother scolding their students for using this vulgar language anymore. Some let it enter the classroom in the form of an educational presentation or by assigning reading material that includes it.

Walk into any classroom and you'll see kids with spiked green hair and eyebrow piercings. You'll see boys with long hair and girls with shaved heads. These are the "alternative" dressers. If the girls don't want to wear baggy jeans and ripped sweatshirts, they're wearing tight Gap blouses and short skirts. New fashions are coming up with different ways to show more skin: low cut tops, bare backs and spaghetti straps. You won't find a skirt without a slit in it. Everybody's wearing Nike, Guess, or Levis. Everybody shops at Old Navy or Le Chateau. Nobody wears the same shirt twice in one week. If you don't buy a new wardrobe each season, you're tacky or out of style.

This is what your teen is exposed to day in and day out, whether it's at a non-Islamic school, or by simply walking down the street, going to the mall or riding the bus. Even inside the house, he is exposed through radio, Internet and TV.

When *Hasan* comes home from school each day, he's already overwhelmed with the contradictions he's facing. Part of him feels disgusted and guilty for the things he sees and hears at school, while the other part wishes he could do it too. He hates standing out as a different kid with a different lifestyle. If only somehow he could feel like he was just another kid in the crowd. He walks in with all of these feelings bottled up inside him. So much of what happens next depends on the reception his family gives him.

Say *Hasan* walks in and finds his mom busy on the phone and his little brother playing in the living room. He kicks off his shoes and drops his school bag at the entrance of the house. Then he flops down on the couch and turns on the TV. His brother leaves his toys and comes over, interested to see what's on: "move over, *Hasan*, I want to sit down too." *Hasan* points to the chair without looking up "You can sit on the chair."

"No, I want to sit on the couch, the chair's not comfortable." His brother *Ahmad* stays standing, waiting for *Hasan* to move. "*Hasan*, he whines, then he comes over and pushes *Hasan*'s feet to sit and *Hasan* shoves him away.

"Get lost!" His mom hangs up the phone and finds them pushing each other.

"*Hasan*, leave your brother alone," she scolds. *Hasan* looks up without moving. "Move," she says, "Didn't you hear me the first time? And stop acting like a baby, for God's sake. You're already 15 and sometimes I wonder if you're still nine. Get off that couch, turn off the TV and go clean up the mess you made. Have you even prayed yet? I just finished cleaning the house before you got here and the minute you walk in, it's like a zoo again!"

Hasan stares at his mom, unsure of where all this anger came from. "What's your problem?" he asks without moving, "what did I do this time?"

"What did you say to me? Do you think you can talk to your mother like that? You must be out of your mind."

Hasan gets up, looking at his mom with anger and frustration. He walks up to his room and slams the door. He throws himself down on the bed and wonders why his life is like this. Last week, he asked his parents to go on the school camping trip over the weekend and they refused. Today, he overheard his friends talking about what a good time they had canoeing and making a bonfire. Two days ago he wasn't allowed to visit his friend Mark or even go with him to the mall. When he asked his dad to buy an Adidas jacket he really wanted, his dad said, "Muslims don't dress like that, you have plenty of clothes."

It seems that every time his dad sees him, all he tells him is, "put your hat on properly. Are you trying to look stupid?" When he brought home his report card, his dad didn't congratulate him on the B he got in English. Instead, he shouted at him for the C he got in Math.

Hasan can't understand why he isn't allowed to do anything. He wishes he had a different family.

In this case, *Hasan* is very vulnerable. He feels rejected and out of place at school. He feels rejected and out of place at home. He wishes his parents could understand him and what he's going through, but he doesn't know how to get them to listen. He knows he can't talk to them about what's happening at school because they're always mad at him.

Hasan is looking for acceptance but he can't figure out how to get it from his parents. At school, he knows that if he acts like the rest of the kids, they'll accept him. As he starts to imitate the kids at school, the gap between him and his parents will continue to grow until there is almost no communication.

Kids like *Hasan* are likely to end up hanging around with the wrong crowd because they need to feel like they are accepted and belong somewhere. They'll smoke, skip school and probably be at risk of using drugs. The sad part is that though the parents cared, they didn't act properly toward their son.

Say *Hasan* walks in, kicks his shoes off and drops his bag. He goes to watch TV and gets in the same fight with his brother, but he gets a different reception from his parents; then the picture will be different.

When *Hasan*'s mom hangs up, instead of focusing on the negative situation, she greets *Hasan* and asks about his day. *Hasan* will see that she is interested in his situation.

Even if he's still too closed up to talk about all his bottled up emotions, *Hasan*'s mom can keep the conversation going by telling him about her day. Then she can ask him if he could get ready for prayer and lead her and his brother in *Salah*. She can tell him that she really enjoys when he's the imam because it makes her feel really good to see her son growing up and leading her in prayer.

It's very important to pay attention to the way *Hasan*'s mom asks something of him. *Hasan* is going through a stage where he is looking for independence and trying to feel like an adult; when his mom tells him that she enjoys having him lead the prayer, this feeds his sense of self-confidence and independence. On the other hand, if she scolds him for not praying right away and orders him to go pray immediately, *Hasan* will feel that she is treating him like a child and become resentful and defensive.

Hasan's mom will sense that he is feeling stressed and confused about something at school. Because of this, she will contain her irritation regarding the fact that he left his shoes and school bag lying around in the entrance and concentrate on getting him to open up and talk about his day. Even if *Hasan* isn't troubled about something today, he'll feel that his mom wants to hear about everyday issues he is facing or maybe he'll talk about something on his mind from before. This will get him into the habit of communicating openly with his parents instead of shutting them out of his life.

Hasan's dad also has to play a major role in his life. Firstly, he needs to make *Hasan* feel that he's a part of his son's life. This can be done by sitting down for dinner as a family and all participating in the conversation. Parents should make a point of being good listeners without jumping in and cutting *Hasan* off with judgmental remarks before he is finished. Another thing *Hasan*'s dad can do is make a point of going up to *Hasan*'s room and seeing him for 10 minutes or so when he gets home from work, asking how his day was, and exchanging meaningful conversation.

Hasan's dad can invite *Hasan* to come with him to the mosque, grocery shopping, or just to run some errands. He can use the time in the car to get to know *Hasan* as a friend. Sometimes, they can go biking or play sports together at the park. This will make *Hasan* feel much closer to his dad since he will find him an approachable person he can laugh with and talk to.

During the teenage stage, the emotional state of an adolescent is very unstable, intense and overactive. Sometimes, this state manifests itself in the form of a rush of emotions directed at a member of the opposite sex. So, if *Hasan* feels that he has a crush on a girl in his class named Lisa, he will feel very preoccupied with his emotions. As a parent, you want to deal with his feelings in the appropriate way.

Parents who understand that this is natural and happens to all teenagers will not be shocked to see it and know how to deal with it in a way that will help their teen.

Hasan's mom or dad needs to open the subject with him in a light hearted way letting him know that his feelings are natural and expected, but that, although they feel very intense and real right now, they're very short-term feelings. As long as *Hasan* doesn't act on his feelings by writing Lisa a note or talking about his crush with his friends, he has nothing to feel guilty about.

Hasan's parents should explain to him that these feelings will go away and he will probably have more crushes in the future, so he needs to remember how to deal with them Islamically. By being approachable, parents are making sure they hear about all that their teen is exposed to and the feelings he is experiencing. They will know where his weaknesses are and be able to help him strengthen himself against them. For example, when *Hasan* expresses his pain or disappointment about not getting to participate in the camping trip, or not being able to hang out at the mall, parents can take this opportunity to calmly explain that *Hasan* has a responsibility to himself regarding how he uses the time Allah (SWT) gave him.

When he expresses his disappointment about not getting to go to a certain movie, his parents can remind him he is accountable for how he uses his senses: what he sees, what he listens to, and so on.

At the same time, when *Hasan*'s parents don't allow him to participate in these activities or other activities they don't find suitable, they need to provide alternative ways for *Hasan* to enjoy himself and socialize. These ways could include family activities, Muslim community activities and youth groups, and general society activities that take place in a healthy environment.

In summary, parents need to be approachable and available to listen to their teens, this includes both the mother and the father. If the teen feels that his parents are there for him, he will come to them instead of seeking help from others who may not give him the right advice or support. This doesn't mean that parents should pay attention to their teen only when he is experiencing trouble, but that communication happens every day

Clear and common vision of *tarbiya* between both parents

This is another very important factor. Both parents must have a common vision for what they want for their children when they grow up. This vision is not limited to the career, but it is mainly a vision for the morals, the values and qualities they want their child to have. Today's children are the adults of the future, and having a vision for the people of the future helps parents to work hard to realize this vision and find solutions for all challenges and hardships preventing them from realizing it. Parents should ask themselves this very important question: what do we want our child to be like when she grows up?

The answer for this question will help you as a parent to take the necessary steps towards achieving this goal. If we tried to answer this question, we would say the following:

We want our child to be a good, balanced, rounded Muslim person who

- Loves Allah SWT and accepts His guidance as a way of life
- Loves the prophet may Allah's peace and blessings be upon him and takes him as a role model
- Realizes that real happiness is in living within the boundaries of Islam
- Feels proud to be a Muslim with a clear purpose in life
- Is able to deal with life matters properly, function, compete and be an active member in society

This is a short list that we think every parent should have in mind as a vision for what he wants his children to be when they grow up and become adults. Write this vision in large letters and keep it in place where you can see it every time you turn around. Hang it on the wall in front of your desk or on the fridge door. Every time you see it think about ways and methods to make sure you can achieve this vision.

Another point to emphasize here is that parents should not keep this vision to themselves, but rather share it with their child. The child should be part of the process and know early enough that this is what is expected from him as he grows. The older the child gets the more parents should explain and talk to him about this important goal in life and the vision they hold for him. A child who buys into such a vision and accepts it as his goal will be much easier for parents to work with to achieve this vision. He will certainly cooperate and be ready to do more because he is convinced that this is his goal in life and that it is a worthwhile goal to work for.

Active participation of both parents in the process of *tarbiya*

According to *Qur'an* and the teachings of our beloved prophet Muhammad may Allah's peace and blessings be upon him, *Tarbiya* is a joint responsibility between both parents as was reported in the following hadeeth:

"On the authority of *Ibn Omar*, may Allah be pleased with him, who narrated that the prophet of Allah, PBUH, has said: "All of you are guardians and are responsible for your wards. The ruler is a guardian of his subjects and the man is a guardian for his family, the lady is a guardian and is responsible for her husband's house and his offspring; and so all of you are guardians and are responsible for your wards." (*Bukhari*)

In *Surah Al-Tahreem*, Allah says

يَٰٓأَيُّهَا ٱلَّذِينَ ءَامَنُوا۟ قُوٓا۟ أَنفُسَكُمْ وَأَهْلِيكُمْ نَارًا وَقُودُهَا ٱلنَّاسُ وَٱلْحِجَارَةُ عَلَيْهَا مَلَٰٓئِكَةٌ غِلَاظٌ شِدَادٌ لَّا يَعْصُونَ ٱللَّهَ مَآ أَمَرَهُمْ وَيَفْعَلُونَ مَا يُؤْمَرُونَ ﴿٦﴾

"O you who believe, save yourselves and your families from a Fire whose fuel is men and stones. Over which are appointed stern and severe angels, who flinch not from executing the command they receive from God, but do precisely what they are commanded." (Q 66, V 6)

It is quite common in families nowadays to witness the absence of one or in some cases even both parents from the *Tarbiya* process. At one extreme, we find a father who tells his wife, "children are your responsibility, I have nothing to do with them." On the other extreme, we find mothers who will not direct or guide their children during the day if they misbehave or do something wrong. They will simply tell them: "Wait until your father comes home and he'll take care of you then." Both attitudes are wrong. *Tarbiya* is a joint responsibility and both parents should be part of the process. This doesn't mean that both will spend exactly the same amount of time with their children, but it means that both will

– Have a common vision
– Agree on techniques to use with their children
– Be aware of the environment around them and its impact on their children
– Agree on the role each will play in the *tarbiya* process
– Never undermine each other's authority in front of the children

We would like to emphasize a very important point here; this is importance of active participation of the fathers in the affairs of their children, especially when the children are boys. Mothers can only do so much with the male children, and their influence decreases past a certain age. After this age, the father figure is very important and boys want to have a role model to imitate. Only the father can provide the right model. Fathers should be a major part of their boys' life. They should listen to them, attend their sports activities and school functions, and go out with them for picnics, hiking and other recreational trips.

A common problem we have seen during our workshops is the lack of participation from the fathers in the life of their boys. This lack of involvement is very serious and the majority of problems facing families in North America with their teens can be attributed to the father's lack of participation in the process of *Tarbiya*. As such, we recommend that fathers take an active role in their children's life. Fathers shouldn't limit their role to earning a living for their families, but they should also fulfill their duty and responsibility towards providing love, guidance and proper training to their children.

The absence of fathers from the life of their boys is a very serious problem. The child/teen is looking for a role model to imitate. If his father is absent from his life, he will find the role model in any of the sports, movies or TV personalities he is exposed to everyday. The boy might start imitating some of their new role model's actions or begin to dress like him. Usually, as soon as the father notices this, he starts scolding the child- sometimes in a humiliating way- for the way he looks or behaves. Then the confrontation starts. As far as the child is concerned, he has now found a way to attract his father's attention. This is attention he is missing because of his fathers' absence from his life. The child will continue to behave in the same way since it is the only way that he knows how to get his father to notice him. If the father continues to scold the child for such behavior, a vicious cycle starts and the relationship between the father and the child quickly deteriorates.

You see, our dear parent, how serious the problem is. We hope that every father will realize the devastating effect his lack of participation in his children's life may bring in this North American environment. We also hope that this realization will motivate fathers to take the necessary steps towards correcting and rectifying this problem. Yes, it may be time consuming. Yes, it may require extra effort on the father's part to drive his son to certain school or community sports activities and give him the support needed to make him feel that he is not less important than any other child. However, it's extremely important to make the child feel that his parents value his life and activities and that he is well loved by them. Yes it may require all of this, but it is worth it because not doing it has serious consequences.

A Strong, Confident Personality for Your Teen, Why and How to Reach it

This is another very important factor that is an essential component of this road map. It may be the most important factor of all. As such, we will fully dedicate the next chapter to this topic, where we will discuss the reasons we want our teens to have this confidence and strength and provide some guidance as to how we can achieve this. However, at this point, we would like the reader to consider the following illustration and decide which of these two cases represents his child? As they say, a picture is worth thousand words.

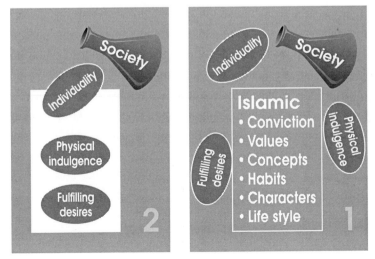

In case number one, we have a child whose parents invested in the early stage of his life to instill Islamic values into his personality, to make him understand certain Islamic concepts and build certain habits. He is convinced that Islam is a complete and comprehensive way of life. His parents made sure that the life he is living represents an Islamic life style. This kind of teen will be very difficult to sway from his Islamic beliefs. He will be able to resist most external influences from his surroundings. If we compare this case to the second case where no concepts or habits were instilled in the child, it is very easy for the external societal influences to mold him because he is empty.

Elevating your Teen from the Level of Islamic Knowledge to the Level of Islamic Conviction

This is the sixth and one of the most important factors on our road map. That is why we will dedicate a separate chapter for the discussion of this factor. We will try to provide some practical ways to help you as parent raise your teen's level from knowledge of Islam to conviction. This means that your teen will be fully convinced that Islam is a complete and comprehensive way of life and achieving happiness in this life and the hereafter can only be realized through living Islam and following the orders of Allah. In that section, we will talk in detail about the conditions to be fulfilled, the circumstances to be considered, and the methods to be used by parents to ensure the success of this operation.

Summary

This chapter drew a road map for every parent to consider in the process of their teen's *tarbiyah* in order to weather the storm of adolescence. The road map consists of six components, namely: an early start, being an approachable friend to your teen, a clear and common vision of *tarbiyah* between both parents, active participation of both parents in the process of *tarbiyah*, helping your teen develop a strong and confident personality, and elevating your teen's level from Islamic knowledge to Islamic conviction.

4. A Strong, Confident Personality for Your Teen, Why and How to Reach it

I t's quite natural for children who grow up in this society to be subject to numerous challenges and dangerous situations, like the ones we discussed in chapter two, especially during their teenage years. This is due to the following reasons:

1. The nature of the adolescent stage of life as explained in the first chapter of this book: Adolescence is a stage where the teen goes through various psychological changes that accompany her fast physical growth. This makes her very sensitive, nervous, and easily angered. Often, she longs for independence, yet at other times, she longs for her parent's attention, love, and care. During this stage, the teen is actually a living struggle, as she continues to search for her identity. Her mind is filled with questions regarding her life and how it relates to the world around her. Who is she? What is the purpose of life in general and her life in particular? Do her parents love her or not? Do her friends really love her or not? Do people her own age accept her? Feeling unaccepted by those her own age is extremely troubling for the teen because she feels an overwhelming need to belong.

2. The nature of North American society and its teen culture and norms: As explained in Chapter two, the current norms of teen culture in North America are completely unacceptable to us as Muslims. The majority of these norms don't agree with our value system and in some cases, they fully contradict Islamic beliefs. A teenager who doesn't follow these norms is viewed as an outcast by mainstream teens. This undoubtedly represents a form of peer pressure to our Muslim teens living in North America.

3. Muslims are a minority in North America, and they feel the same pressures that all minorities feel. In addition to this, the division among

various Muslim groups is another factor that contributes negatively to the feelings of Muslim teens. They feel helpless and some tend to follow the crowd in order to be accepted.

Why

The reasons stated above all represent a great source of pressure for our Muslim teens. Unless we succeed in training our teens to have strong personalities and be confident in themselves and their belief system, we may very well lose them in the whirlwind of western culture. It will be very difficult for teens who don't believe strongly in their values to resist the temptation of following the crowd. A teen needs this strong personality and belief to be able to stand against the flow and say no to certain situations. The clash is eminent, it will happen, and when it happens he needs this confidence and strong personality.

A teen that is confident in his way of doing things will not be shaken if his peers do not agree with him about the way he talks or dresses. When he is invited to a mixed party where alcohol and wine will be served, he needs to say NO in an assertive and confident way. When she is asked to smoke a cigarette or to take drugs, she needs to say NO with pride and conviction. For the teen, saying no needs to be a source of pride and victory rather that a source of defeat and failure.

That is why it is very important for parents to use ways and means of tarbiya that help Muslim teens to have strong personality. Parents need to use the methods that will ensure that their teen be confident in her ability to do the right thing all times and make the correct decision when she is faced with a specific situation.

How

Following are some methods parents can use to help their teen have a strong personality:

1. Knowing and believing in Allah can be a great source of confidence and support for the teen. This means that he believes that Allah's word is the truth and this life is very short compared to the hereafter, which is eternal. He believes that Allah's reward is so great that it is easy to sacrifice temporary joy in this short life. This beautiful reward of paradise will always be before his eyes and in his mind to the extent that it will provide him with the strength he needs to say no to the temptations he faces.

Parents should try to link the teen to His creator using the methods we described in our book " Meeting the Challenge of Parenting in the West, An Islamic Perspective" starting from a young age. This is an ongoing process that should never stop. It should continue through the teenage years using reminders, as indicated by the hadeeth of the prophet PBUH, narrated by *Ibn Abbas* may Allah be pleased with him who said, "One day I was riding behind the prophet PBUH when he said: O' my dear son, I wish to instruct you with some words. Adhere to the orders of Allah and safeguard the commandments of Allah, He will protect you. Safeguard His rights, and he will be ever with you. When you beg, beg of Him alone; and when you stand in need of his assistance, supplicate Allah alone for help. Remember that if all people desire to benefit you, they will be unable to bestow anything upon you except that which Allah has preordained for you. And if all of them agree to do you harm, they will not be able to afflict you with anything except that which Allah has predestined against you. The pens have been lifted and put aside and the ink of the book of predestination has dried up." (*At-Termithy*)

Reminders such as this one will help the teen feel that Allah is with him, constantly supporting him and watching over him. He will always try his best to do the right thing wherever he is. The intimate knowledge and love of Allah and following His orders is definitely the prime source of all support. During the migration of the prophet PBUH from Makkah to Madinah, after he made all the plans and arrangements humanly possible for his trip, he fully put his trust in Allah SWT. When the disbelievers came up to the opening of cave *Thawr* where the prophet PBUH was hiding with *Abu Bakr*, may Allah be pleased with him, *Abu Bakr* was very concerned about the prophet's safety, but the prophet PBUH assured him that Allah would protect them. The prophet's knowledge and love of Allah as well as his complete obedience to Allah's orders provided him with tranquility, a great sense of self confidence, and a feeling of security even in the most difficult situations.

2. Another source of confidence for your teen would be to know the prophet PBUH and take him as a role model. Once your teen has done this, she will love him and feel honored to be his follower. She'll believe that whatever he tells her is the truth and that it's the best thing for her in this life and the hereafter. This belief can come from reading a comprehensive and authentic biography of the prophet PBUH.

It is the parents' job to help their teen find the right source of knowledge about the prophet's life and the lives of his companions. These biographies are the most important element in motivating your teen and making her learn about these wonderful heroes who sacrificed their lives for the sake of spreading the truth and making the word of Allah supreme. Examples of courage and bravery in the prophet PBUH's life and the lives of his companions, may Allah be pleased with them, are limitless and are all sources of confidence for your teen. Make sure your teen joins the right study circles and listens to scholars who motivate and explain Islam as a complete way of life, a mission, and a movement. Don't limit your teen's exposure to just memorizing *Qur'an* and *hadeeth* without understanding what she is memorizing and without explaining how these verses and ahdeeth fit into her everyday life.

3. The teen should feel that his parents love him, understand his needs, know that he is facing a lot of peer pressure, and care about his well being. Parents should try their best to help him face his problems by giving their support. They should make him feel like he can relate to them and they can relate to him by doing simple things like calling him by a nickname he likes and sharing jokes. They should speak to him in the most loving and compassionate way. They should be sensitive to his needs and try to satisfy them. They should make him feel that his presence is welcomed and that he is wanted at all times.

4. The teen should feel that she is valuable, capable, and skilled in various areas where she is similar to her mainstream North American peers. She can participate in several activities related to her age group. She can drive a car, work on a computer, play certain sports and so on. This will require hard work and effort on the parents' part in their teen's life to train her to acquire these skills. Of course, this has to start early in the child's life.

5. Parents have to make sure that the teen's life style is an active one. They can help fill his life with useful, entertaining, and exciting activities. He doesn't feel like it's boring and tedious, just because it's different from the mainstream. Parents can get their teen involved in Muslim activities and have him attend regular study circles where he meets with Muslim friends of the same age group. They can memorize *Qur'an* together, and learn about the life of the prophet PBUH and his companions in an

interesting and attractive way. He can attend the *Jama'ah* prayer in the Mosque with his father or, if the Mosque is not close by, they can pray *Jama'ah* as a family at home. He can play certain types of sports and go out with his family or community members on organized hiking trips and nature outings. He can attend regular Islamic camps, conferences, retreats and conventions. In a nutshell, he can put his energy towards useful activities and no spare time is left unfilled. If it is not filled with good things, it can't be left empty, or it will be filled with bad things. As it was said, "If you don't occupy yourself with good things, it will make you busy with bad things."

6. The teen has to learn how to make decisions and decide what is good for her. After all, life is all about making the right choice and taking the right decision and the prophet PBUH said, "Be keen about what is good for you and seek help from Allah." Parents have to provide this training to make the right choice within the family from an early age. For example, at the age of three, rather than dressing their daughter in a certain outfit when they are going out, parents should show the child two acceptable sets of clothes and ask her which one she would like to where going to the Mosque. When she grows a little older, at the age of six or seven, parents should give her the choice on how she wants to spend her spare time on the weekend. Rather than saying, "we will do this and that on the weekend," they can ask her which she would prefer: to go and visit another Muslim friend, or go on a picnic with the family. Starting from age nine and ten, they should consult with her on various family affairs and issues. They should make her part of the decision making process rather than imposing things on her or simply informing her that the family has decided to do so and so. At age twelve, they should start training her how to handle certain responsibilities such as letting her make up the family budget for the week, and so on.

When you train your child at various ages to make her own decisions, she will be able to make the right one, *insha' Allah*, when she becomes a teenager and is faced with choices. She won't just follow her peers blindly, rather, she will asses and evaluate situations, weigh the negatives and the positives and, insha' Allah, choose the right choice because she has been through the training and it isn't the first time she is making a choice. But if the family hasn't provided such training, the chances are that their teen may follow the crowd because she doesn't know how to choose and say NO. This is an important element in building a strong personality and confident teen.

7. The parent should train the teen to be independent by giving him the skills needed to serve himself and survive in his environment rather than being dependent on his parents for everything. For example, give him some guidance in how to do it, and then allow him to shop for himself.

8. Parents should be supportive and empathize with their teen. Be accepting and understanding of her view rather than critical and ridiculing. A parent who can guide through discussion, listen attentively, and allow his teen to express her point of view freely without getting angry, no matter how wrong it might be from parents perspective, can help dramatically in boosting his teens self esteem and self confidence.

9. Another way of building a strong personality for a teen and increasing his self-confidence is for parents to give reasons for what they ask of him rather than simply saying, "case closed. Do as I say and don't ask questions." Your teen needs a parent who doesn't feel insulted whenever he asks you "Why?" but, instead, uses the opportunity to explain, encourages him to ask more, trains him to ask in a polite, proper, and respectful way, and shows the wisdom behind orders and issues. This goes a long way in building a strong personality and self-confidence for your teen.

10. Empower your teen through making her feel good about herself. When she feels good about herself, she won't be oversensitive as to how others view her behavior or think of her actions. She will be able to stand out from the mainstream and confidently say NO to things she shouldn't do. Of course, this process has to be done in a careful way to make sure that the teen is not boasting or becoming arrogant. You need her to be proud of who she is and what she believes in without being arrogant and looking down on others.

11. Allow him to ask questions, no matter what the subject is and train him for in depth and critical thinking. *Qur'an* encourages in depth thinking in every area of life. In *Surah Abasa*, when *Qur'an* talks about food, it says,

$$\text{فَلْيَنظُرِ ٱلْإِنسَٰنُ إِلَىٰ طَعَامِهِۦٓ ۞ أَنَّا صَبَبْنَا ٱلْمَآءَ صَبًّا ۞ ثُمَّ شَقَقْنَا ٱلْأَرْضَ شَقًّا ۞ فَأَنبَتْنَا فِيهَا حَبًّا ۞ وَعِنَبًا وَقَضْبًا ۞ وَزَيْتُونًا وَنَخْلًا ۞ وَحَدَآئِقَ غُلْبًا ۞ وَفَٰكِهَةً وَأَبًّا ۞ مَّتَٰعًا لَّكُمْ وَلِأَنْعَٰمِكُمْ ۞}$$

"Then, let men look at his food. We pour forth water in abundance. And We split the earth in clefts. And We cause therein the grain to grow, and grapes and clover plants, and olives and Date palms, and gardens dense with many trees, And fruits and herbage to be a provision and benefit for you and your cattle" (Q 80, V 24-32).

It is very clear that *Qur'an* didn't just provide a simple answer to the question of food, it went into great details to describe the food production cycle. This is to teach us in depth thinking and not to stop at the superficial level of things, but always look beyond the immediate and obvious answer. Also in *Surah Al-kahf,* we were told the story/parable of the two men. One of them was given two gardens and was very arrogant. During the dialogue between them we notice that his companion responds to his arrogant attitude in this way:

$$\text{قَالَ لَهُۥ صَاحِبُهُۥ وَهُوَ يُحَاوِرُهُۥٓ أَكَفَرْتَ بِٱلَّذِى خَلَقَكَ مِن تُرَابٍ ثُمَّ مِن نُّطْفَةٍ ثُمَّ سَوَّىٰكَ رَجُلًا ۞}$$

"His companion said to him during the talk with him, "Do you disbelieve in Him Who created you out of dust, then out of *Nutfah* (mixed semen drops of male and female discharge), then fashioned you into a man?" (Q 18, V 37)

This way, he is reminding him of his origin and bringing more in depth thinking into the discussion that may trigger a positive change in the other person's attitude.

Here are some examples of how to use this principle to help your teen build a strong and confident personality

1. When your teen comes to you with a question that may be related to Islam that he couldn't answer to one of his peers, rather than answering the question for him directly, a better way is to identify some references for him and ask him to research the answer. When he comes up with the answer, ask him about it and give constructive criticism. At the same time, provide some suggestions to make his answer more comprehensive and complete. A good way to think of a more complete answer is to use "what if" questions and try to respond to them.

2. Occasionally ask your teen to critique an article in the paper or a book she has just finished reading. Try to help her through providing a list of questions as guidelines to the critique process.

These are all ways to help your teen in having an analytical mind that questions and examines the things that are presented to him. He will not follow a trend just because it's the popular thing to do. Instead, he will see if this idea is sound, and has merits and basis. Doing this, *insha' Allah*, will help him to have a strong and confident personality.

12. Avoid lowering your child's self esteem. Parents should be aware of how they can unknowingly discourage their children in their efforts. Among ways, they can do this are through being perfectionists, through being overprotective, and through humiliating. Here are some examples taken from our book "Meeting the Challenge of Parenting in the West, An Islamic Perspective" to illustrate this fact

a. Perfectionism

It was reported that the prophet, PBUH has said:

"The hasty one, neither covers the desired distance, nor spares the back of his means of transportation."[*Albazzar*]. The "hasty one" was explained by the scholars as the one who lost the companionship of his fellow travelers because he has caused the beast he was riding to be fatigued. Perfectionist is similar to the hasty one; he or she asks others to do more than what they can bear, and in the process he causes them to be fatigued. This is not a healthy behaviour especially with children.

Here are two examples of perfectionism from the parents towards children:

1. When *Hoda* showed Dad her seven A's and one B report card, he said, " I know you can do better than a B, *Hoda*, I want to see all A's next time." He then laid the report card down with no comment on the higher marks.

2. *Aly*'s grandfather sent him a gift on the occasion of *Eid*, so he used Dad's computer and produced a thank you note. When it was finished, he showed it to his mother. " This is okay , but the last paragraph is crooked, *Aly*," she said. "Do it over."

Here we see that perfectionist parents tear down their children's self-esteem by never seeming to be satisfied with their accomplishments. Yes, it is good to do fine tuning of some of the children's actions and it is desirable when parents are sure the child's self-esteem can handle it. It is important that childrens' efforts be applauded.

Here is what *Hoda*'s Dad should have said, "I'm so proud of you, *Masha'a Allah*, seven A's, dear. I'm sure you must be happy about this result as I am. You see, Allah always rewards those who work hard and those who try to perfect their work. Allah blessed your efforts and you got these great marks. Congratulations honey." Later *Hoda*'s father could discuss with her in a gentle way what could be done to improve that B.

Aly's mom too could have encouraged him by saying, "A thank you note for Grandpa? How thoughtful of you . I'm sure it will make him very happy."

Without such comments *Hoda* and *Aly* may think nothing they do is acceptable and that will have a negative impact on their self-esteem. Parents should be very careful about being perfectionists.

b. Overprotection

Here are two examples of overprotection by parents towards their children:

1. *Ahmed* is 5 years old. He wants to take skating lessons with his friends, but Dad said, "That's too dangerous, you remember what happened to my knee when I tried to skate, maybe you should wait until you become little bit older."

2. Two Muslim families asked *Noha* to baby-sit, but her mom said no: "Caring for younger children is a big responsibility, *Noha*. What if something happens to them?."

Here we see in their attempts to protect *Ahmed* and *Noha*, parents crossed the thin line between protection and discouragement. The father used his bad experience as an excuse to deprive *Ahmed* from skating lessons. Yes, caution is necessary sometimes, depending on the circumstances, but children may believe that Mom or Dad think they are stupid or incapable. In the case of *Noha*, her parents should have given her the chance and equip her with the tools such as allowing her to baby-sit with certain precautions like having to check on her every hour by phone to make sure that everything is OK as well as make a list of contact available for her in case of emergency.

Parents should remember that bruised knees will heal, but low self-esteem can last a lifetime.

c. Humiliation

When Allah SWT tells us in Sura 49, verse 11

"Do not call each others names or humiliate one another." This applies to everyone. It applies more to us for the way we deal with our children. Humiliation destroys the child's self-esteem. Here are two examples of humiliation by parents towards their children:

1- *Fatima*, a grade fiver cannot watch TV until her homework is finished. She knew that part of her project was due the next day, but she wanted to watch her favorite figure skating show. So she lied to her mother. The next day her teacher called to ask about the assignment, and *Fatima*'s mother was furious. She stormed to the driveway where she was skipping rope with her friends. "*Fatima* you are such a liar!," she yelled. " You ought to be ashamed of yourself!"

Fatima wanted to crawl under a rock as her buddies snickered.

2- *Faisal* gained weight between third and fourth grade, and his mother started calling him "Chub." " *Faisal*, you need to stop eating so much so you can be slim like other boys," said his mom. "Your brother is older than you and he doesn't weigh as much as you do." *Faisal* hung his head and cried.

The mother of both *Fatima* and *Faisal* thought they were motivating and correcting their children, but they really were humiliating them. Humiliation is a common way to rob a child of self-esteem."

Do not be critical or point fingers

The prophet PBUH has taught us the etiquette and proper way of giving advice: It should be in private, not in public. If it has to be in public, we should not point fingers at the individual who made the mistake, rather the advice should be given in general terms, "Why are certain people doing so and so?"

This rule should be observed by parents when they deal with children's mistakes, especially if they have more than one child. It is very important not to accuse or chide your child, particularly in the presence of his friends or peers. This makes him more defensive. Talking in private is much more effective, as it gives the child the chance to think about the actual situation and not about the embarrassment he is feeling. The disadvantages of criticizing in public certainly outweigh the advantages. It is humiliating and embarrassing for your teen and it will certainly not help him to have a strong and confident personality. But if we follow the advice of the prophet PBUH, *insha' Allah* we can help our teen to achieve the strong confident personality we all want for him.

Recognize your teen's need to belong and be accepted

Belonging and feeling accepted is a basic need for every human being. In the early stages of a child's life, this need is mainly satisfied through the immediate family. The common activities practiced by the family create and sustain a strong bond and feeling of attachment among all family members. This basic need to belong stays with the individual through all stages of life, early school years, adolescent years and even adulthood years. This fact was very clear even in the life of the prophet PBUH and his companions. When they migrated from Makkah to Madinah, it was reported in many incidents that most of the companions felt homesick for Makkah and some of them even wrote poetry expressing their feelings and how much they missed Makkah and their life their. This shows that they were so attached to the place and to the experience they felt living in Makkah. It was reported that the prophet PBUH said, "By Allah, you are the most beloved land to me. It is only because your people have driven me away from you that I have left; otherwise I would have never left you."

There is a lesson here for parents when they reflect on this fact. Parents should appreciate their children's great need to be accepted and to feel like they belong. It is of paramount importance to fulfill this need for their teens.

Following are some practical examples of how to ensure that this need is being fulfilled in your teen's life but that, at the same time, the basic principles of Islam are not being compromised:

1. Encourage your teen to watch good sports games on TV such as figure skating competitions, hockey games, Olympic events, etc. This will give her something clean to talk about the next day at school with her peers rather than completely feeling isolated from her schoolmates.

2. Allow your teen to participate in some useful extra curricular activities such as the computer club, the yearbook committee, etc.

3. Once in a while, allow your teen to be part of a committee that prepares for certain school activities such as field days, sports competitions, or the end of year graduation ceremony.

This will raise your teen's level of confidence because he will be able to participate with other kids and relate to them. As a result, he will not feel isolated or inferior to his peers.

13. Provide Active life style.

Here is how our daughters, together expressed their appreciation to the active and positive life style we provided for them when they were growing. They wrote the following piece, framed it and presented it to us as a gift on the occasion of the marriage of one of them

Mama & Baba

Writing this to let you know that we remember all you've done and all you do for us that we notice the on-going sacrifices, big and small, that we're thankful you stayed home with us, despite the prestigious career awaiting and the hours of invested studying that we appreciate Soccer Saturdays at St. Joseph's and Sundays at the kitchen table, the bicycle training, the emergency hospital trips when our daredevilish sides had gotten the best of us that we appreciate the *Eid* brunches at Tucker's, the *Ramadan Iftar* readings, the driving training, the emergency exam trips when our sleep-deprived student side had gotten the best of us That we remember the clothes wars, and hair wars, and bedtime wars, and we thank you for never losing sight of your objective and our nature.

To thank you for the time you took to *Dahdah*[1] us and guide us, to teach us and cuddle us, to nurse us and baby us, to love us and cherich us.

To let you know we're glad you chose the house next to the mosque over the one with the swimming pool.

---

1. *Dahdah* is a word that was invented by our family which indicates rough and tumble play that all the kids enjoyed very much

To thank you for the *halaquas*, for the *khutbas*, for the camps, for the picnics, for the schools, for the workshops, for the weekends you never took after your 60 hour work weeks.

To thank you for the trips to Egypt, for the family road trips to Niagra Falls and Marine Land and MAYA and ISNA, for the *Beshir* family car choir.

To thank you for the endless list which cannot be expressed on paper here, for the things we know about and those we do not know about, to thank you for being who you are.

To assure you that, though we are now, one by one, moving out of your home, we are not and will not move out of your life, *Insha'a Allah*.

To let you know that, just as you welcomed and nurtured us for so many years with great generosity in your home, you are welcome to come, stay, and honour us with all you are in our homes, always and forever.

Summary

In this chapter, we discussed how important it is for your teen to have a strong and confident personality. We recommended numerous ways to aid your teen in achieving such a personality. By not being critical and judgmental as well as by recognizing your teen's need to belong and feel accepted, you can help your teen attain this desired personality

5. From Knowledge to Conviction

As promised, we need to discuss in detail the way to achieve the task of elevating your teen from the level of knowledge to the level of conviction. In this chapter, we will discuss important conditions and circumstances that parents should set in place to help them in performing this significant task and achieving the required results. In addition to these conditions and circumstances, parents should use certain methods and follow certain principles to ensure the successful achievement of this goal. This will also be discussed during the chapter.

This is not an easy task by any stretch of the imagination. Most parents depend on instructing children and telling them 'you have to do this and that because you're Muslim.' They think that just by passing on the Islamic information to their children, the children will automatically become good Muslims and perform all their religious duties towards Allah. Knowledge alone is not enough to convince individuals to follow the straight path. A very clear example of this would be a University professor who teaches Islam as a subject. He definitely has lots of knowledge about the religion, yet he is not convinced enough to adopt it as his own way of life.

When the father tells his son to pray because praying is one of the pillars of Islam, the son now knows this piece of information, but is he at the stage of deep belief and conviction that prayer is very important and should not be missed? Is he at the same level of conviction as his father, who has had this feeling ingrained in his mind and heart for many years? Of course not. As such, the son may miss some prayers unless his parents remind him. Also, he might pray quickly just to get it out of the way, but his heart won't be there.

The same is true when the mother tells her daughter not to lie or not to watch certain questionable TV programs because they are *haram*.

The mother might tell her daughter that Allah sees her all the time and always knows what she's doing. The daughter might still do these things secretly because she hasn't reached the level of conviction yet. Even though she has been told, she doesn't really realize that Allah is with her all the time.

The real challenge facing all parents is how to instill deep Iman and conviction in their teens. This is a rather complicated and compounded process that takes a long time and requires gradual introduction of concepts accompanied by ensuring the presence of the right conditions and using the proper methodology and principles. Let us start with discussing what we mean by the right conditions, and then elaborate on the proper methodology and the needed principles to be observed and followed in the rest of this chapter. As for the concepts we will discuss them in the next chapter insha' Allah.

Conditions and Circumstances

A pleasant and loving family atmosphere

Parents should provide a family atmosphere that is cozy, warm, pleasant and friendly, an atmosphere which everyone loves and feels comfortable in. When you talk with your teen, talk in a nice, gentle, and loving way. Your teen should feel that you care for her. Be full of compassion, mercy and gentleness toward your teen. A sense of humor proves to be a great asset in creating a strong bond between teens and their parents. Joking and talking with your teen in a casual, simple, and funny way makes her feel at ease and ensures a strong and open channel of communication.

To the children, the home represents Islam. If the family atmosphere at home is negative and the relationship between the parents is unhealthy, this will reflect on your teen's perception of Islam. She will see it as a hurtful aspect of her life and find the non-Muslim environment outside much more appealing. Because of this, it is very important to provide a positive and friendly family atmosphere so your teen will associate happiness and positive settings with Islam, become more willing to learn more about it, and accept it as a way of life.

Helping your teen out with everyday situations and coming to his rescue sometimes if he's caught in a difficult position strengthens the family ties and makes him more attached to the values of Islam. It goes long way in enhancing the positive image you are trying to build to him about the Muslim home. It makes your teen appreciative of the kind and gentle relationship he has with his parents. Here is a real life situation as narrated by our daughter *Sumaiya*. It illustrates the point we are trying to make in a very vivid way.

"It was early Saturday morning. My shift at work was to begin at 8:30 am and I still had to get ready and bus down to the shopping center. I was glad I was fasting because then I wouldn't have to spend time preparing and eating breakfast. When the alarm clock rang at 7:15 am, I hit the snooze button to catch a little more sleep. When it rang for the second time, I knew I had to get up if I didn't want to be late for work. So, reluctantly, I got out of bed. I moped down the hall sleepily and saw my older sister's vacant bed inviting me to sleep in it. 'Just five minutes,' I told myself as I crawled under the warm covers in my sister's empty room. The next thing I knew, I woke up and the time on my watch read 8:20 am. What was supposed to be a five minute snooze had turned into an hour-long nap and I knew there was no way I would be able to get ready and bus down to work in 10 minutes. I was stuck. Or so I thought. I went downstairs and saw my mother there. I explained to her what had happened and she offered to drive me to work so I could get there on time. My mother had done it again; she had come to the rescue.

Both of us got ready as quickly as we could, and she happily drove me to work without complaining or lecturing me about missing the bus or carelessly sleeping in. My mother understood that accidents happen and people make mistakes. As long as I wasn't continuously missing buses or sleeping in, my mother understood that we are, after all, only human. The ride down was also nice because it gave my mother and I a chance to talk, which is very important, but, unfortunately, can sometimes be forgotten in a busy, hectic schedule.

The story I have just related to you is just one example of when my mother or my father has come to the rescue. This is not an isolated incident. Often, if I have a big project due or a test coming up and I've stayed up late putting on the final touches, my mother will wake up early and make my breakfast and sit with me as I eat. During the exam period, my mother or father will give me a ride to school or make me breakfast which can really help me out a lot. All of these small gestures on their part make a world of a difference to me. It shows me that they love me and care about me and my life.

It's important that children learn independence. I'm glad I was raised up knowing how to make my own breakfast and lunch and how to bus to school, work and many other places on my own. However, it is also important that parents are there for their children for the little things, like driving them to school if they're late or making them breakfast while they study for an exam. A little compassion can go a long way."

I don't think there is any need for us to comment on this incident and its impact in providing the nice family atmosphere we are talking about. We will leave you to reflect on it.

Regular and continuous follow up

Allah the Almighty tells us in *Surah Taha,*

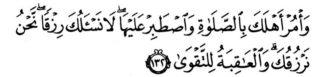

"And enjoin thy people (family) with prayer and be constant in it." (Q 20, V 132)

This great verse establishes the importance of continuous and regular follow up by parents when they instruct their children to do certain things or to fulfill religious duties. It also emphasizes being patient on the parents' part during the process of training and coaching their children, so as to ensure achieving the required results through this training. The word *"Wastaber"* in the Arabic language used in the above verse not only takes its root from the word sabr, but it is also expressed with very strong emphasis. This indicates that parents should never give up. They should try every possible way to train their children to do the right thing and adhere to Islamic values. If one method of training hasn't worked, they have to think of other methods and keep trying without giving up.

It should be noted here that the methods used by parents should suit their children's age. For example, with younger children, story telling in a casual, informal and warm atmosphere is very well suited to teaching them certain values and moral characteristics. Follow up with the children on the characteristic they have just learned from the story is a must; otherwise, they may not implement what they have learned.

Let's illustrate this with a practical example; say the children have just been taught about the characteristic of respecting others. If parents notice that their child is behaving in a disrespectful way towards adults, such as talking to his father in a sharp tone or using unacceptable expressions like, "I don't care" etc. what should they do? They should follow up using these steps:

– Firstly, whoever is dealing with the situation should try not to react directly to the child's behavior. He should keep quiet for a while, try to control his anger and become calm. Never react out of anger.

– Secondly, he should call his son to a private area of the house and speak to him in a firm, assertive, but not angry tone. He should explain to him that the way he behaved is improper. All of this should be done in a polite and respectful manner, and the father should point this out to his son, he might even ask him, "Am I speaking to you in a rude way right now? No. I'm speaking to you calmly and respectfully." He should also remind his son of the saying of Prophet Muhammad PBUH, "He is not from us the one who does not respect our elders and the one who has no mercy on our young ones." The father should ask his son to ask Allah's forgiveness for his sin. Then he should tell him to please repeat the situation in a proper way without using unacceptable expressions or a rude tone of voice.

– Thirdly, when the son does as he is told, his father should thank him and remind him not to repeat the disrespectful behavior or there will be consequences.

– Fourthly, after the child modifies his behavior, it is important that parents not insult or humiliate over the incident. It is also important not to remind him of his mistakes regularly.

– Fifthly, if the same behavior recurs, parents should repeat the process, and this time, they may add certain disciplinary measures to follow up on their promise that actions have certain consequences and bad behavior can't go unpunished. These measures could include depriving him from certain privileges, such as not allowing him to visit his friend for a week or not letting him go to the community picnic, etc.

You should also use some tools to help you, as parent, in the process of follow up. These could be follow up charts displayed in an agreed-upon location in the house (such as on the fridge), written contracts, etc. Refer to chapter nine for samples of these tools.

Utilizing what is best in all your dealings with your teen

In *Surah Fussilat* Allah says,

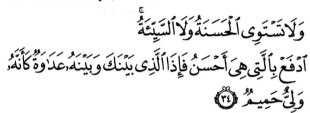

"The good deed and the evil deed can't be equal. Repel the
evil with one which is better, then verily, he between whom
and you there was enmity will become as though close
friends." (Q 41, V 34)

This indicates that Allah ordered the faithful believers to be patient at
the time of anger and to excuse those who treated them badly.

Using the best method in handling situations is also recommended
when we enter into debate with the people of the book. In *Surah Al-
Ankabut*, Allah says,

$$\text{﴿ وَلَا تُجَـٰدِلُوٓاْ أَهْلَ الْكِتَـٰبِ إِلَّا بِالَّتِي هِيَ أَحْسَنُ إِلَّا}$$
$$\text{الَّذِينَ ظَلَمُواْ مِنْهُمْ ۖ وَقُولُوٓاْ ءَامَنَّا بِالَّذِىٓ أُنزِلَ إِلَيْنَا وَأُنزِلَ}$$
$$\text{إِلَيْكُمْ وَإِلَـٰهُنَا وَإِلَـٰهُكُمْ وَٰحِدٌ وَنَحْنُ لَهُۥ مُسْلِمُونَ ﴾}$$

"And argue not with the people of the scripture (Jews and
Christians), unless it be a way that is better, except with
such of them as do wrong." (Q 29, V 46)

This means that we have to use good words and good manners in
inviting them to Islam.

It was narrated by *Abu Zarr Jundob Ibn Junadah* and *Mu'az Ibn
Jabal* may Allah be pleased with them both that the messenger of Allah,
may Allah's blessings and peace be upon him, said, "Have *Taqwa* towards
Allah wherever you are. Follow a bad deed with a good one so it may
erase it. And conduct yourself with people in good manners."
(*At-Termithy*)

The above verses and teachings of the prophet, may Allah's peace and blessings be upon him, establish a decent pattern of behavior for faithful believers to follow. This pattern is one of good manners and high moral fibers in all their dealings and affairs. This indicates that we always should try to use the best way in completing tasks or fulfilling duties. It also means that if one option is good and the second option is better our choice should be always to use the one that is better.

According to the above verse of *Surah Fussilat*, if we use what is best, even with those who have enmity towards us, they will become close friends. Imagine how much our situation would improve with our own children if we began to use what is best (*ALLATY HEIA AHSAN*) with them. They will definitely be even closer than close friends are. They'll love their families and their homes and will always be keen to please them. They'll think twice before doing anything that could upset their parents. They'll try their best to adhere to the right value set and hesitate to commit any sins. The atmosphere will encourage them to feel that Islam is the right way of life and help to convince them that following Islam in totality is the best thing that anybody can do. This will help them to move one notch closer to the level of conviction.

Fulfilling their spiritual needs and touching their soul

The North American environment, with its materialistic focus, does not promote spiritual feelings or enhance closeness to Allah. TV programs, media promotions and the moral norms in North America are quite low and we should not measure our commitment and moral values against them.We should measure our moral values and religious commitment to the level of the sahaba, may Allah be pleased with them.

To make sure that this level is achieved, parents have to ensure the proper environment for their children to enhance them spiritually. One way of achieving this is to provide spiritual trips for their children. These trips can be done in the form of hiking trips or overnight camping trips to watch the skies, stars, rivers, lakes, and trees and enhance spiritual feelings. Teens can witness the fascinating creation of Allah and read or listen to verses from the *Qur'an* describing nature. During these trips, they should be taught various *dua'a*s for various times of day, including the early morning *dua'a* before sunrise and the evening *dua'a* just before sunset. They should also learn prayers that protect them from evil creatures such as "in the name of Allah, where nothing will harm with His name in earth or in Heavens." The prophet PBUH use to tell the *sahaba* to say *Allahu Akbar* when they climbed a mountain and say *Sobhan Allah* when they walked through a valley. This was to link the beauty of nature to the power of Allah and enhance their *Iman*. As such, it is important for parents to make sure to say these prayers and words of praise for Allah whenever they arrange a trip for their children.

In North America, there are lots of wonderful natural trails and beautiful scenic routes that parents can drive through with their children while remembering Allah. Take, for example, the time of fall in the northeastern part of North America. The leaves on the trees change color, providing an amazing view of the landscape, showing everyone the beautiful creation of Allah. Trips to watch this change of color for young youth are great sources of spiritual enhancement.

This spiritual training shouldn't be done in isolation. It should be part of a complete *tarbiya* plan that deals with the teen as a whole and meet all his needs, physical, mental, emotional and above all spiritual. During the adolescent years, a teen is usually searching for the truth. She has many questions in her mind and is trying to find a meaning for her life. When your teen finds you guiding her and helping her to find answers to these questions, she is content and satisfied. When you don't provide satisfactory answers for these questions, she is confused and restless, and may try to fulfill her spiritual needs in the wrong way. She may fall prey to any of the many cults or confused spiritual groups and join one of them hoping to satisfy her spiritual needs through them. This is very dangerous and no parent wants his teen to fall into such trap.

As such, it is parents' responsibility to try their best to fulfill their teen's spiritual needs. Parents should also take the opportunity to answer their teen's questions related to the hereafter, the day of resurrection, the reward of those who do good, and the punishment for those who do evil while on those spiritual trips.

Also at this stage, teens are longing for models and they love stories of courage and heroism. It is very important for parents to read such stories with their teens and subject them to the right kind of heroes: the brave companions of the prophet PBUH who sacrificed their lives to support the *deen* of Allah; the great Muslim scholars who fought injustice and tyrant dictators; the leaders of Muslim armies at various times during our history; and the intelligent Islamic movement leaders who revived Islam and worked very hard to raise all Muslims' level of awareness as to what was going on around them and make sure they understand Islam as it was understood by the companions of the prophet PBUH as a complete and comprehensive way of life.

Learning about those great Muslim heroes and satisfying your teen's spiritual needs will also contribute to raising his level of conviction. It will, *insha' Allah*, help move his conviction level up another notch and make him feel that living within the boundaries of Islam is indeed a source of real happiness and great satisfaction. However, if parents fail to present these heroes to their teens, the teens will try to find heroes in today's movie or sport's stars, who may not be good role models.

Helping him to understand the logical reasons for what is happening around him

This is another very important condition to help your teen move from a state of knowledge to a state of conviction. Your teen is going through a mental state of growth. He is trying to find explanations for everything he sees or experiences. Due to his lack of experience, he may end up misinterpreting certain events or phenomena happening around him. For example, when the teen sees that his Muslim community is suffering from a lack of experts and resources, he may think that this is because Islam doesn't promote knowledge or hard work, but this is exactly the opposite of the truth. Islam actually encourages people to learn and gain all kinds of useful experience. It is the parents' responsibility to explain the real reasons for the community's shortcomings to their teen. If the parents can't do it, they should seek the help of learned individuals in the community; otherwise the teen will attribute these shortcomings to Islam, although the two are completely unrelated.

As for another example, say the teen grows up in a family where the father is harsh and abusive. The father treats his wife and children in an unkind manner, but still claims to be a good Muslim. He prays regularly and dresses in white thawb, thinking that this is part of the Islamic dress code. To the teen, it may seem that her father is abusive because of Islam. On the contrary, Islam asks men to be very good to their families and to treat them kindly. As a matter of fact, the prophet PBUH was reported to have said, "The best of you is the best to his family, and I am the best to my family."

It is really important that somebody explain clearly to this teen that her father's behavior has nothing to do with Islam, or she will continue to associate Islam with mistreating family members, and may be driven away from it.

A third example is the poor state of Muslims across the globe. A teen will look around him and find that Muslims are being aggressed upon in every part of the world, that injustices are being committed against Muslim countries, and that many of the most underdeveloped countries in the world are Muslim. He may then attribute the miserable condition most Muslims are living in to Islam due to his lack of experience and knowledge. It's very necessary that you as parent or some learned individual in the community explains to him that what is happening has nothing to do with Islam. On the contrary, these conditions are occurring because many people are not fully adhering to Islam, as well as for other reasons.

Helping teens to understand the logical reasons for what's going around them is very important in the process of moving them from a state of knowledge to a state of conviction. As such, discussing, listening to their questions and responding to their queries is very important. When this is done successfully, the teen, *insha' Allah,* will again move another notch closer to the conviction state and realize that Islam is the *deen* of Allah and the *deen* to be followed.

Providing opportunities to make her feel like she is part of the bigger *Ummah* of Islam

This is another important factor to help your teen move from a state of knowledge to one of conviction. Most of our Muslim youth living in North America feel like they're a minority and that they are different from the mainstream. They feel that nobody else shares their values and beliefs. This leaves them under tremendous amounts of pressure. Having the opportunity to feel that others share their same views and live the same lifestyle they do contributes positively to their well-being. It helps them to feel like they're part of a bigger Community which has the same beliefs, follows the orders of Allah and abides by the guidance of Islam represented in *Qur'anic* injunctions and in the teachings of the prophet PBUH. It is the parents' duty to ensure that this happens. It can be done through the following means:

- Allow your teen to attend Muslim Youth camps and participate in organizing activities with other Muslims on a regular basis
- Form sports teams, organize structured sports activities for youth, and arrange for intercity exchange visits. This provides a very healthy and supportive environment for teens and make them feel like they're not alone
- Make sure your teen accompanies you to various Islamic conferences and conventions. Keep in touch with the organizers of these functions and ask them to have suitable programs for youth included as part of the convention program
- Take your teen for *umrah* trips whenever possible. If you can't do it on   your own, contact some of the Islamic national organizations who organize such trips and make sure to send your teen to some of them
- Once every few years visit your own home country – if you are an immigrant. If you are originally from North America, try to visit a country where Muslims are a majority and spend a few weeks there
- Never isolate yourself or your family to only those from your own ethnic community. Islam is universal and when you lock your teen into one ethnic community, you deprive him from feeling this wonderful aspect of Islam. Always mix with Muslims from different parts of the world and build your relations based on Islam not ethnicity.

All of the above techniques provide a wonderful environment for your teen and make her feel that she is not alone and that others are following the same way of life. This supportive mechanism is very needed and will help your teen move from the level of knowledge to the level of conviction, *insha' Allah.*

Evaluating your *tarbiya* plans, reassessing progress and adjusting to achieve required goals

Parents should regularly evaluate the progress in their teen's development and respond to any difficulties or negative influences that may impede progress in the right direction. Some of the steps needed may prove to be hard to take, but parents should always put the mental, emotional and spiritual well-being of their child ahead of any other objectives in life. Your child is a trust from Allah and he is your biggest investment. As such, you should deal with him accordingly. Here are some examples of hard decisions parents may have to make to ensure that their teen is being placed in the right environment and getting the care and attention needed to grow up as a well balanced and rounded Muslim person:

– A father may have to change his working hours to make sure that he can spend enough time with his teen. In some extreme cases, he may even have to change his work/career if it proves to be fully impeding his ability to provide his family with the needed care.

– A family may have to move to another city to ensure the presence of a healthy environment and good company for their teens.

– A family may have to move from one part of a city to another to enroll the child in a good school or to live close to a good Islamic center where youth activities are offered.

We understand that these are hard choices to make, but in some cases we have to ensure that our priorities are right. We can't continue business as usual and end up losing our children to mainstream North American society. Our children are much more valuable to us than anything else and we should do what it takes to ensure their well-being.

Methods and ways

In addition to ensuring the presence of the above conditions, it is important to use certain methods when we discuss with our teens to help them move from a state of knowledge to a state of conviction. Among these methods are active listening, reasoning, allowing open discussion, and using proper Islamic ways for conflict resolution. Let us now discuss these methods in detail.

Active listening

The teen's primary need is to communicate and to be understood. To succeed in meeting this need, first and foremost, you must learn to listen effectively. Be an "active listener" as explained in our book "Meeting the Challenge of Parenting in the West, An Islamic Perspective." This means

LISTEN

To the verbal messages and the body language. Less than 20% of what is understood comes from the actual words used. We respond far more to tone of voice, eye contact, facial expressions, body position, etc. (Taping some family times together, with the permission of everyone involved, can be informative.)

REFLECT

(i.e., repeat back) what you believe your teen was saying and feeling without judging or trying to solve the problem. Allow the teen to elaborate.

CLARIFY

Whether your understanding is correct or whether you have misinterpreted. Are there important details that you have overlooked?

EMPATHIZE

By trying to put yourself in the other person's position. It may help to try to recall a similar incident you have experienced. Tell your teen you understand and care about how she feels.

Remember, if your teen asks and seems to want help in dealing with a particular situation, then you may try to SOLVE THE PROBLEM by asking her what she thinks might help and if there is anything you can do. Be careful; don't impose the idea on her. Make a suggestion, and give your teen the choice to accept or reject it.

This sort of effective listening will not only ensure that you really hear what your teen is saying, it will signal to him that you can accept and understand all those other things he has wanted to share, and the real communication will begin.

When your teen feels that you're keen to listen to him and suspend your judgment, he will be more attentive when you try to advise him on something or provide him with certain guidance. He will try his best to understand and implement the guidance learned. This is very helpful to him in reaching the stage of conviction.

Reason and discuss

Qur'an and the teachings of the prophet PBUH have always explained and reasoned with believers and disbelievers alike when discussing any issue. In *Surah Baqarah,* Allah asks the unbelievers to bring proof for their argument:

$$وَقَالُوا۟ لَن يَدْخُلَ ٱلْجَنَّةَ إِلَّا مَن كَانَ هُودًا أَوْ نَصَـٰرَىٰ ۗ$$

$$تِلْكَ أَمَانِيُّهُمْ ۗ قُلْ هَاتُوا۟ بُرْهَـٰنَكُمْ إِن كُنتُمْ$$

$$صَـٰدِقِينَ ۝١١١$$

"And they say, 'None shall enter Paradise unless he be a Jew or a Christian.' These are their own desires. Say, 'Produce your proof if you are truthful'" (Q 2, V 111)

In *Surah AL-Nisa'* Allah SWT says,

$$\text{يَٰٓأَيُّهَا ٱلنَّاسُ قَدْ جَآءَكُم بُرْهَٰنٌ مِّن رَّبِّكُمْ وَأَنزَلْنَآ إِلَيْكُمْ نُورًا مُّبِينًا} \ (١٧٤)$$

"O mankind, verily there has come to you convincing proof from your Lord and We send down to you a manifested light." (Q 4, V 174)

In other places in the *Qur'an*, we find the same trend in seeking proof and encouraging explanations and reasoning. The teachings of Prophet Muhammad PBUH also encourage this concept. "It was reported that when a young man came to the prophet PBUH asking him permission to fornicate, the prophet PBUH told him, "Would you like it for your mother?"

The young man said, "No."

The prophet then asked him, "Would you like it for your sister?"
He said "No."

The prophet then asked him, "Would you like it for your aunt?"
He said "No."

The prophet then asked him "Would you like it for your cousin?"
He said "No."

Then the prophet PBUH told him, "Likewise, people would not like it for their female relatives," and he put his hand on the young man's chest and prayed that Allah grant him chastity."

You see the reasoning of the prophet PBUH with this young man. He explained in a very clear and detailed way. In another example, It was narrated by *Abu Hurairah* may Allah be pleased with him that a man complained, "O Allah's Messenger, my wife has given birth to a black son."

The prophet asked, "Have you any camels."

The man replied, "Yes."

The prophet asked, "What is their color?"

The man replied, "They are red."

The prophet asked, "Is there a dusky one among them?"

The man replied, "Yes."

The prophet asked, "How has that come about?"

The man replied, "It is perhaps a strain to which it has reverted."

The prophet said, "It is perhaps a strain to which this son has reverted" (agreed upon).

The above examples are very clear indications that we should always reason and explain issues clearly. As such, when we deal with our children, especially our teenagers, we should always reason and explain things to them. It is not enough to tell your teen, 'do this and that because you're Muslim," you have to explain why he should do it and what the benefits of doing it are. This way, he will be convinced that every thing we are asked to do in Islam is for a good reason. Without this, he will feel that Islam is just one restriction after another. This may require us parents to raise our level of understanding of Islam, but this is a very important step in helping our teens move from the state of knowledge to the state of conviction.

Following is how one of our daughters, *Hoda* valued our reasoning with her on various subjects and how important it was to her,

"The process of reasoning has always played a very important part in my life, in my relationships, and in my understanding of concepts. My parents reasoned with me whenever introducing rules, discussing, and even during disagreements. I remember endless hours of reasoning with my parents through which I could come to understand their perspective and respect the rules with which they presented me.

I remember that when I was in junior high, at about thirteen years old, I approached my mother and asked her if it would be okay for me to go to the dance that they were having at school. Now, this probably came as a surprise to her, because several dances had already passed that year and I had never shown any desire to attend any of them. I had explained to my friends that I don't go to dances because I don't socialize with boys so I shouldn't dance at all. After a few dances, my friends told me that they really don't dance at the dances; they just stand around and talk amongst themselves and don't really socialize with the boys either.

"*Hoda*," they asked me, "come to the next dance and we won't talk to the boys at all. We'll stand at the wall far away from the boys' side and we'll just talk together. It'll be fun."

In my opinion at the time, it seemed like a reasonable solution. I wasn't sure if my mom would go for it though, because there would still be music blasting through the gym. Something inside of me kept telling me "Go *Hoda*. You won't really be doing anything wrong and you'll finally get to see what these dances are like. Look how much your friends were willing to give up just to have you there with them. Come on, go." So I asked my mom.

My mom didn't panic or get upset with me, but she wasn't about to let me go to the dance either. Instead, she took the opportunity to teach me a very important and basic Islamic concept: blocking any paths that lead to evil. She explained to me that the purpose of a dance was for boys and girls to meet and become attracted to each other (that I agreed with, but I argued that that wasn't why I was going there).

"You may not be going with that intention, *Hoda*," she explained, "but if that's the purpose of the gathering and you go to it anyway, then you're taking one small step in the wrong direction. Once you get accustomed to being there in that environment, then, slowly, other things that are happening there won't seem so bad after all. Bit by bit, you could be pulled in without noticing. By not going to the dances at all, you keep a clear line between what's right and what's wrong and you aren't getting into any paths that lead you to wrongdoings."

She was patient with me and she answered my questions in many different ways. Having had this kind of discussion with my mom, I could approach my friends confidently and tell them that I would not be going to the dance, because in the case that they would ask me "why not?" (Which I was sure they would), I had a full answer prepared.

Fasting during *Ramadan* was also explained to me in very explicit terms. My parents told me about those living in poverty. We would not really be able to understand them by simply talking about them, but to experience the feeling of hunger day after day would bring us much closer to their reality. Also, when we refrain from eating and drinking and we keep in mind those who do not have food and water regularly, those who do not have the emotional security that the fridge is full and that it is only a matter of time before they eat, we can *insha' Allah* come closer to a true appreciation of Allah's bounties on us. This way, we learn not to be wasteful through developing a deep sense of gratitude for all that we are given, every last drop and every last crumb. Fasting is not only about refraining from food or water, but also refraining from any bad words and bad actions. Of course, *Ramadan* is a great time to start stopping the bad habits we may have, like name calling or yelling, but it is not the only time. After *Ramadan* is over, we must continue practicing what we have learned to do during Ramadan, so that this will be a process of continual self-improvement *insha' Allah*.

Another very important thing that my parents used reasoning in, was the concept of the *hijab*. This was something we discussed before I wore my hijab and, of course, after I wore it as well. Because the hijab makes the difference between Muslims and non-Muslims so obvious, I often asked my parents why we wore the *hijab*. Their answer was always detailed, multi-leveled, and left open for further discussion. They never only said, "Because Allah told us to". Don't get me wrong. That Allah has commanded us to do something is of great importance, but, at that stage of my life, I couldn't possibly be fully satisfied if that was where the answer had stopped. They told me that Allah told us to wear *hijab* because He loves us and He knows what is best for us. Allah knows that when we wear the *hijab* it will protect us from committing bad deeds that are related to boy-girl interactions. The *hijab* is a tool that will help us and the people around us focus on our personality and not on our looks. This way, instead of worrying about how a pair of jeans fit on me, how I should do my hair today, or putting on makeup to cover up skin blemishes, I can concentrate on improving my character. Those around me, also, will have to judge me based on my personality and not my looks. This way, I can be respected for who I am, *Alhamdulillah*.

When my parents reasoned with me about the hijab and about *Ramadan*, it made it easy for me to wear the hijab and to fast when the time came. It wasn't like I was faced with a decision in completely foreign territory. No, I already knew what this was about, so it wasn't as scary as the unknown. Another benefit of the reasoning process with my parents was that it made me realize that they really knew what they were talking about. They didn't just pull these rules out of a hat and order me to follow them. For almost every rule my parents had, I would ask them why. For every time I asked why, I received an answer that was as long and detailed as I required it to be. This gave me the confidence and trust in my parents' judgment that made it easier for me to respect and appreciate their rules. In turn, this eased the pressure off me when I was confronted on the street or in school by questions from non-Muslims. If the issue that they brought up was one that I had already discussed with my parents, then, chances were I had an answer and was previously prepared for the confrontation *Alhamdulillah.* If the particular question that they brought up was a new one to me, then at least I had the fortune of knowing that when I went home that night, because of the trust developed between my parents and I, I would tell my parents about the incident, together we would discuss it, and they would provide me *insha' Allah* with the answers that Allah has provided us with."

Proper Islamic conflict resolution

Proper conflict resolution is very important to follow when there is a difference of opinions or any conflict between parents and their teens. Parents have to abide by the teachings of the prophet PBUH and allow the teen to present his case and his point of view while they are attentively listening. Then they can try to reach an agreement, which is acceptable to every body. When they reach the agreement, the teen will honor his part of the agreement because he feels that he has participated in the decision making process. On the other hand, if parents try to impose their own point of view without giving the teen a fair chance to present his case, the teen may not be eager to implement the final decision. Also, by using proper conflict resolution, parents are training their teen in how to resolve conflicts in a positive way.

Islam provides a wonderful framework and valuable guidelines for conflict resolution as well as disciplining techniques. This is important for parents to learn, since even with the most successful parents, conflicts do happen between them and their teens. Using proper conflict resolution methods and techniques, which are based on *Qur'anic* teachings as well as the teachings of Prophet Muhammad PBUH, will ensure a higher rate of success with our teens. It will also help in keeping a strong bond between parents and teens, a healthy family atmosphere, and an open channel of communication. These are very important factors without which parents would not find it easy to work with their teens and instill the important concepts we will discuss in the next chapter. This is another crucial reason for parents to familiarize themselves with the Islamic methodology of dealing with conflicts. We try to address this issue in the next few pages.

Islamic Guidelines for conflict resolution

A successful Islamic conflict management and resolution technique utilizes a combination of an open mind and heart, accommodation, suspension of judgment, forgiveness, gentleness, calmness, and above all anger control. It also tries to get to the core of the problem and find the proper, permanent solution rather than providing superficial treatment, which deals only with the symptoms of the problem. Let us now discuss some conflict resolution guidelines in detail and see how we can benefit from them as parents.

Take initiative

Whenever a conflict takes place between two Muslims, the one who takes the initiative to resolve the problem and starts by greeting the other party is considered the better person, according to the teachings of Prophet Muhammad, may Allah's peace and blessings be upon him. *Abu Ayub*, may Allah be pleased with him, relates that the messenger of Allah said, "It is not proper for a Muslim to keep away from his Muslim brother for more than three days so much so that when they meet they move away from each other. The better of them is the one who is first to salute the other" (*Bukhari and Muslim*)

It was also reported by *Abu Hurairah*, may Allah be pleased with him, that the messenger of Allah, may Allah's peace and blessings be upon him said, "It is not lawful for a Muslim to be angry with his brother for more than three days. If one remains angry with his brother for more than three days, and he dies during this interval, he will go to hell" (*Abu Dawoud*)

Forgive and forget

In *Surah Al-Imran*, Allah says,

وَسَارِعُوٓاْ إِلَىٰ مَغْفِرَةٍ مِّن رَّبِّكُمْ وَجَنَّةٍ عَرْضُهَا السَّمَـٰوَٰتُ وَٱلْأَرْضُ أُعِدَّتْ لِلْمُتَّقِينَ ﴿١٣٣﴾ ٱلَّذِينَ يُنفِقُونَ فِى ٱلسَّرَّآءِ وَٱلضَّرَّآءِ وَٱلْكَـٰظِمِينَ ٱلْغَيْظَ وَٱلْعَافِينَ عَنِ ٱلنَّاسِ وَٱللَّهُ يُحِبُّ ٱلْمُحْسِنِينَ ﴿١٣٤﴾

"And be quick in seeking forgiveness from your Lord and a Heaven whose width is as the width of the earth and sky, which is prepared for those who exercise *Taqwa*, those who spend at easy as well as at difficult times, those who control their anger, and those who pardon people. Allah certainly loves those who exercise Ihsan." (Q 3, V 133-134)

In *Surah AlShura,* Allah says,

فَمَآ أُوتِيتُم مِّن شَىْءٍ فَمَتَٰعُ ٱلْحَيَوٰةِ ٱلدُّنْيَا وَمَا عِندَ ٱللَّهِ خَيْرٌ وَأَبْقَىٰ لِلَّذِينَ ءَامَنُوا وَعَلَىٰ رَبِّهِمْ يَتَوَكَّلُونَ ۝ وَٱلَّذِينَ يَجْتَنِبُونَ كَبَٰٓئِرَ ٱلْإِثْمِ وَٱلْفَوَٰحِشَ وَإِذَا مَا غَضِبُوا هُمْ يَغْفِرُونَ ۝

"...But that which is with Allah is better and more lasting for those who believe in the Oneness of Allah and put their trust in their Lord. And those who avoid the greater sins and Al-Fawahish, and when they are angry, forgive." (Q 42, V 36-37)

In *Surah Al-Aa'raf,* Allah says,

خُذِ ٱلْعَفْوَ وَأْمُرْ بِٱلْعُرْفِ وَأَعْرِضْ عَنِ ٱلْجَٰهِلِينَ ۝

"Show forgiveness, enjoin what is good and turn away from the foolish (i.e. don't punish them)." (Q 7, V 199)

These verses clearly illustrate the importance of forgiving others. It considers those who do such acts as the Mutaqeen. It also indicates that Allah loves them and promises them a great and lasting reward in the hereafter.

The teachings of Prophet Muhammad, may Allah's peace and blessings be upon him, further emphasize the importance of forgiving and pardoning in human relations in general and particularly when it involves family members.

It was reported by *Anas Ibn Malik,* may Allah be pleased with him, that the messenger of Allah, may Allah's peace and blessings be upon him, has said, "Neither nurse mutual hatred, nor envy, nor abandon each other, and be fellow brothers and servants of Allah. It is not lawful for a Muslim that he should keep his relation estranged with his brother beyond three days" (agreed upon).

Also It was reported by *Abu Hurairah* may Allah be pleased with him that a man said to the messenger of Allah, may Allah's peace and blessings be upon him, "I have relatives with whom I have tried to reunite, but they continue to sever their relationship with me. I try to treat them kindly, but they treat me badly, with them I am gentle, but with me they are rough."

The prophet PBUH replied, "If you are as you say, you will not be without supporters against them from Allah as long as you do so." (*Muslim*)

It was also narrated by *Ubada Ibn Al-Samad*, may Allah be pleased with him, that the messenger of Allah PBUH said, "Shall I tell you about what would elevate your ranks and increase your honor?"

Those with him replied, "Yes, oh messenger of Allah."

He said, "Exercise forbearance with the one who is ignorant with you, forgive the one who has wronged you, give to the one who didn't give you, and establish good relations with the one who severs his relations with you." (*At-Tabarani*)

Forgetting and forgiving plays a great role in keeping healthy relations between family members. Here is how one of our teens; *Sumaiya* describes the importance of this factor in her relationship with her mother.

"Quarrels, arguments, disputes, controversies, or squabbles, however it is you label disagreements, they're all the same in the end. In a healthy relationship, it's only natural to have differences of opinion that can result in a disagreement. What's important is that this disagreement doesn't result in a grudge. My mother and I, *Alhamdulillah,* have a great relationship. We discuss almost everything with each other and confide in each other a lot. But, naturally, we also get into disputes or small quarrels with each other. So, how do we maintain such a strong relationship year in and year out when we have these controversies? The answer lies in the way we deal with them. The most important thing is that we won't let them escalate or pile up. The key idea is that we don't hold grudges. We drop it and start a new. Simply put, we forgive and forget."

Control your anger

Among the great advice of the prophet, may Allah's peace and blessings be upon him, is the advice not to be angry.

On the authority of *Abu Hurairah*, may Allah be pleased with him, who narrated that a man asked the Messenger of Allah, may Allah's peace and blessings be upon him, to give him a piece of advice, he said, "Don't be angry." The man repeated his question several times and the prophet replied, "Don't be angry." (*Bukhari*)

In another agreed upon *hadeeth*, the prophet, may Allah's peace and blessings be upon him, defined the strong person as the one who controls himself in a fit of rage, and not the one who wrestles others.

On the authority of *Mu'ath Ibn Anas*, may Allah be pleased with him, who narrated that the prophet, may Allah's peace and blessings be upon him, said, "The one who swallows up anger will be called out by Allah, the Exalted, to the forefront of the creatures on the Day of Resurrection and will be put to option about any pure-eyed virgin, he will like." (*Abu Dawoud and At-Termithy*)

Not only did the prophet, may Allah's peace and blessings be upon him, warned us against getting angry, but he also taught us the best anger management techniques:

– Seek refuge with Allah from Satan: On the authority of *Suliman Ibn Surd*, may Allah be pleased with him, that two people began to quarrel with each other in front of the prophet, may Allah's peace and blessings be upon him. One of them was so angry that his face had turned red and the veins on his neck were swollen. The messenger of Allah said, "I know of a phrase that, if he were to utter it, his fit of rage would be relaxed, and that phrase is: I seek refuge with Allah from Satan, the accursed." So the companions said to him, "the messenger of Allah said, 'seek refuge with Allah from Satan, the outcast'" (agreed upon).

– Change your position: It was narrated that the messenger of Allah, may Allah's peace and blessings be upon him, said, "if one of you gets angry while he's standing, let him sit down, and if he is still angry, let him lie down." (*Ahmad*)

– Perform wudu': It was narrated that the prophet, may Allah's peace and blessings be upon him, said, "anger is from Satan and Satan is created from fire, and fire is extinguished by water; so if one of you becomes angry let him perform wudu'." (*Abu Dawoud*)

– Be silent: It was narrated that the prophet, PBUH, said, "If one of you gets angry let him be silent." (*Ahmad*)

Parents should make use of all these wonderful techniques in managing their anger when they're in a conflict with their children. Parents should not be quick to react when they are upset with their teens, but should use one of the above strategies instead. It may be difficult at first, and it does take training but these techniques are very helpful and make it a lot easier to avoid unnecessary added problems. Parents should also teach their children these anger management techniques, and train them to exercise these methods.

No name-calling

Allah SWT tells us in *Surah Al-Hujorat,*

يَـٰٓأَيُّهَا ٱلَّذِينَ ءَامَنُوا۟ لَا يَسْخَرْ قَوْمٌ مِّن قَوْمٍ عَسَىٰٓ أَن يَكُونُوا۟ خَيْرًا مِّنْهُمْ وَلَا نِسَآءٌ مِّن نِّسَآءٍ عَسَىٰٓ أَن يَكُنَّ خَيْرًا مِّنْهُنَّ وَلَا تَلْمِزُوٓا۟ أَنفُسَكُمْ وَلَا تَنَابَزُوا۟ بِٱلْأَلْقَـٰبِ بِئْسَ ٱلِٱسْمُ ٱلْفُسُوقُ بَعْدَ ٱلْإِيمَـٰنِ وَمَن لَّمْ يَتُبْ فَأُو۟لَـٰٓئِكَ هُمُ ٱلظَّـٰلِمُونَ ﴿١١﴾

"Do not call each others names or humiliate one another." (Q 49, V 11)

This applies to everyone, but it applies even more to us in the way we deal with our children. Humiliation destroys the teen's self-esteem and we don't want our teens to end up having weak personalities. We all want strong and confident teens to be able to face the challenges of this society as we discussed in the previous chapter. Also, the prophet PBUH was described as a person who never used foul language or cursed others.

The use of active listening techniques described earlier in this chapter is also helpful in conflict resolution and tends to keep problems from escalating.

Following the above guidelines and being accommodating to others' views helps greatly in ensuring that parents are being objective and dealing with the root of the problem and not only the symptoms. This will ensure a win-win situation and the teen will feel that he is part of the process. As such, he will tend to honor his part of the agreement.

Next is a real-life example of a small conflict we had about brand name clothing, and how following these guidelines of reasoning and controlling anger helped to solve our problem and keep everyone happy while we did. This is expressed by our youngest daughter *Sumaiya*:

"I stared longingly at the green and white Adidas jacket hanging in the store window. It looked really comfortable and the word "Adidas" printed across it diagonally was so strategically placed. I thought about how nice that Adidas jacket would look on me. I was in grade seven at the time and almost all my classmates wore some sort of brand name item at least from time to time. Brand names are always going to be around bombarding a teenager. In the younger years, they're Adidas, Nike, or Fila; as you grow older, they change to Gap, Guess, Tommy Hilfiger, Club Monaco, Jacob, Old Navy etc. Before my eyes met this jacket, I really hadn't thought or cared much for brand names, but I had started to notice all my friends' wardrobes changing to accommodate brand names. Now I even knew this one girl who had Nike jewellery as well as the jacket, pants and shoes. Seriously, this girl had Nike earrings and a Nike ring. I decided to ask my parents if they could buy me the jacket as a present, for Eid. However there was one problem, this spring jacket was somewhere in the vicinity of $60; which was probably more money than my parents had ever paid for one of their spring jackets and I was only 13! My parents had always stressed the importance of being careful and responsible with your money, no matter how rich or poor you might be. They often mentioned the Prophet Muhammad PBUH's hadeeth about how we will be accountable for how we used the blessings that Allah has endowed us with, including money. At dinner that evening, I told my parents about the jacket that, to me, appeared so beautiful and asked them if they could buy it for me as my *Eid* present as *Eid* was soon approaching. And then the inevitable question was popped: they wanted to know how much this wonderful Adidas jacket cost and I dreaded having to respond. Very hesitantly, I answered "Umm…sixty dollars."

I braced myself, Oh no! Were they going to yell at me for even suggesting such a crazy thing, wasting $60 on a spring jacket when that money could most definitely be put to much better use. Well, no such response came. On the contrary, my parents were actually very calm as they explained to me that $60 was a lot of money and that it was probably that much just because it was a brand name jacket. But that response was not enough for me; it didn't satisfy that inner crave and desire for the jacket. The response was absolutely logical but I didn't want logic at that time, I wanted that beautiful Adidas jacket that hung so nicely in the store window.

My parents could tell I was not convinced and I told them that I really wanted that jacket. I don't quite know why it was so important to me then. Maybe it was because all my friends had some brand name clothes and to me that jacket represented a sense of belonging or maybe I just really liked the jacket. Whatever it was, it wasn't going away and my parents realized that. My mom put the time an effort in to make the trip to the store with me and take a look at this jacket that she'd heard so much about. This was very important to me because it showed that my feelings and needs (though this was not a need per say) mattered to her. She cared about my desires, as absurd as they may be, and didn't make me feel bad about them. In the back of my mind, though I didn't want to admit it to myself, I knew that buying that jacket would be a waste of money and that I could get a non-brand name jacket of the same quality for half the price of this one. But did that matter to me at the time? Did that really matter to me as a 13 year old girl in junior high school? The jacket to me was a halal way of fitting in, of not standing out too much from the rest of my friends since there were already many things I did and wore differently that set me apart from the rest. My mother seemed to understand why I wanted this expensive jacket so badly. She explained, however, that brand names don't increase the worth of a person but that if I wanted it so badly, I must contribute to it's cost. So we made a deal that we'd split the cost. My parents would pay for half of the jacket as a present for me for *Eid* and I would pay for the other half. Now, I paid for some of it using money from my allowance but you must remember that I was only 13 and wasn't exactly swimming in money. So my mother told me that I could do extra work around the house to pay for my share of the jacket.

So I worked, I cleaned, I washed, I scrubbed, I fixed, all for my wonderful jacket. Through my labors, I understood the value of money and I realized that it was really something not to be taken for granted, no matter how much of it you had. I developed an appreciation for the work my father did everyday, and he had much more to pay for than half the price of my Adidas jacket. When I had finally earned enough money, I went out and bought the jacket. Excited, I wore it to school the next day, but I realized that having a brand name printed across my back was not going to help me be a better person.

Ultimately, Adidas didn't care if I was the most or least popular girl at school, they just wanted my money. My friends didn't treat me any differently because now I had an Adidas jacket, sure I got a few compliments about my new jacket here and there but Adidas did not make me any nicer, smarter, or funnier – that was up to me."

For another example illustrating the implementation of conflict resolution, along with the use of behavioral contracts, see *Safiya*'s case in chapter nine.

Other principles to follow to raise your teen from a level of knowledge to a level of conviction: Avoid greater harms by selecting the lesser harms

This is a great rule in Islamic jurisprudence that was deduced by the scholars from the practices of the prophet PBUH and the teachings of *Qur'an*. This rule should be understood properly and used and applied wisely by parents in the North American environment. We have come across a great number of cases where committed Muslim parents failed miserably to use this rule and ended up driving their children away from Islam. Some of those children became completely lost to the mainstream North American society while others are at an unacceptable level of Islamic commitment and practice. On the other hand, we have also come across some parents who were wise enough to use this rule properly and, with the help of Allah, ended up protecting their children from deviating from Islam. Most of those children are at a very good level of commitment to Islam and are very good practicing Muslims now alhamdulillah. Let us illustrate what we mean by an example.

When it comes time for a young woman to wear a *hijab*, some parents insist that she wears long, loose dresses (*Jilbab*) or skirts and a long khimar right away. While this may be closer to the full hijab, it is often an extreme change for the young woman to make and she may not feel ready for it. In some cases we have seen, this has caused the young woman to completely deviate from Islam. This is the greater harm. Other parents see that the daughter does not feel ready to make a complete change, and allow her to start by wearing loose pants and loose, long-sleeved shirts with her headscarf. While this is the minimum for hijab, it is better that the young woman starts off gradually, and makes the change to looser clothing when she is ready. This way, we have avoided the greater harm of deviation by allowing the lesser harm of a temporary lower level of *hijab*. While the young woman is in this first stage of wearing *hijab*, the parents should help her to strengthen her belief so that she may eventually feel ready to move on to the next level.

Following this principle will help teens to feel that Islam makes sense and doesn't enforce or impose things on people without preparing them and making them ready to carry huge responsibilities. This will help in elevating your teen's level from knowledge to conviction *insha' Allah*.

Use examples that they can relate to

The prophet PBUH always used to use examples from the immediate environment to make sure that the audience he was addressing clearly understood what he meant. It was reported that the prophet PBUH said, "If the hour is to happen and one of you has a small plant in his hands and he is able to plant it, let him plant it."

It was also reported by *Abu Musa Al Ash'ari*, may Allah be pleased with him, that the prophet, may Allah's peace and blessings be upon him, said, "The example of a Muslim who studies *Qur'an* is like the orange which is aromatic and delicious. And the example of a Muslim who doesn't recite *Qur'an* is like a dried date, which has no aroma but is sweet. The example of a hypocrite who recites *Qur'an* is like a basal which is scented, yet tastes bitter, and the example of a hypocrite who doesn't recite *Qur'an* is like a fruit which has no aroma and is better in taste" (agreed upon).

You see how the prophet PBUH used various types of fruits and produce in this hadeeth that were known to the Arabs and grew in their environment. This was to bring the meaning close to their hearts and minds. This was to make them understand the concept clearly and learn the lesson he was trying to teach.

Using examples from the immediate environment brings closeness among people. As such, it is important for parents to use examples from their environment while they are interacting with their children—

especially teenagers – to make it easier for them to relate. This imposes a great responsibility on parents in terms of understanding the North American environment, knowing what it calls for, adopting what is good in it, and rejecting what is bad. The following are few examples to illustrate this principle:

a) If you have a quiz coming up, how long would you take to prepare for it? If you have a test, how long would you study for it. If you have an exam, how long would you need to study? Think of the Day of Judgment as the biggest exam you will ever face, and think of this life as the time you have to prepare for it.

b) When you want to tell them that consistency is important, and that we have to regularly do the right thing, even it's in little doses as we were told by the prophet PBUH, "The best of deeds are the ones which are continuous even if they are little," It may be a good idea to give them the example of regular physical fitness training.

You may say, "If you want to be strong and participate in a sports competition you need to train every day even if you train only a little bit. If you train only once, no matter how intense it is, you won't have the endurance required for the competition."

There is no doubt that this will bring the ideas close to home and help the teen in her quest for moving from the state of knowledge to the state of conviction.

Touch their soul and awaken their conscience

In an authentic hadeeth that was narrated by both *Bukhari* and *Muslim*, Two men came to the prophet PBUH to resolve a dispute that occurred between them. The prophet PBUH told them both, "I am a human being like you and when you ask my judgment in an issue, and perhaps one of you is more eloquent and expressive while presenting his case, I may judge in his favor because of this although the right may be with his counterpart. If I do this, I am giving him a piece of fire and he is free to take it or leave it." Upon hearing this, both companions started crying and both of them wanted to forfeit his right and leave it to his brother. You see how the prophet PBUH awakened their consciences to the extent that they were even willing to sacrifice some of their rights to avoid being unjust or ending up having piece of hell fire.

The best way to touch the soul of your teens -and for this matter any human being- is to use the wonderful methodology of the *Qur'an*. The Qur'an is the word of The Creator, and The Creator knows His creation and what affects them most and touches their hearts and souls. As such, *Qur'anic* methodology tends to have a great effect on people. The simplest and the most direct and effective way to explain a subject or to try to influence and affect the views of somebody to use the language and methodology of the *Qur'an*. For example, some people insist on talking about Islamic creed (*Aqeeda*) or explaining the attributes of Allah SWT in a very technical and academic way, using dry expressions and confusing language. Neither the *Qur'an* nor the prophet PBUH ever presented Aqeeda or the attributes of Allah in this way. For example, when Qur'an talks about Allah's attribute of being "*Alqader*", which translates into the ability to do anything, it touches the souls and the hearts of the readers by illustrating this attribute using a deep story. This is clearly illustrated *Surah Baqarah,*

أَوْ كَالَّذِى مَرَّ عَلَىٰ قَرْيَةٍ وَهِىَ خَاوِيَةٌ عَلَىٰ عُرُوشِهَا قَالَ أَنَّىٰ يُحْىِۦ هَٰذِهِ ٱللَّهُ بَعْدَ مَوْتِهَا ۖ فَأَمَاتَهُ ٱللَّهُ مِائَةَ عَامٍ ثُمَّ بَعَثَهُۥ ۖ قَالَ كَمْ لَبِثْتَ ۖ قَالَ لَبِثْتُ يَوْمًا أَوْ بَعْضَ يَوْمٍ ۖ قَالَ بَل لَّبِثْتَ مِائَةَ عَامٍ فَٱنظُرْ إِلَىٰ طَعَامِكَ وَشَرَابِكَ لَمْ يَتَسَنَّهْ ۖ وَٱنظُرْ إِلَىٰ حِمَارِكَ وَلِنَجْعَلَكَ ءَايَةً لِّلنَّاسِ ۖ وَٱنظُرْ إِلَى ٱلْعِظَامِ كَيْفَ نُنشِزُهَا ثُمَّ نَكْسُوهَا لَحْمًا ۚ فَلَمَّا تَبَيَّنَ لَهُۥ قَالَ أَعْلَمُ أَنَّ ٱللَّهَ عَلَىٰ كُلِّ شَىْءٍ قَدِيرٌ ﴿٢٥٩﴾

"Or like the one who passed by and it had tumbled over its roof. He said, "How will Allah ever bring it to life after its death?" So Allah caused him to die for a hundred years, then raised him up again. He said," How long did you remain (in slumber)?" He (the man) said, "Perhaps I remained a day or a part of a day". He said, "you have remained (dead) for a hundred years, look at your food and your drink, they show no change; and look at your donkey! And thus we have made of you a sign for the people. Look at the bones, how we bring them together and clothe them with flesh". When this was clearly shown to him, he said, "I know that Allah is Able to do all things"" (Q 2, V 259).

Another example is given in *Surah Mariam* illustrating the stories of *Zakaria* PBUH and the story of the miraculous birth of Isa PBUH (Q 19, V 7-9 and V 16-34).

When the *Qur'an* wants to illustrate the attribute of "*Al-Aleem*", which translates into the one who knows everything, again it touches the hearts of the readers with its eloquent language and wonderful presentation. For example, in *Surah Al-ana'am*, Allah says,

$$\text{۞ وَعِندَهُ مَفَاتِحُ ٱلْغَيْبِ لَا يَعْلَمُهَآ إِلَّا هُوَ وَيَعْلَمُ مَا فِى}$$
$$\text{ٱلْبَرِّ وَٱلْبَحْرِ وَمَا تَسْقُطُ مِن وَرَقَةٍ إِلَّا يَعْلَمُهَا وَلَا حَبَّةٍ}$$
$$\text{فِى ظُلُمَٰتِ ٱلْأَرْضِ وَلَا رَطْبٍ وَلَا يَابِسٍ إِلَّا فِى كِتَٰبٍ مُّبِينٍ ﴿٥٩﴾}$$

"And with Him are the keys of the *Ghaib*, (all that is hidden), none know them but He. And He knows whatever there in (or on) the earth and the sea; not a leaf falls but He knows it. There is not a grain in the darkness of the earth, nor anything fresh or dry, but is written in a clear record." (Q 6, V 59)

Here is an example of how to use this with your teen

1. During picnics, or hiking trips try always to allocate time to enjoy nature and observe the wonderful creation of Allah. Trees, flowers, ants and bees. Always make the right comment and praise Allah for His wonderful creation. This will soften their hearts and make them close to Allah's creation.

Illustrate consequences in a vivid way

The prophet, may Allah's peace and blessings be upon him, used to illustrate the consequences of bad deeds in a very vivid way. This was to get the attention of Muslims and emphasize how bad these deeds were so they would not commit them. Following are some examples illustrating this principle:

1. *Ibn Abbas*, may Allah be pleased with him, reported that the messenger of Allah PBUH said, "A man who takes back his charity is like a dog who eats its own vomit" (agreed upon).

2. *Nu'man Ibn Basheer*, may Allah be pleased with him, narrated that the prophet PBUH said, "The likeness of the man who remains passive in the prescribed crimes of Allah and the man who commits them is like people who have got on board a ship after casting lots, some of them on its lower and some of them on its upper deck. Those who are on its lower deck would have to pass by those who are on the upper deck every time they want to bring water and thus they have troubled them. They said, "If we dig a hole in our share (the bottom of the ship), we won't have to go to the upper deck every time we need water." If those in the upper deck left them to dig the hole, they would destroy them and also destroy themselves. If they prevented them, they will save them and save themselves." (*Bukhari*)

3. *Ibn Abbas*, may Allah be pleased with him, reported that the messenger of Allah PBUH saw a person with a gold signet ring on his hand. He pulled it off and threw it away saying, "One of you is bringing a piece of fire from Hell and putting it on his hand." It was said to the man after Allah's messenger PBUH had left, "take your ring and derive benefit out of it," whereupon he said, "I would never take it where Allah's messenger has thrown it away." (*Muslim*)

The above examples show clearly that the prophet PBUH illustrated the consequences of bad deeds in a very vivid way to have a lasting impact on his companions and stay alive in their minds. This ensured strict adherence by the companions to the instructions and guidance of the prophet PBUH.

Parents should try to use this principle with their teens, rather than just telling them, "No, you can't do this" or, "this is haram." Here is an example on how to apply this principle with your teen:

If your teen becomes lazy and doesn't do his homework properly or complete his assigned tasks, you can sit down with him and discuss the issue in a quiet way, trying to convince him that it is important for his future to work hard so he can be a person of value and be able to hold down a job in the future. If his behavior still isn't up to par, you can take him with you downtown and show him some of the homeless people on the streets. Ask him if this is how he would like to be in the future. Tell him this might be what happens if he neglects his work and doesn't do what it takes to become a successful person.

Utilize opportunities

The story of prophet *Yousef*, may Allah's peace and blessings be upon him, with his inmates is a very clear illustration for this principle.

وَدَخَلَ مَعَهُ ٱلسِّجْنَ فَتَيَانِ قَالَ أَحَدُهُمَآ إِنِّىٓ أَرَىٰنِىٓ أَعْصِرُ خَمْرًا وَقَالَ ٱلْأَخَرُ إِنِّىٓ أَرَىٰنِىٓ أَحْمِلُ فَوْقَ رَأْسِى خُبْزًا تَأْكُلُ ٱلطَّيْرُ مِنْهُ نَبِّئْنَا بِتَأْوِيلِهِۦٓ إِنَّا نَرَىٰكَ مِنَ ٱلْمُحْسِنِينَ ٣٦ قَالَ لَا يَأْتِيكُمَا طَعَامٌ تُرْزَقَانِهِۦٓ إِلَّا نَبَّأْتُكُمَا بِتَأْوِيلِهِۦ قَبْلَ أَن يَأْتِيَكُمَا ذَٰلِكُمَا مِمَّا عَلَّمَنِى رَبِّىٓ إِنِّى تَرَكْتُ مِلَّةَ قَوْمٍ لَّا يُؤْمِنُونَ بِٱللَّهِ وَهُم بِٱلْأَخِرَةِ هُمْ كَٰفِرُونَ ٣٧ وَٱتَّبَعْتُ مِلَّةَ ءَابَآءِىٓ إِبْرَٰهِيمَ وَإِسْحَٰقَ وَيَعْقُوبَ مَا كَانَ لَنَآ أَن نُّشْرِكَ بِٱللَّهِ مِن شَىْءٍ ذَٰلِكَ مِن فَضْلِ ٱللَّهِ عَلَيْنَا وَعَلَى ٱلنَّاسِ وَلَٰكِنَّ أَكْثَرَ ٱلنَّاسِ لَا يَشْكُرُونَ ٣٨ يَٰصَٰحِبَىِ ٱلسِّجْنِ ءَأَرْبَابٌ مُّتَفَرِّقُونَ خَيْرٌ أَمِ ٱللَّهُ ٱلْوَٰحِدُ ٱلْقَهَّارُ ٣٩ مَا تَعْبُدُونَ مِن دُونِهِۦٓ إِلَّآ أَسْمَآءً سَمَّيْتُمُوهَآ أَنتُمْ وَءَابَآؤُكُم مَّآ أَنزَلَ ٱللَّهُ بِهَا مِن سُلْطَٰنٍ إِنِ ٱلْحُكْمُ إِلَّا لِلَّهِ أَمَرَ أَلَّا تَعْبُدُوٓا۟ إِلَّآ إِيَّاهُ ذَٰلِكَ ٱلدِّينُ ٱلْقَيِّمُ وَلَٰكِنَّ أَكْثَرَ ٱلنَّاسِ لَا يَعْلَمُونَ ٤٠ يَٰصَٰحِبَىِ ٱلسِّجْنِ أَمَّآ أَحَدُكُمَا فَيَسْقِى رَبَّهُۥ خَمْرًا وَأَمَّا ٱلْأَخَرُ فَيُصْلَبُ فَتَأْكُلُ ٱلطَّيْرُ مِن رَّأْسِهِ قُضِىَ ٱلْأَمْرُ ٱلَّذِى فِيهِ تَسْتَفْتِيَانِ ٤١

"And there entered with him two young men in the
prison. One of them said, "Verily I saw myself (in a dream)
pressing wine." The other said, "Verily I saw myself (in
a dream) carrying bread on my head and birds eating
thereof." (They said) Inform us of the interpretation of this.
Verily we think you are one of the good doers. He said,
"No food will come to you but I will inform its interpretation before it comes. This is of that which my Lord has
taught me. Verily I have abandoned the religion of a people
that believe not in Allah and are disbelievers in the
hereafter, and have followed the religion of my fathers
Ibraheem, Ishaq, and Ya'qoob and never could we attribute
any partners whatsoever to Allah. This is from the grace of
Allah to us and to mankind, but most men thank not. O two
companion of prison, are many lords (gods) better or Allah
the One, the Irresistible? You don't worship but only names
that you have named (forged)- you and your fathers for
which Allah has sent no authority. The command is for none
but Allah. He has commanded that you worship none but
Him. That is the true straight religion, but most men know
not. O two companion of the prison, as for one of you, he
will pour wine for his master to drink; and as for the other
he will be crucified and birds will eat from his head. Thus
is the case judged concerning that which you inquired."
(Q 12, V 36-41)

You see how he used the opportunity to make *Da'wa* to them when
they asked him to interpret their dreams. He didn't answer their inquiry
directly, but first he talked to them about the issue that concerned him, the
Oneness of Allah. He had their attention and was able to deliver his
message in the most effective way to them.

It was also reported that Prophet Muhammad PBUH was walking
with his companion and saw a dead sheep, he asked them, "Who amongst
you would buy this sheep with a *Derham*[1]?"

They responded, "None of us."

The prophet PBUH said, "Likewise is the value of this worldly life;
it is the same like the value of this dead sheep." You see how the prophet
PBUH used the occasion to emphasize the fact that the value of this life

---

[1] *Derham* is the lowest denomination of the Arabic currency at that time.

is very little compared to the bounties prepared by Allah in the hereafter. These bounties are for those who do righteous deeds and live this life in accordance with the injunctions of Islam to please Allah.

Here are some examples for parents to illustrate how to use this principle on various occasions:

1. When your teen comes back from the school upset because of a less-than- expected mark in one of her tests, saying, "I did my best. I even made lots of *dua'a* to Allah to help me get a high mark." This is an opportunity for you to explain the concept of *dua'a* in Islam and teach your teen that Allah responds to it in different ways: Allah could grant you your wish right away, or could protect you from a harm that was going to fall on you, or reserve it for you in the hereafter and give you more rewards. You can also use the occasion to help your teen understand that in addition to *dua'a* one has to work hard and do her best to have high marks.

2. When the death of loved ones takes place, or a close friend suffers from a long illness, this is an opportunity to talk to your teen about the fact that life is a test and we could all face these kinds of hardships. What matters is how we respond to it. We should do our best to alleviate it, and if we can't, we should accept it, try to live with it, and help the sick person to cope with it.

Don't force them to pick up where you left off

Parents have to take into consideration what stage their child is at. They should not ask him to do things that are beyond his current level. *Aisha*, may Allah be pleased with her, is reported to have said, "Take into consideration the young girl's age." Some parents, in their zeal and enthusiasm to have their children behave, act, and dress as Muslims, insist on forcing their teens to do exactly as they do. For example, a mother might ask her teenaged daughter to dress exactly as she does in a full *Jilbab* and *Khimar*. There is nothing wrong with accepting loose clothing and a scarf as the daughter's *hijab* at this stage, even if it isn't exactly like her mom's clothing. As long as it meets Islamic requirements, parents should accept it. The basic requirements call for the clothes to cover the whole body, not to be tight or transparent, and to cover the head. Another common example is when the father asks his son to pray all extra prayers, such as full taraweeh during *Ramadan*, and to dress in his country's traditional dress, thinking that this is the only way to apply

Islam. There is nothing wrong with accepting only the compulsory duties from the young man and helping him to grow and strengthen his belief gradually in the meantime. This way, the son will be able to do extra without feeling that it is too much of a burden on him. In some situations, insisting on forcing the teen to do more and more without real conviction may turn him away from Islam. We have to take the child's age into consideration and give him enough room to grow.

One way which may help parents exercise this principle is to try to remember whether or not they fully applied Islam when they were their child's age. Of course, the answer to this question by most parents would be NO. As such, you should give your teen enough time to grow, develop, and improve day after day. When you encourage and praise your teen's positive actions instead of being critical towards him, he will do more and more things correctly, *insha' Allah*. This is exactly what the prophet PBUH did with his companions. He accepted what they did according to their level, and then helped them to improve. Not only this, but he also applauded and praised their positive actions, even if the actions were little or seemed irrelevant.

It was reported that a man came to the prophet, PBUH, and asked him about Islam. The prophet told him about the basic pillars of Islam (five daily prayers, *Zakat*, fasting, and *Hajj*). The man said he would do only this and nothing more. The prophet PBUH said that this man would achieve prosperity if he implemented what he said he would.

Also in *Surah Al-Baqarah*, Allah says,

$$\text{لَا يُكَلِّفُ ٱللَّهُ نَفْسًا إِلَّا وُسْعَهَا}$$

"that He does not burden any soul beyond its capability."
(Q 2, V 286)

The prophet PBUH also said,
"Whatever I order you to do, do as much as you can. And whatever I forbid you, avoid completely" (agreed upon).

Utilizing this gradual approach is very important and is a fundamental method used by Islam to introduce new concepts and change social habits. It is much easier for teens to do things in a gradual way than to make an abrupt change. Following all of the principles mentioned above will no doubt help your teen in building her confidence and in moving from the state of knowledge to the state of conviction. Here is how one of our daughters valued our use of these principles with her during the high school years

"I am grateful to Allah SWT and to my parents that I was left to explore my friendships and then come to my own realization. I'm sure that if my parents had made a rule that I couldn't have a non-Muslim friend under any condition, I would have been very resentful. My parents allowed me to explore my world as long as I was within the boundaries of Islam, and that allowed me to come to my own realization, which I am much more confident in than any rule that they could have held me to."

These words summarized how a high school student came to her own realization regarding the concept of friendship. Yes, she needed her parent's guidance, but she also needed some room to move from knowledge to conviction. This was written by one of our daughters who is, *masha' Allah*, a committed Muslim, very confident about her Islamic identity and involved with Muslim community activities and the society at large. Here she writes about what helped her through her journey from knowledge to conviction.

"I didn't realize how distinct teen culture was until I had finished high school. I had been surrounded by this culture for five years and had built a protective wall of distance around myself in order to deal with it. Of course, this was only after my many trials to find a group or a friend that was different than the rest of the school. In the midst of a culture in which dating, drinking, drugs, concerts, and parties are the focus, where the every-day conversations are centered around the new movie and music releases and sprinkled with at least two swear words in every sentence, I was looking for a girls-only group of friends that I had enough in common with to spend the lunch period.

In grade nine, I had my friends from junior high school and a few people that I met in high school who didn't drink, do drugs, or party. They dated and sometimes swore. By grade ten, my grade nine group was centering their discussions around boys. Feeling awkward, I knew it was time to move on. I shouldn't listen to this kind of talk. I looked for another place to spend my lunch hour. At the same time, I met a girl who was new to the city and to the school. She didn't know anybody at school and I became one of her only friends. We started hanging out together regularly at school. We got involved in intellectual and conceptual discussions and we compared this society's perspective with the Islamic perspective on many topics. *Masha' Allah*, she had a big heart and a clear head and she could see my points and my views. She wasn't caught up in partying and boys, or at least that was what I thought. As the year went on and she got to know more people, she was invited to more parties and quickly was accepted into the "in group". Though she still respected me and we still enjoyed each other's company, we couldn't spend time together at school anymore because her group of friends had many boys and I mix only with girls. Her activities now centered around skipping class, doing drugs, and going to bars and parties.

In my grade 11 year, it seemed that absolutely everybody was into boys, swearing, and drinking, and that most of the school was into drugs and parties as well. So you can imagine my delight when I found a big group of girls who shunned drinking and drugs and didn't talk about boys too much. Unfortunately, some of them still swore, but seeing my different options, I felt they were the group that I could fit into the most. I still had to use the technique of trying to change the topic whenever they talked about boys, and excused myself to leave when the swear words got irritating. I spent the whole of my grade 11 year with them and looked forward to returning to the same no-drinking, no-smoking, and no-drugs group next year.

Grade 12 caught me by surprise; I couldn't believe how my grade 11 group had transformed over the summer. At the beginning of the year, I went to meet one of the girls at her locker. When I saw that her locker was decorated with pictures of beer and vodka, I said to her, "Wait a second. What happened? I thought you hated drinking and all that stuff?"

"Yeah," she grinned, "that was before I tried it, man."

To my dismay, the innocent no-parties group that I had known last year was no more. Over the summer, a few boys had joined the group and one of them had a large house and parents who were often out of town. His house became party central and my friends became party animals. Now the girls talked about last weekend's party until Wednesday and about next weekend's party from Thursday on and, of course, partied and drank all weekend.

So grade 12 left me searching for someone new to spend my lunch hours with again. History repeated itself; I got to know a girl who was new to both the city and the school until I felt comfortable with her and then she got to know the school and went off with the people who partied and drank.

In Grade 13, I came in with a different attitude, an attitude of distance and distinctions; yes, I told myself, I go to school with these girls and I spend the majority of my year interacting with them, but that doesn't mean that my soul-mate has to be here at school. They have completely different mentalities and different value systems and these effects trickle down to every part of our lives. Who we hang out with, how we talk, what we talk about, all these are simple examples of things that distinguished me from the girls around me and sometimes made it impossible for us to spend time together. I also came into grade 13 with an attitude of people instead of groups. All through my time at school I had gotten to know some people who were wonderful to spend time with as individuals, but not when they were with their groups. With this attitude and the understanding that I was not looking for a soul-mate among the girls, but I was looking instead for pleasant companions that I could spend time with and share some experiences with, grade 13 was easier to get through. Sometimes I think to myself, "I wish I had the same attitude throughout all of high school. Then it would have been a much better experience." The truth is that I could not have had this attitude before. All throughout my life, I had heard people talk about how it is not possible for a non-Muslim to be a Muslim's closest friend. Hearing this from my parents and others didn't stop me from wanting badly to have a close friend at school. I had to come to the same realization on my own. Now it is not just a piece of information I know, it is rather a real conviction that I would not compromise."

To clarify some of the points that may have crossed your mind while reading the above high school experience, please read the following questions and answers, answered by our daughters:

Questions:

1. What are the conditions under which you were allowed to have and visit non-Muslim friends?

We were allowed to have non-Muslim friends as long as being their friend didn't compromise our Islam. This means that we were careful in choosing our friends and picked people who had values and morals and respected our values and morals. We were allowed to visit our non-Muslim friends only if we were sure that it was a safe household and only while the mother was at home. If they had an older brother, we could only visit them if the brother was out. When we were little, our parents always arranged to meet their parents before we were allowed to go over to their houses. As we grew older and had better judgment, sometimes our parents would depend on our judgment without having to meet them. If we were allowed to visit a friend, we would always leave her address and telephone number at home for our parents. Our parents would know when we were expected back and how we would be returning home. When we were young, we were reminded to follow safety rules while we were there. This included not sitting with any boys at the house, locking the door when we went to the washroom, and always calling home when we arrived and before we left. If, at any time, for any reason, we found out that we shouldn't be at the house, we called our parents to come pick us up right away. We would often invite our friends over to our house if the above criteria could not be met.

2. Did you ever attend any school dances?

No, we never attended any school dances. If the dance was during school hours we would bring a note from home saying that we could not attend the dance. At times, the teachers would excuse us and allow us to leave the school. Other times we would be sent to the library, cafeteria, or computer lab to pass the time.

3. Were you ever invited to a party by one of your schoolmates? Did you accept the invitation?" If not, what was your response to your schoolmate?

Yes, we were often invited to parties by our friends. However, most of these parties, we knew, would include boys, drinking, gambling and maybe drugs. Those parties, obviously we did not attend. We only attended parties if we were certain (and this would include checking with the host) that there would be nothing haram there. When we did not accept the invitation to a party because we knew it would not be Islamic, we would explain to the person who invited us the reasons we could not come. We told them about our religion and religious rules.

Even though it was often hard to refuse because we knew all our friends would be there, it would be the talk of the week after, and we wouldn't be part of that, intellectually, we understood the reasons why we couldn't go. Because of this, when we'd explain it to our friends, we didn't say it grudgingly or say that our parents would not let us, but we presented it to them with a logical explanation and with conviction. This way, our friends accepted our rules just as much as we did because they saw that it was part of us, not something being forced upon us. Sometimes, when we would decline an invitation to a party we would suggest to the friend who invited us an alternative activity that wouldn't include any of the haram activities that we were trying to avoid, such as going out to a restaurant either alone or with a group of friends, or having a dinner party.

4. How did you feel not going to the party?

It wasn't always easy declining the invitation and knowing that all our friends would be gathered in one spot socializing and we would not be there. The first few times are the hardest to say no to because you want to be part of the group, but after the parties are over and you hear about all the ridiculous stuff that people (who are usually drunk) did there, it becomes a lot easier to appreciate the rules that protect you from this insanity. Eventually, you realize that these parties are a complete waste of time and that the people who go often end up getting hurt, whether it is emotionally or physically. Again, a way to compensate for the effects of missing the party is to participate in alternative things with your friends as well as getting involved in Islamic activities.

Summary

In this chapter, we discussed how to elevate the level of your teen from knowledge of Islam to complete conviction in it. We indicated that particular conditions have to be fulfilled, and the specific ways and methods to be followed as well as certain principles to be observed, to fulfill these conditions. Among these conditions are; the pleasant and loving family atmosphere, regular and continuous follow- up, utilizing what is best in dealing with your teens, fulfilling their spiritual needs and touching their souls, and helping them to understand the logical reasons for what is happening around them. The methods and principles to observe include active listening, reasoning and discussing, touching their souls and awakening their conscience, illustrating consequences in a vivid way, utilizing opportunities, not forcing your teens to pick up where you left off, and using the proper Islamic methods for conflict resolution. Detailed guidelines for Islamic conflict resolution were presented, which cover taking initiative, forgetting and forgiving, controlling anger and humiliation or name-calling.

6. Basic Concepts
– How to instill them in Your Teen

This chapter is devoted to the discussion of some very important Islamic concepts which every parent should strive to instill in his teen to help him live as a righteous, upright, rounded personality who can contribute to himself, his family, the Muslim community, and humanity in general. These concepts, if ingrained properly in your teen, will help him resist most temptations to deviate from the Straight Path and live a fruitful and productive life. These concepts include the following;

– Allah Loves you,
– Our real home is in the hereafter,
– Life is a test
– Allah is with you at all times,
– Patience is a great virtue,
– Islam is a complete way of life,
– We will all meet Allah as individuals on the day of judgment,
– We are accountable for whatever we hear, we see, or we think of,
– Select friends carefully

Throughout the chapter, we will mention each concept, discuss its sources from the *Qur'an* and the teachings of Prophet Muhammad PBUH, and then elaborate on its importance in your teen's life. We have intentionally gone into great detail in listing the sources of each concept; this is to make sure parents have enough information and material from the verses of *Qur'an* and the sayings of the prophet to use in fulfilling the task at hand.

To be able to instill these concepts in your teen and make her live by it, you should follow the guidelines and principles presented in the previous three chapters. These include starting early, providing a happy, pleasant, healthy, warm and positive family atmosphere, using the best methods (*ALLATY HEYA AHSAN*) in dealing with your teens, especially during conflicts, reasoning, discussing your decisions, providing her with logical answers to her questions, and allowing her to express her views. These are the general guidelines to use with all the concepts.

In addition, with each concept, we will try to add specific methods and ways that you may use to introduce and ingrain this particular concept in your teens' life and personality.

Now, here are some important concepts that parents should strive to instill in their children in general and particularly when they approach teenage years:

Allah loves you

Source

Teens have to understand that Allah SWT loves them, especially when they behave properly and live according to Islam. First, they have to remember that Allah SWT has fashioned all human beings in the best form;

$$\text{لَقَدْ خَلَقْنَا ٱلْإِنسَـٰنَ فِىٓ أَحْسَنِ تَقْوِيمٍ ٤}$$

"We certainly have created human being in the best state" (Q 95, V 4).

$$\text{ٱللَّهُ ٱلَّذِى جَعَلَ لَكُمُ ٱلْأَرْضَ قَرَارًا وَٱلسَّمَآءَ بِنَآءً}$$
$$\text{وَصَوَّرَكُمْ فَأَحْسَنَ صُوَرَكُمْ وَرَزَقَكُم مِّنَ ٱلطَّيِّبَـٰتِ}$$
$$\text{ذَٰلِكُمُ ٱللَّهُ رَبُّكُمْ فَتَبَارَكَ ٱللَّهُ رَبُّ ٱلْعَـٰلَمِينَ ٦٤}$$

"It is He who fashioned you in the best form and provided you with good things, ..." (Q 40, V 64).

Also, He has equipped us with all the tools, senses, and faculties we require to be able to live, perform, and fulfill our duties in this life in the most efficient and enjoyable manner we can. There are so many places in the *Qur'an* in which this has been illustrated.

$$\text{قُلْ هُوَ ٱلَّذِىٓ أَنشَأَكُمْ وَجَعَلَ لَكُمُ ٱلسَّمْعَ وَٱلْأَبْصَـٰرَ وَٱلْأَفْـِٔدَةَ}$$
$$\text{قَلِيلًا مَّا تَشْكُرُونَ ٢٣}$$

"Say, it is He Who has created you, and endowed you with hearing (ears) and seeing (eyes) and hearts. Little thanks do you give." (Q 67, V 23)

Not only this, but Allah SWT has subjected various things for us to make our lives easier and more manageable.

اللَّهُ ٱلَّذِى سَخَّرَ لَكُمُ ٱلْبَحْرَ لِتَجْرِىَ ٱلْفُلْكُ فِيهِ بِأَمْرِهِۦ وَلِتَبْتَغُوا۟ مِن فَضْلِهِۦ وَلَعَلَّكُمْ تَشْكُرُونَ ۝ وَسَخَّرَ لَكُم مَّا فِى ٱلسَّمَٰوَٰتِ وَمَا فِى ٱلْأَرْضِ جَمِيعًا مِّنْهُ إِنَّ فِى ذَٰلِكَ لَءَايَٰتٍ لِّقَوْمٍ يَتَفَكَّرُونَ ۝

"Allah, it is He who subjected to you the sea that ships may sail through it by His command, and that you may seek of His Bounty, and that you may be thankful. And He has subjected to you all that is in the heavens and all that is in the earth; it is all as a favor and kindness from Him. Verily, in it are signs for a people who think deeply" (Q 45, V12-13)

اللَّهُ ٱلَّذِى جَعَلَ لَكُمُ ٱلَّيْلَ لِتَسْكُنُوا۟ فِيهِ وَٱلنَّهَارَ مُبْصِرًا إِنَّ ٱللَّهَ لَذُو فَضْلٍ عَلَى ٱلنَّاسِ وَلَٰكِنَّ أَكْثَرَ ٱلنَّاسِ لَا يَشْكُرُونَ ۝

"Allah, it is He who has made the night for you that you may rest therein and the day for you to see. Truly Allah is full of bounty to mankind; yet most of mankind gives no thanks." (Q 40, V 61)

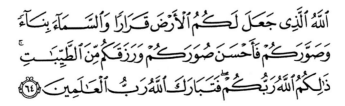

اللَّهُ ٱلَّذِى جَعَلَ لَكُمُ ٱلْأَرْضَ قَرَارًا وَٱلسَّمَآءَ بِنَآءً وَصَوَّرَكُمْ فَأَحْسَنَ صُوَرَكُمْ وَرَزَقَكُم مِّنَ ٱلطَّيِّبَٰتِ ذَٰلِكُمُ ٱللَّهُ رَبُّكُمْ فَتَبَارَكَ ٱللَّهُ رَبُّ ٱلْعَٰلَمِينَ ۝

"Allah, it is He who has made for you the earth as a dwelling place and the sky as a canopy, and has given you shape and made your shape good (looking) and has provided you with good things. That is Allah your Lord: so blessed is Allah, the Lord of *A' lamin* (mankind, jinn and all that exists)." (Q 40, V 64)

In addition, Allah SWT gave us so many bounties to the extend we can not count them, even if we try

$$\text{اللَّهُ ٱلَّذِى خَلَقَ ٱلسَّمَـٰوَٰتِ وَٱلْأَرْضَ وَأَنزَلَ مِنَ ٱلسَّمَآءِ}$$
$$\text{مَآءً فَأَخْرَجَ بِهِۦ مِنَ ٱلثَّمَرَٰتِ رِزْقًا لَّكُمْ ۖ وَسَخَّرَ لَكُمُ}$$
$$\text{ٱلْفُلْكَ لِتَجْرِىَ فِى ٱلْبَحْرِ بِأَمْرِهِۦ ۖ وَسَخَّرَ لَكُمُ ٱلْأَنْهَـٰرَ}$$
$$\text{(٣٢) وَسَخَّرَ لَكُمُ ٱلشَّمْسَ وَٱلْقَمَرَ دَآئِبَيْنِ ۖ وَسَخَّرَ لَكُمُ}$$
$$\text{ٱلَّيْلَ وَٱلنَّهَارَ (٣٣) وَءَاتَىٰكُم مِّن كُلِّ مَا سَأَلْتُمُوهُ ۚ وَإِن}$$
$$\text{تَعُدُّوا۟ نِعْمَتَ ٱللَّهِ لَا تُحْصُوهَآ ۗ إِنَّ ٱلْإِنسَـٰنَ لَظَلُومٌ}$$
$$\text{كَفَّارٌ (٣٤)}$$

"Allah is He who has created the heavens and the earth and sends down water (rain) from the sky, and therefore brought forth fruits as provision for you. And He has made the ships to be of service to you, that they may sail through the sea by His command; and He has made rivers (also) to be of service to you. And He has made the sun and the moon, both constantly pursuing their courses, to be of service to you; and He has made the night and the day to be of service to you. And He gave you of all that you asked for, and if you count the blessings of Allah, never will you be able to count them. Verily, man is indeed an extreme wrongdoer, a disbeliever." (Q 14, V 32-34)

Allah SWT has provided all of these favors and bounties for all human beings. He creates them in the best form, He equips them with all the tools they require to live on this earth, He provides for them, He subjects for them various things in order to help them live their life. As for the believers, there are even more favors granted specifically for them when they follow the way of Allah.

وَهُوَ ٱلَّذِى يَقْبَلُ ٱلتَّوْبَةَ عَنْ عِبَادِهِۦ وَيَعْفُواْ عَنِ ٱلسَّيِّـَٔاتِ وَيَعْلَمُ مَا تَفْعَلُونَ ۞ وَيَسْتَجِيبُ ٱلَّذِينَ ءَامَنُواْ وَعَمِلُواْ ٱلصَّـٰلِحَـٰتِ وَيَزِيدُهُم مِّن فَضْلِهِۦ وَٱلْكَـٰفِرُونَ لَهُمْ عَذَابٌ شَدِيدٌ ۞

"It is He who accepts repentance from His servants and forgives sins and knows what you do. He also responds to those who attain to faith and do good deeds and provides extra for them from His grace. As for those who disbelieve, they will have severe punishment." (Q 42, V 25-26)

وَلَا تُفْسِدُواْ فِى ٱلْأَرْضِ بَعْدَ إِصْلَـٰحِهَا وَٱدْعُوهُ خَوْفًا وَطَمَعًا إِنَّ رَحْمَتَ ٱللَّهِ قَرِيبٌ مِّنَ ٱلْمُحْسِنِينَ ۞

"Certainly Allah's mercy is near unto the good doer." (Q 7, V 56)

۞ وَٱكْتُبْ لَنَا فِى هَـٰذِهِ ٱلدُّنْيَا حَسَنَةً وَفِى ٱلْأَخِرَةِ إِنَّا هُدْنَا إِلَيْكَ قَالَ عَذَابِىٓ أُصِيبُ بِهِۦ مَنْ أَشَآءُ وَرَحْمَتِى وَسِعَتْ كُلَّ شَىْءٍ فَسَأَكْتُبُهَا لِلَّذِينَ يَتَّقُونَ وَيُؤْتُونَ ٱلزَّكَوٰةَ وَٱلَّذِينَ هُم بِـَٔايَـٰتِنَا يُؤْمِنُونَ ۞ ٱلَّذِينَ يَتَّبِعُونَ ٱلرَّسُولَ ٱلنَّبِىَّ ٱلْأُمِّىَّ ٱلَّذِى يَجِدُونَهُۥ مَكْتُوبًا عِندَهُمْ فِى ٱلتَّوْرَىٰةِ وَٱلْإِنجِيلِ يَأْمُرُهُم بِٱلْمَعْرُوفِ وَيَنْهَىٰهُمْ عَنِ ٱلْمُنكَرِ وَيُحِلُّ لَهُمُ ٱلطَّيِّبَـٰتِ وَيُحَرِّمُ عَلَيْهِمُ ٱلْخَبَـٰٓئِثَ وَيَضَعُ عَنْهُمْ إِصْرَهُمْ وَٱلْأَغْلَـٰلَ ٱلَّتِى كَانَتْ عَلَيْهِمْ فَٱلَّذِينَ ءَامَنُواْ بِهِۦ وَعَزَّرُوهُ وَنَصَرُوهُ وَٱتَّبَعُواْ ٱلنُّورَ ٱلَّذِىٓ أُنزِلَ مَعَهُۥٓ أُوْلَـٰٓئِكَ هُمُ ٱلْمُفْلِحُونَ ۞

". ...And My Mercy embraces all things. That (Mercy) I
shall ordain for those who have *Taqwa*, those who pay
Zakat, and those who believe in Our signs and proofs.
Those who follow the messenger, the prophet who can
neither read nor write..." (Q 7, V 156-157)

إِنَّ ٱللَّهَ مَعَ ٱلَّذِينَ ٱتَّقَواْ وَّٱلَّذِينَ هُم مُّحْسِنُونَ ﴿١٢٨﴾

" Allah is with those who have *Taqwa* and those who do
Ihsan." (Q 16, V 128)

۞ قُلْ يَعِبَادِيَ ٱلَّذِينَ أَسْرَفُواْ عَلَىٰٓ أَنفُسِهِمْ لَا تَقْنَطُواْ مِن
رَّحْمَةِ ٱللَّهِ إِنَّ ٱللَّهَ يَغْفِرُ ٱلذُّنُوبَ جَمِيعًا إِنَّهُۥ هُوَ ٱلْغَفُورُ ٱلرَّحِيمُ
﴿٥٣﴾ وَأَنِيبُوٓاْ إِلَىٰ رَبِّكُمْ وَأَسْلِمُواْ لَهُۥ مِن قَبْلِ أَن يَأْتِيَكُمُ
ٱلْعَذَابُ ثُمَّ لَا تُنصَرُونَ ﴿٥٤﴾ وَٱتَّبِعُوٓاْ أَحْسَنَ مَآ أُنزِلَ
إِلَيْكُم مِّن رَّبِّكُم مِّن قَبْلِ أَن يَأْتِيَكُمُ ٱلْعَذَابُ
بَغْتَةً وَأَنتُمْ لَا تَشْعُرُونَ ﴿٥٥﴾

"Say oh my servants who have transgressed against themselves (by committing evil deeds and sins), despair not from
Allah's mercy. Allah forgives all sins. Truly, He is Oft-
Forgiving, Most Merciful. And turn in repentance and
obedience in true faith to your Lord and submit to Him (in
Islam) before the torment comes upon you (and) then you
will not be helped. And follow the best of that which is sent
down to you from your Lord, before the torment comes on
you suddenly while you perceive not." (Q 39, V 53-55)

It was narrated by *Aby Hamzah Anas Ibn Malik*, the supporter of
the prophet and his servant, may Allah be pleased with him, that the
messenger of Allah PBUH said, "Certainly Allah is Happier with the
repentance of His servant than a person who rides a camel in a waterless
desert. The man lies down to sleep during his journey, and when he

wakes, he finds that the camel is gone with all his food and drink. Soon, he loses all hope and sits on the sand waiting to die. He falls asleep again only to wake up and find the camel before him. The man is so excited that he blurts out in boundless joy: O' Lord, you are my servant and I'm your Lord. He confuses his words out of extreme joy." (*Muslim*)

It was also narrated by *Abu Mosa,* may Allah be pleased with him, that the messenger of Allah PBUH said, "Allah SWT stretches out His hands during the night so the sinners of the day will repent. And He SWT stretches out His hands during the day so the sinners of the night will repent until the sun rises from the west." (*Muslim*)

It was also narrated by *Aby Abderahman Abdullah Ibn Omar Ibn Al Khattab*, may Allah be pleased with them both that the messenger of Allah PBUH said, "Allah accepts the repentance of His servant as long as his soul hasn't reached the point of no return (until the death-rattle starts in his throat)." (*At-Termithy*)

Not only this, but out of His mercy and love to the believers, Allah will always reward any attempt of a believer to draw near to Him with success and more closeness from Allah. *Anas*, may Allah be pleased with him, reported that the messenger of Allah PBUH said, "Allah says: When a servant of Mine advances towards Me a foot, I advance towards him a yard. And when he advances to Me a yard, I advance towards him the length of both arms spread out. When he comes to Me walking, I turn to him running."(*Bukhari*)

Muslims should do their best in trying to follow the injunctions of Allah and the teachings of Prophet Muhammad. They should have great hope in Allah's Mercy. It was reported by *Abu Hurairah*, may Allah be pleased with him, that he heard Allah's messenger PBUH saying, "When Allah created the creation, He ordained for Himself and this document is with Him: Verily, My mercy predominates My wrath. In another version is: My mercy dominates my wrath" (agreed upon).

Importance of this concept

This concept is quite important in the life of your teen. When she understands that Allah loves her, she will be more comfortable and willing to follow Allah's instructions and commandments, even if she doesn't fully understand the wisdom and the logic behind His orders. This is not an invitation to force our teens to blindly follow Islam. On the contrary, it is the parents' responsibility to try to understand the logical reasoning for Islamic instructions and explain them in simple terms to their children.

When teens believe that Allah SWT loves them, it will be easier for them to accept Allah's orders as a source of goodness for them even if they know that applying these orders and following these instructions will make them stand out. It will help their endurance level and their ability to stand in the face of peer pressure and the fact that they will act and look different from the rest of their age group.

How to instill it in your teen

In addition to the use of the general methods we presented in the previous chapters, parents can also use the following specific methods to introduce and instill this important concept in their teen's personality:

1. From an early age, parents should teach their child to repeat the various *dua'a*s the prophet PBUH taught us. One very important *dua'a* to remember is the one we say when we stand in front of a mirror, "Oh Allah, as you have shaped and fashioned me in the most beautiful way, please also make my character as good."

2. Use everyday events. For example, when you are with your child and you see a disabled person, you should immediately mention the *dua'a* of the prophet PBUH, "Praise be to Allah Who has made us healthy and didn't subject us to the illnesses that He tested others with."

3. Train your child to appreciate the bounties of Allah through the exercise of imagining that she has lost one of these bounties through illness or an accident. For example, ask your child, maybe once a week or on a frequent basis, to imagine that she has lost her sight. Let her close her eyes for five minutes and imagine how her life would be if this happened. Or ask her to imagine that she has lost her ability to move for five minutes and let her live the experience. This type of exercise will definitely help her to appreciate the bounties of Allah and feel His love and mercy towards her.

4. Take your child with you to visit the sick and elderly in hospitals. Ask her to volunteer with programs for sick or elderly people.

5. Use the prophet's teachings related to *Sujood Al Shokr.* The prophet PBUH taught us to prostrate thanking Allah when we receive good news or experience success and prosperity. Modeling this to your child on happy occasions will teach her to appreciate the bounties of Allah.

Here is a piece by our daughter *Sumaiya*, indicating her understanding of the above concept that Allah's love and support is the most important thing in the world and that without it, we are lacking something essential:

> As I was walking in the park one evening
> I spotted a beautiful lone flower
> Standing tall with its petals perfectly shaped
> And its array of colors glowing in the evening sunset
> It looked strong and proud with the sun's rays
> Beaming down on it, like nothing could stop it
> Could knock it down.
> I continued my promenade until the sun
> Had completely set
> And my flashlight had to be taken out.
> As I was returning home, I searched for that
> Beautiful flower I had seen before
> The one that seemed so powerful, so strong,
> Yet so charming at the same time.
> As I surveyed the grounds,
> I could not spot it,
> Instead I saw a weak stem blowing in the wind
> Lingering where the flower used to be.
> As I came close, I noticed some petals
> Scattered nearby, wrinkled and weak,
> As if they were stepped all over.
> Was this the same flower I had seen before?
> Was this what had become of it?
> The flower had seemed so strong in the sunlight
> During the security of the day
> But as soon as the dark night settled in
> Its petals were captured by the wind
> And became slaves to the darkness,
> Obeying its every command.

The flower that had once seemed so fine
Had broken down into virtually nothing
It hit me now,
This flower was a mere pretender
Masking its reality with its beauty during the day
And crumbling by nightfall
For its only protector was the sun.

"This piece is a metaphor for our lives, paralleling deceit and reality. If we put our trust and faith into something false and take something false as our protector, we'll be setting ourselves up for failure and disappointment. We must put our trust in Allah and have faith that He will protect us and guide us on the straight path. Islam may not seem thrilling and everyone these days seems to be looking for a thrill, something to excite them and make them happy. Movie stars and athletes have become glorified and are taken as role models. On the surface, to the untrained eye, they appear happy, beautiful, and perfect, but away from the cameras and deep in the night, they question their purpose and fill their void with drugs and alcohol. Much like the flower, they are weak and ungrounded.

Following Islamic rules may not seem thrilling and exciting on the surface, but it is a foolproof way to achieve long term happiness and peace of mind, unlike the instant gratification that may put a smile on someone's face for a minute, but eat away at his heart for a lifetime."

Our real home is in the hereafter

Source

In *Surah Baqarah*, when Adam and Eve disobey Allah SWT and eat from the tree that He asked them not to eat from, He tells them,

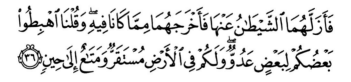

" On earth will be your dwelling place, and your means of livelihood for a time". (Q 2, V 36)

Also in *Surah Al Hadeed,* verse number 20, Allah SWT says,

$$اَعْلَمُوٓاْ اَنَّمَا الْحَيَوٰةُ الدُّنْيَا لَعِبٌ وَلَهْوٌ وَزِينَةٌ وَتَفَاخُرٌ بَيْنَكُمْ وَتَكَاثُرٌ فِى الْاَمْوَالِ وَالْاَوْلَادِ كَمَثَلِ غَيْثٍ اَعْجَبَ الْكُفَّارَ نَبَاتُهُ ثُمَّ يَهِيجُ فَتَرٰىهُ مُصْفَرًّا ثُمَّ يَكُونُ حُطَامًا وَفِى الْاٰخِرَةِ عَذَابٌ شَدِيدٌ وَمَغْفِرَةٌ مِّنَ اللّٰهِ وَرِضْوَانٌ وَمَا الْحَيَوٰةُ الدُّنْيَا اِلَّا مَتَاعُ الْغُرُورِ ﴿٢٠﴾$$

"Know that the life of this world is but play and amusement, pomp and mutual boasting and multiplying, (in rivalry) amongst yourselves, riches and children. Here is a similitude: How rain and the growth it brings forth delights the hearts of the tillers; soon it withers; thou will see it grow yellow; then it becomes dry and it crumbles away. But in the hereafter is a penalty severe (for the devotees of wrong). And forgiveness from God and (His) good pleasure (for the devotees of God). And what is the life of this world, but goods and chattels of deceptions." (Q 57, V 20).

This indicates that our life in this earth is a temporary one and not our permanent home. Every human being will live for a predetermined period of time on this earth and then die. Life on earth is not eternal, and we Muslims should understand this fact and act accordingly.

The teachings of Prophet Muhammad PBUH emphasize this concept more and more in various ways. It was reported on the authority of *Abdullah Ibn Omar* may Allah be pleased with him that the messenger of Allah PBUH took hold of his shoulder and said, " Be in this life/world as if you are a stranger or wayfarer." *Ibn Omar* may Allah be pleased with him used to say, "When you survive until the evening do not expect to be alive until the morning. And when you survive until the morning, don't expect to live until the evening. During health prepare for illness and while you are alive prepare for death." (*Bukhari*).

In another *hadeeth* reported by *Imam Muslim,* Prophet Muhammad

PBUH describes this worldly life as the jail of a believer and the paradise of the disbeliever. The prophet PBUH also emphasizes the actual value and worth of this earthly life by saying, "If this earthly life was to be equal in the sight of Allah to a mosquito's wing, He would have never given a disbeliever a sip of water out of it." (*At-Termithy*)

It was also reported on the authority of *Mustawrid Ibn Shadad* may Allah be pleased with him that the messenger of Allah PBUH said, "This world in comparison with the world to come is like one putting his finger in the sea. Let him consider what it returns with." (*Muslim*)

Importance of the concept

This concept is very important in the life of your teen. If you succeed in infusing this concept in your teen's mind and heart, he will not give much importance or pay much attention to many of the trivial things that the majority of teenagers in North American society consider important. Your teen will look at life for what it is really worth. He will be always looking forward to his real home after death. As such, he will use this life as a way to prepare for the hereafter. Your teen will work hard to earn a place in his ultimate home. He will have long-term objectives to fulfill and no matter what happens in this life, it will not discourage him from reaching his goals. This puts things in perspective and makes it easier for him to find explanations for things happening around him.

A person who doesn't believe in the hereafter will find it very difficult to understand, let alone explain, so many of the disparities that happen in this life. He will find himself preoccupied with difficult questions he won't be able to answer: why are so many people suffering? Why do some people get away with wronging others? Why does it seem like the bad-guy always wins? etc.

How to instill it in your teen

1. Use an event such as death to your advantage. Whenever a family member or a close friend dies, make sure you talk about this absolute fact with your teen. Emphasize that everybody is going to die and that no one will live forever. Make sure to link this to the fact that this life is just transitory in nature and that the real, eternal life is when we meet our Lord and we are admitted into paradise. That is what everyone should aspire for and work hard toward in order to ensure that on the Day of Judgment

he will be one of the winners and his abode will be paradise.

2. Take your children to visit their relative's graves frequently and let them think about how those same people who are now buried and covered with earth used to live like we do everyday. They had homes, families, and businesses like we do. They used to laugh, joke and enjoy this life as we do. They used to have dreams, ambitions and lofty goals to achieve in this life. Now look where they are. They lived their life, and when the time came, they died. This life is not eternal and can't continue forever. Our real home is waiting for us, as long as we live our life according to Allah's guidance and follow the teachings of our beloved prophet Muhammad PBUH. Our real home is paradise, which is the final abode for those who believe and do righteous deeds. May Allah make us from them.

Life is a test

Source

In *Surah Almolk,* Allah SWT says,

$$ ٱلَّذِى خَلَقَ ٱلْمَوْتَ وَٱلْحَيَوٰةَ لِيَبْلُوَكُمْ أَيُّكُمْ أَحْسَنُ عَمَلًا وَهُوَ ٱلْعَزِيزُ ٱلْغَفُورُ ﴿٢﴾ $$

"It is He Who has created death and life, that He may test which of you is best in deed: and He is the all mighty, the Oft-Forgiving" (Q 67, V 2).

Also in *Surah Al-ankabut* Allah says,

$$ الٓمٓ ﴿١﴾ أَحَسِبَ ٱلنَّاسُ أَن يُتْرَكُوٓا۟ أَن يَقُولُوٓا۟ ءَامَنَّا وَهُمْ لَا يُفْتَنُونَ ﴿٢﴾ $$

"Alif-Lam-Mim. Do people think that they will be left alone because they say, "We believe," and will not be tested." (Q 29, V 1,2)

The same concept is also mentioned in *Surah Baqarah,* Allah says,

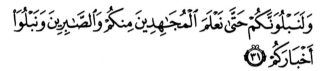

"Or do you think that you shall enter Paradise (the Garden (of Bliss)), without such (trials) as came to those who passed away before you? They encountered suffering and adversity, and were so shaken in spirit that even the apostle and those of faith who were with him cried, "When (will come) the help of God?" Ah! Verily the help of God is (always) near." (Q 2, V 214)

Also in *Surah Muhammad,* Allah SWT says,

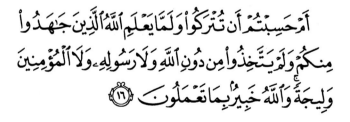

"And We shall try you until we test those among you who strive their utmost and those who persevere in patience; and We shall try your facts." (Q 47, V 31)

In *Surah Tawbah,* the same concept is emphasized again. Allah SWT says,

"Or do you think that you shall be left alone, while Allah has not yet tested those among you who have striven hard

and fought and have taken none for friends and protectors except Allah, His apostle, and the community of believers? But Allah is well acquainted with all that you do."
(Q 9, V 16)

The Prophet's companion, *Khabab Ibn al-Arat*, said, "A group of us once appealed to Allah's Messenger while he was resting in the shade of the *Ka'bah*, and said, 'Would you care to appeal to Allah to help us? Would you care to pray for us?' He replied, 'In days gone by, believers like yourselves used to be put in ditches and have their heads sawed in half, and have their flesh scraped of the bone with iron combs, to dissuade them from their religion, but they would never waver, I swear that Almighty Allah will establish this religion [Islam] so that a man can travel from *Sana'a* [in western Yemen] to *Hadramawt* [in eastern Yemen] fearing nothing but Allah or the wolf for his sheep. But you are so impatient!' " (*Bukhari, Abu Dawoud and Nesa'ee*)

All these verses of *Qur'an*, as well as the teachings of Prophet Muhammad PBUH indicate that life is one test after another and that we should perceive it as such. Also, the life of Prophet Muhammad PBUH illustrates this concept very clearly. He and his companions were tested frequently during both the Makkan and Madinan stages. They had to prove their sincerity and show their real love for Islam no matter how difficult it was for them. Their families and tribes boycotted them and some even inflicted physical punishment on some of the believers like *Bilal Ibn Rabah* and *Ammar Ibn Yaser* may Allah be pleased with them all.

Importance of the concept

This concept is another very important one in your teen's life. Together with the previous concept, our real home is in the hereafter, it can play a very essential role in the way your teen perceives things and deal with them in this life. When she understands that life is a test, your teen will try to do her best in utilizing her time properly and making sure it is not wasted on minor and trivial matters. When you have a test, you study hard for it and time becomes of great value if you want to succeed.

Here is how one of our daughters, *Noha*, views the importance of this concept in her life. "This concept is extremely important because it's a constant reminder of how a Muslim should view life. It's easy to feel discouraged or give up hope in a difficult situation, and many people do.

I myself have always been a worrywart, but I find it assuring to bear in mind that life isn't supposed to be perfect, since it is a test and our final reward will come in the hereafter. Another very encouraging aspect is that Allah tests those servants whom he loves most. It's very comforting to remember this at a time of struggle, when everything looks hopeless and overwhelming.

Also, when I think of a test, I think of how I will get checkmarks for my correct answers and X's for my wrong ones. Being a studious person who always wants to do well on tests and assignments in school, it's a very helpful analogy for me to keep me on track."

How to instill it in your teen

Here is an example of how you, as a parent, can instill and ingrain this concept in your teen in a very subtle and gentle way, as remembered by *Noha* herself. "My mother once said this in a very helpful way at a *halaqa* (study circle) and I have never forgotten it. She asked all the girls sitting in the circle how much time they would give themselves to study for a little quiz at school. Most said they would study the night before. Then she asked how much time they would take to prepare for a big test. Most said three or four days. Then she asked us how long we took to prepare for an exam. The answer was about one to two weeks. Then she took a long look at us and told us, 'think of your life as the biggest test or exam you will ever have. Bigger than your final exams, bigger than your university entrance tests, bigger than a really important job interview. It's easy to forget about this exam because we don't see it in front of us. We don't write this exam in a quiet room, sitting in uncomfortable chairs with big papers in front of us. We don't know exactly when this exam is going to come up, so we have to be studying for it all the time.' For me, this put a very tangible light on a very abstract idea. It was much easier for me to imagine an enormous test and how much I would need to prepare for it than something as seemingly distant and vague as death."

Islam is a total way of life

Source

The fact that Islam is a total, comprehensive way of life is something that can't be denied. The life of the prophet PBUH is clear evidence of this fact. He advised his companions in every aspect of life. He taught them how to deal with every thing in this life. He taught them how to be successful individuals in their relations with Allah, The Lord of the worlds. At the same time, he taught them how to deal with other individuals in the community, with their family members, with their neighbors, and with the opposite sex. He taught them how to behave in the Mosque, in the market, and even during battles and wars. He was able to build a whole society based on the teachings of the *Qur'an* by enjoying what was good and forbidding what was bad and evil, a just society which has never previously or since been experienced throughout history. The teachings of Islam cover all aspects of life: social, economical, political and spiritual. In Surah Baqarah, the *Qur'an* tells us

$$يَٰٓأَيُّهَا ٱلَّذِينَ ءَامَنُوا۟ ٱدْخُلُوا۟ فِى ٱلسِّلْمِ كَآفَّةً وَلَا تَتَّبِعُوا۟ خُطُوَٰتِ ٱلشَّيْطَٰنِ إِنَّهُۥ لَكُمْ عَدُوٌّ مُّبِينٌ ﴿٢٠٨﴾$$

"Oh you who believe enter Islam in totality." (Q 2, V 208)

In the same, *Surah,* the *Qur'an* condemns the people of the book because they practice parts of their scripture and leave other parts

$$ثُمَّ أَنتُمْ هَٰٓؤُلَآءِ تَقْتُلُونَ أَنفُسَكُمْ وَتُخْرِجُونَ فَرِيقًا مِّنكُم مِّن دِيَٰرِهِمْ تَظَٰهَرُونَ عَلَيْهِم بِٱلْإِثْمِ وَٱلْعُدْوَٰنِ وَإِن يَأْتُوكُمْ أُسَٰرَىٰ تُفَٰدُوهُمْ وَهُوَ مُحَرَّمٌ عَلَيْكُمْ إِخْرَاجُهُمْ أَفَتُؤْمِنُونَ بِبَعْضِ ٱلْكِتَٰبِ وَتَكْفُرُونَ بِبَعْضٍ فَمَا جَزَآءُ مَن يَفْعَلُ ذَٰلِكَ مِنكُمْ إِلَّا خِزْىٌ فِى ٱلْحَيَوٰةِ ٱلدُّنْيَا وَيَوْمَ ٱلْقِيَٰمَةِ يُرَدُّونَ إِلَىٰٓ أَشَدِّ ٱلْعَذَابِ وَمَا ٱللَّهُ بِغَٰفِلٍ عَمَّا تَعْمَلُونَ ﴿٨٥﴾$$

"Then, do you believe in parts of the scripture and reject the rest? Then what is the recompense of those who do this among you, except disgrace in the life of this world, and on

the Day of Resurrection they shall be consigned to the most
grievous torment. Allah is not unaware of what you do."
(Q 2, V 85)

Importance of this concept

This concept is very important because you want your teen to understand
Islam properly and know that it regulates all aspects of his time, from the
moment he wakes up in the morning until he gets into his bed again at
night. You want your teen to feel that whatever he does should be within
the realm of Islam and agree with its injunctions. You don't want your
teen to limit Islam to certain timely rituals such as prayers, fasting and
zakat. You want him to behave properly at school or university. You want
him to conduct himself in the best manner in every situation and on every
occasion.

If teens don't understand that Islam is a complete way of life, it will
not be reflected in their behavior during various situations. They'll think
that they're doing enough by praying and performing certain Islamic rituals, but it will not reflect on other activities.

How to instill it in your teen

1. Learn as many of the *dua'as* that prophet Muhammad may Allah's
peace and blessing be upon him said during various occasions and teach
them to your child. You should repeat these *dua'as* with your teen on
every occasion: when you wake up in the morning, when you look in the
mirror, when you put on a new outfit, and when you leave your home to
go out. Also when you ride your car or your bike, when you sit down for
dinner, when you meet somebody, before you go to bed at night, etc.

2. Your behavior as a parent is very crucial in instilling this concept
in your teen. If you, as parent, observe your prayer regularly, but you
don't pay attention to whether your financial dealings adhere with Islamic
injunctions, it will be difficult for your teen to believe that Islam is a total
way of life. If you, as parent, fast the month of *Ramadan*, but you don't
adhere to the Islamic dress code of modesty for men and *Hijab* for
women, it will be difficult for your teen to understand that Islam is a
complete way of life. If you as parent pay your *Zakat*, but at the same
time, you don't visit the sick or help in community projects, it will be
very hard for your teen to believe that Islam is a complete way of life.
If you read *Qur'an* occasionally (when you visit the mosque, when you

buy a new house, or when somebody dies) but you don't care about the affairs of the Muslim *Ummah* as a whole, it is impossible for your teen to understand that Islam is a complete way of life. You have to set the example. If you practice Islam in totality, then your teens will understand that Islam is a complete way of life. Modeling is the best teacher.

The prophet PBUH used modeling to instill almost every concept in his companions' personality. When he told them to practice five daily prayers, he himself was practicing them as well as extra voluntary prayers such as *Sunan*, *Nawafel*, and night prayers. When he instructed his companions to fast the month of *Ramadan*, he himself was fasting the month of *Ramadan* as well as extra voluntary fasting such as Mondays, Thursdays, and the three days in the middle of the Arabic month. When he asked his companions to give charity, he himself was giving much more than anybody to the extent that he was described as 'Swift Wind' (giving everything) when it came to charity. He was doing this to give an example and be a model to his companions. This is what you as parent have to do. You have to learn the way of the prophet PBUH and then try to be the model for your children.

We are accountable for whatever we hear, see, or think of

Source

In *Surah Israa'*; Allah says,

$$ وَلَا تَقْفُ مَا لَيْسَ لَكَ بِهِۦ عِلْمٌ إِنَّ ٱلسَّمْعَ وَٱلْبَصَرَ وَٱلْفُؤَادَ كُلُّ أُوْلَٰٓئِكَ كَانَ عَنْهُ مَسْئُولًا ۝ $$

"And pursue not that of which you have no knowledge; for every act of hearing, or of seeing, or of (feeling in) the heart will be inquired into (on the day of Reckoning)" (Q 17, V 36)

This verse indicates that every individual is responsible for what she does. Allah entrusted us with our senses to use them in the proper way, to use them to carry out our responsibility as vicegerent of Allah on this earth. If we use them in ways that will not please Allah, we will certainly be held responsible. This concept is emphasized in other verses of *Qur'an*. Allah describes believers as those who avoid vain talk. In *Surah Almo'minon*, Allah says,

قَدۡ أَفۡلَحَ ٱلۡمُؤۡمِنُونَ ۝ ٱلَّذِينَ هُمۡ فِى صَلَاتِهِمۡ خَٰشِعُونَ ۝ وَٱلَّذِينَ هُمۡ عَنِ ٱللَّغۡوِ مُعۡرِضُونَ ۝

"Successful indeed are the believers. Those who offer their prayers with all solemnity and full submissiveness. And those who turn away from *Al-Laghw* (dirty, false, evil, vain talk, falsehood, and all that Allah has forbidden)." (Q 23, V 1-3)

In *Surah AlQasas,* Allah says,

وَإِذَا سَمِعُوا ٱللَّغۡوَ أَعۡرَضُوا عَنۡهُ وَقَالُوا لَنَا أَعۡمَٰلُنَا وَلَكُمۡ أَعۡمَٰلُكُمۡ سَلَٰمٌ عَلَيۡكُمۡ لَا نَبۡتَغِى ٱلۡجَٰهِلِينَ ۝

"And when they hear Al-Laghw (vain talk), they withdraw from it and say, "To us our deeds and to you your deeds. Peace be to you. We seek not the way of ignorant." (Q 28, V 55)

Allah also orders the believers to lower from their gaze. In *Surah Alnoor,* Allah says,

قُل لِّلۡمُؤۡمِنِينَ يَغُضُّوا مِنۡ أَبۡصَٰرِهِمۡ وَيَحۡفَظُوا فُرُوجَهُمۡ ذَٰلِكَ أَزۡكَىٰ لَهُمۡ إِنَّ ٱللَّهَ خَبِيرٌۢ بِمَا يَصۡنَعُونَ ۝ وَقُل لِّلۡمُؤۡمِنَٰتِ يَغۡضُضۡنَ مِنۡ أَبۡصَٰرِهِنَّ وَيَحۡفَظۡنَ فُرُوجَهُنَّ وَلَا يُبۡدِينَ زِينَتَهُنَّ إِلَّا مَا ظَهَرَ مِنۡهَا وَلۡيَضۡرِبۡنَ بِخُمُرِهِنَّ عَلَىٰ جُيُوبِهِنَّ وَلَا يُبۡدِينَ زِينَتَهُنَّ إِلَّا لِبُعُولَتِهِنَّ أَوۡ ءَابَآئِهِنَّ أَوۡ ءَابَآءِ بُعُولَتِهِنَّ أَوۡ أَبۡنَآئِهِنَّ أَوۡ أَبۡنَآءِ بُعُولَتِهِنَّ أَوۡ إِخۡوَٰنِهِنَّ أَوۡ بَنِىٓ إِخۡوَٰنِهِنَّ أَوۡ بَنِىٓ أَخَوَٰتِهِنَّ أَوۡ نِسَآئِهِنَّ

أَوِ ٱلتَّبِعِينَ غَيْرِ أُوْلِى ٱلْإِرْبَةِ مِنَ أَوِ مَا مَلَكَتْ أَيْمَنُهُنَّ
ٱلرِّجَالِ أَوِ ٱلطِّفْلِ ٱلَّذِينَ لَمْ يَظْهَرُوا عَلَىٰ عَوْرَٰتِ ٱلنِّسَآءِ
وَلَا يَضْرِبْنَ بِأَرْجُلِهِنَّ لِيُعْلَمَ مَا يُخْفِينَ مِن زِينَتِهِنَّ وَتُوبُوٓا
إِلَى ٱللَّهِ جَمِيعًا أَيُّهَ ٱلْمُؤْمِنُونَ لَعَلَّكُمْ تُفْلِحُونَ ﴿٣١﴾

" Tell the believing men to lower their gaze (from looking
at forbidden things) and protect their private parts (from
illegal sexual acts). That is more pure for them. Verily,
Allah is All Aware of what they do. And tell the believing
women to lower their gaze (from looking at forbidden
things) and protect their private parts (from illegal sexual
acts) and not to show of their adornment except only that
which is apparent." (Q 24, V 30-31)

The teachings of Prophet Muhammad PBUH also emphasize this
concept in many ahadeeth. *Abu Hurairah* may Allah be pleased with him
relates that prophet Muhammad PBUH said, "A man commits adultery
with his eyes when he looks at strange women. Adultery of the ears is
listening to sexual dialogue; adultery of the tongue is talking about sex;
the adultery of the hand is to inflict harms on others unlawfully; and
adultery of the feet is to walk towards unlawful sex. The heart ardently
desires adultery; and the sexual organ confirms or contradicts the act."
(*Muslim*).

Also *'Uqba Ibn Amir* may Allah be pleased with him reported that
prophet Muhammad PBUH said: Avoid visiting strange women. A man
among the *Ansar* asked: O messenger of Allah! What if the visitor is the
husband's brother or an in-law from the other gender? He said: These are
death (agreed upon).

Abu Sa'id Al-khudry may Allah be pleased with him relates that
prophet Muhammad PBUH said, "Avoid sitting in public roads."

They said, "o messenger of Allah, we have no choice but to sit there.
It is where we discuss our affairs."

The prophet PBUH said, "If you have to do this, make sure you
observe the rights of public road."

They said, "and what are these rights?"

He said, "lower your gaze; don't harm anybody; salute others with peace; enjoin what is good and forbid what is evil" (agreed upon).

Abu Sa'id Al-khudry may Allah be pleased with him relates that prophet Muhammad PBUH said, "A man must not look towards a man's private parts, nor a woman should look at another women's private parts; nor should two naked men or two naked women cover themselves under one cover." (*Muslim*)

Importance of this concept

The importance of this concept in your teen's life can't be over emphasized. It is this concept that will make your teen be very careful about what she selects to watch on TV, in videos, or in movies. This is what will make her careful of which books she reads and what type of music she listens to on the radio. This concept will make your teen very selective about the type of friends she hangs around with, the things she hears, the things she watches, and even things she thinks of doing. It is this concept when ingrained in your teen that will make her turn the TV off when there is an indecent scene or foul language on. It will help your teen to avoid being part of any slander or vain talk. If your teen finds herself in a sitting where her friends are talking about boys, this is the concept that will convince her to get up and leave.

How to instill it in your teen

There are a few ways that you as parent can use to instill this concept in your teen. As we mentioned in the beginning of this chapter, to be successful you should start early with all the concepts, and this one in particular. Here are some techniques to use

1. Make sure you join your children in watching some useful TV programs together. Whenever there is a bad scene in the program or commercials you are watching, make sure that they switch the channel or turn the TV off for few seconds then turn it on again.

2. Don't tolerate the use of foul language, backbiting, slanderous talk, or vain talk (*Laghw*) at any time. If any of your children/teens engages in any of the above, stop her at once and remind her that Muslims don't use this type of language. Teach your teen the proper language to use in various occasions. Remember to use the proper language and voice tone

suitable to your child's age. Also remember to be calm while doing this. Don't turn it into a shouting match between you and your teen/child.

3. When your children/teens want to go to the movies, make sure you do enough research to help them select a proper movie that doesn't include indecent scenes or foul language. Read the reviews about the movie as well as check with those who may have seen the movie. Be very specific in your questions, especially if you are checking with somebody who may not share the same value system you do. Don't ask general questions such as whether the movie is good or decent. The frame of reference is not the same, so 'good' and 'decent' for them may be totally different from good and decent for you. Rather, ask whether the movie includes kissing scenes or scenes with other sexual situations. Ask whether the movie includes foul language such as swear words. Be specific.

4. Train your children to regularly say the *dua'as* of each occasion as well as to love Allah and remember His bounties. This way, they will always be thinking about Allah and how to please Him. As such, their thoughts will be clean and focused on useful matters.

Allah is with you all the time

Source

In *Surah Al-Imran* Allah says,

$$\text{إِنَّ ٱللَّهَ لَا يَخْفَىٰ عَلَيْهِ شَيْءٌ فِى ٱلْأَرْضِ وَلَا فِى ٱلسَّمَآءِ ﴿٥﴾}$$

"From Allah, verily nothing is hidden on earth or in the heavens."(Q 3, V 5)

Also in *Surah Tawbah*, Allah says,

$$\text{أَلَمْ يَعْلَمُوٓا۟ أَنَّ ٱللَّهَ يَعْلَمُ سِرَّهُمْ وَنَجْوَىٰهُمْ وَأَنَّ ٱللَّهَ عَلَّٰمُ ٱلْغُيُوبِ ﴿٧٨﴾}$$

"Know they not that Allah knows their secret (thoughts) and their secret counsels, And Allah knows well all things unseen." (Q 9, V 78)

Also in *Surah Yunus,* Allah says,

وَمَا تَكُونُ فِي شَأْنٍ وَمَا تَتْلُواْ مِنْهُ مِن قُرْءَانٍ وَلَا تَعْمَلُونَ مِنْ عَمَلٍ إِلَّا كُنَّا عَلَيْكُمْ شُهُودًا إِذْ تُفِيضُونَ فِيهِ وَمَا يَعْزُبُ عَن رَّبِّكَ مِن مِّثْقَالِ ذَرَّةٍ فِي ٱلْأَرْضِ وَلَا فِي ٱلسَّمَاءِ وَلَا أَصْغَرَ مِن ذَلِكَ وَلَا أَكْبَرَ إِلَّا فِي كِتَبٍ مُّبِينٍ ﴿٦١﴾

"In whatever business you may be, and whatever portion of *Qur'an* you may be reciting, and whatever deed you (mankind) may be doing, We are witness thereof when you are deeply engrossed therein. Nor is hidden from your Lord (so much as) the weight of an atom on the earth or in heaven. And not the least, and not the greatest of these things but are recorded in a clear record." (Q 10, V 61)

Also in *Surah Al-Sha'raa'* Allah says,

ٱلَّذِى يَرَىٰكَ حِينَ تَقُومُ ﴿٢١٨﴾ وَتَقَلُّبَكَ فِي ٱلسَّٰجِدِينَ ﴿٢١٩﴾

"Who sees you standing forth (in prayer) and your movement among those who prostrate themselves." (Q 26, V 218-219)

Also in *Surah Ghafer*, Allah says,

يَعْلَمُ خَآئِنَةَ ٱلْأَعْيُنِ وَمَا تُخْفِي ٱلصُّدُورُ ﴿١٩﴾

"Allah knows the treachery of the eyes and all that the hearts of people conceal." (Q 40, V19)

Also in *Surah Al-Hadeed* Allah says,

هُوَ ٱلَّذِى خَلَقَ ٱلسَّمَوَتِ وَٱلْأَرْضَ فِى سِتَّةِ أَيَّامٍ ثُمَّ ٱسْتَوَىٰ
عَلَى ٱلْعَرْشِ يَعْلَمُ مَا يَلِجُ فِى ٱلْأَرْضِ وَمَا يَخْرُجُ مِنْهَا وَمَا يَنزِلُ مِنَ
ٱلسَّمَآءِ وَمَا يَعْرُجُ فِيهَا وَهُوَ مَعَكُمْ أَيْنَ مَا كُنتُمْ وَٱللَّهُ بِمَا تَعْمَلُونَ
بَصِيرٌ ﴿٤﴾

"And He is with you where so ever you may be and Allah sees well all that you do." (Q 57, V 4)

Also in *Surah Al-Fajr* Allah says,

إِنَّ رَبَّكَ لَبِٱلْمِرْصَادِ ﴿١٤﴾

"For your Lord is watchful." (Q 89, V14)

Also in *Surah Al-Mujadala* Allah says,

أَلَمْ تَرَ أَنَّ ٱللَّهَ يَعْلَمُ مَا فِى ٱلسَّمَوَتِ وَمَا فِى ٱلْأَرْضِ مَا يَكُونُ
مِن نَّجْوَىٰ ثَلَثَةٍ إِلَّا هُوَ رَابِعُهُمْ وَلَا خَمْسَةٍ إِلَّا هُوَ سَادِسُهُمْ
وَلَا أَدْنَىٰ مِن ذَلِكَ وَلَا أَكْثَرَ إِلَّا هُوَ مَعَهُمْ أَيْنَ مَا كَانُوا ثُمَّ يُنَبِّئُهُم
بِمَا عَمِلُوا يَوْمَ ٱلْقِيَمَةِ إِنَّ ٱللَّهَ بِكُلِّ شَىْءٍ عَلِيمٌ ﴿٧﴾

"Haven't you seen that Allah knows all that is in the heavens and on the earth? There is not a secret consultation between three, but He is the fourth of them, nor between five, but He is the sixth, nor between fewer nor more, but He is with them, where so ever they be. On the Day of Judgment He will tell them what they did. For Allah has full knowledge of all things." (Q 58, V 7)

There are so many other verses in *Qur'an* that illustrate the same message and warn all of us that Allah is with us where ever we may be.

The teachings of Prophet Muhammad PBUH are full of the same instructions. They emphasize the importance of having (*Taqwa*) towards Allah where ever we may be, in every place and at every time and all times. Among these teachings are the following ahadeeth: On the authority of *Abu Zarr Jundub Ibn Junada*, and Abu Abderrahman Mu'ath Ibn Jabal (may Allah be pleased with them both), the messenger of Allah PBUH said, "Fear Allah wherever you are, and follow up a bad deed with a good one and it will erase it, and behave well towards people." (*At-Termithy*)

On the authority of *Omar Ibn Al-Khattab* (May Allah be pleased with him), who said, " One day while we were sitting with the messenger of Allah PBUH, there appeared before us a man whose clothes were exceedingly white and whose hair was exceedingly black; no signs of journeying were to be seen on him and none of us knew him. He walked up and sat down in front of the prophet PBUH, resting his knees against the phrophet's knees and placing the palms of his hands on his thighs, he said, "O Muhammad, tell me about Islam."

The messenger of Allah PBUH said, "Islam is to testify that there is no God but Allah and that Muhammad is the messenger of Allah, to perform the prayers, to pay the *Zakat*, to fast in *Ramadan* and to make the pilgrimage to the House if you are able to do so."

The man said, "You have spoken rightly", and we were amazed at him asking the prophet PBUH and then saying that he had spoken rightly. He said, "Then tell me about *Iman*."

The prophet PBUH said, "It is to believe in Allah, His angels, His books, His messengers, and the Last Day, and to believe in divine destiny, both the good and the evil thereof."

The man said, "You have spoken rightly." Then he said, "tell me about *Ihsan*."

The prophet PBUH said, "It is to worship Allah as though you are seeing Him, and while you see Him not, truly He sees you."

The man said, "Then tell me about the Hour."

The prophet PBUH replied, "The questioned about it knows no better than the questioner."

The man said, "Then tell me about its signs."

The prophet PBUH said, "That the slave girl will give birth to her master and that you will see the barefooted, naked, destitute herdsmen competing in constructing lofty buildings."

Then the man left and I stayed for a time. The messenger of Allah PBUH said, "O *Omar*, do you know who the questioner was?"

I said, "Allah and His messenger know best."

The prophet PBUH said, "It was *Gabriel*, who came to you to teach you your religion." (*Muslim*)

Importance of this concept

This concept is very important in the life of your teen. If you succeed to instill it in him, it will help him in two ways. Firstly, the feeling that Allah is with him all the time will provide him with a source of continuous support. He will feel that the source of all power, all strength, all wisdom and all knowledge (Allah) is with him and that all he has to do is stay on the right path and observe his duties towards Allah in order to be subject to His Mercy and receive His support and guidance.

The second way this concept benefits your teen is very clear. When your teen really feels that Allah knows everything, that He sees him at all times and in every place, when he understands that secrecy is a relative and limited term and that nothing is hidden or unknown to Allah, he will always ask himself, before everything he does, is this the right thing to do or not? Regardless of whether or not you as a parent are there to watch over your teen, he will do the right thing because he understands that Allah sees everything.

Here is how one of our daughters (*Noha*) describes the importance of this concept to her life:

"This was one of the main concepts that directed my behavior while growing up and still directs my behavior now. The reason this concept is so important is because it helped me understand that though I was trying to do the right things to please my parents, I was ultimately doing those things to please Allah. I think that many children get stuck here if they aren't reminded daily of the reasons for their actions. Many children keep doing things just to make their parents happy and so they don't develop their own decision-making skills.

"Another reason this concept is so important is because it is very encouraging. When you're going through a difficult time, it's easy   to stop trying and feel as though you are getting no support. However, by remembering that Allah is always with you no matter what and that Allah is the most powerful, it is easier to keep trying. It is also a reminder that Allah tests those He cares about most, which is something to take solace in when things are not going well.

Lastly, this concept is important because it instills a high level of self-control. I always knew that even if no one else was looking, Allah could still see me, and knowing that helped me monitor my behavior more."

How to instill it in your teen

Here is how *Noha*, the same daughter remembers what we did with her to instill this concept and make it part of her personality; "One of the ways my parents helped me to understand this concept was through story-telling. By hearing the stories of the prophets when I was little, there was always the assurance that even when things looked impossible, Allah would find a solution. One of my favorite stories while growing up was the story of prophet Youssuf, because he had been through so much but Allah had never left him.

Another method my parents used was to gently remind me and my sisters that Allah could always see us and that we should fear and love Allah more than anything or anyone else in the world. For example, if we had done something bad and wouldn't say, my mother might tell us that Allah knew the truth and that this was what mattered the most. This way, she wasn't accusing us in case we hadn't actually been bad, she was just keeping us aware so that we would be careful not to repeat the act another time."

<u>Patience is a great virtue</u>

Source
The word patience or its derivatives has been mentioned in *Qur'an* over 100 times in various locations and on various occasions. Here are some of these verses that encourage the believers to exercise patience.

In *Surah Al-Baqarah*, Allah says,

$$\text{وَلَنَبْلُوَنَّكُم بِشَىْءٍ مِّنَ ٱلْخَوْفِ وَٱلْجُوعِ وَنَقْصٍ مِّنَ ٱلْأَمْوَٰلِ}$$
$$\text{وَٱلْأَنفُسِ وَٱلثَّمَرَٰتِ وَبَشِّرِ ٱلصَّٰبِرِينَ ﴿١٥٥﴾}$$

"Be sure that We shall test you with something of fear and hunger, some loss in goods, lives and the fruits (of your toil), but give glad tiding to those who patiently persevere." (Q 2, V 155)

Also in the same *Surah*, Allah says,

يَٰٓأَيُّهَا ٱلَّذِينَ ءَامَنُوا ٱسْتَعِينُوا بِٱلصَّبْرِ وَٱلصَّلَوٰةِ إِنَّ ٱللَّهَ مَعَ ٱلصَّٰبِرِينَ ۝

"O you who believe, seek help with patient perseverance and prayer, for Allah is with those who patiently persevere." (Q 2, V 153)

In *Surah Al-Imran,* Allah says,

يَٰٓأَيُّهَا ٱلَّذِينَ ءَامَنُوا ٱصْبِرُوا وَصَابِرُوا وَرَابِطُوا وَٱتَّقُوا ٱللَّهَ لَعَلَّكُمْ تُفْلِحُونَ ۝

"O you who believe persevere in patience and constancy; vie in such perseverance; strengthen each other; and fear Allah that you may prosper." (Q 3, V 200)

In the same *Surah,* Allah also says,

لَتُبْلَوُنَّ فِىٓ أَمْوَٰلِكُمْ وَأَنفُسِكُمْ وَلَتَسْمَعُنَّ مِنَ ٱلَّذِينَ أُوتُوا ٱلْكِتَٰبَ مِن قَبْلِكُمْ وَمِنَ ٱلَّذِينَ أَشْرَكُوٓا أَذًى كَثِيرًا وَإِن تَصْبِرُوا وَتَتَّقُوا فَإِنَّ ذَٰلِكَ مِنْ عَزْمِ ٱلْأُمُورِ ۝

"You shall certainly be tried and tested in your possessions and in yourselves; and you shall hear much that will grieve you, from those who received the book before you and from those who worship partners besides Allah. But if you persevere patiently, and guard against evil, then that indeed is a matter of resolution." (Q 3, V 186)

Also in *Surah Az-Zumar,* Allah says,

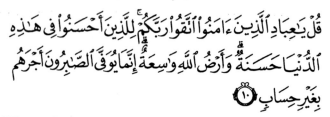

"Those who patiently persevere will truly receive a reward without measure." (Q 39, V 10)

Also in *Surah Al-Mu'min,* Allah says,

بِحَمْدِ رَبِّكَ بِالْعَشِيِّ وَالْإِبْكَارِ ۝

"Patiently, then persevere: for the promise of Allah is true: and ask forgiveness for your fault, and celebrate the praises of your Lord in the evening and in the morning." (Q 40, V 55)

Also in *Surah Al-Shura,* Allah says,

وَلَمَن صَبَرَ وَغَفَرَ إِنَّ ذَٰلِكَ لَمِنْ عَزْمِ الْأُمُورِ ۝

"But indeed if any shows patience and forgives, that would truly be an affair of great resolution." (Q 42, V 43)

Also in *Surah Al-Ahqaf,* Allah says,

بَلَٰغٌ فَهَلْ يُهْلَكُ إِلَّا الْقَوْمُ الْفَٰسِقُونَ ۝

"Therefore patiently persevere, as did all messengers of firm resolution; and be in no haste about the unbelievers. On the day that they see the punishment promised them it will be as if they have not tarried more than an hour in a single day...." (Q 46, V 35)

Also in *Surah Muhammad*, Allah says,

وَلَنَبْلُوَنَّكُمْ حَتَّىٰ نَعْلَمَ ٱلْمُجَٰهِدِينَ مِنكُمْ وَٱلصَّٰبِرِينَ وَنَبْلُوَاْ
أَخْبَارَكُمْ ٣١

"And We shall try you until we test those among you who strive their utmost and persevere in patience; and We shall try your reported (mettle)." (Q 47, V 31)

Also in *Surah Al-Muzzammil*, Allah says,

وَٱصْبِرْ عَلَىٰ مَا يَقُولُونَ وَٱهْجُرْهُمْ هَجْرًا جَمِيلًا ١٠

"And have patience with what they say, and leave them with noble dignity." (Q 73, V 10)

The teachings of Prophet Muhammad May Allah's blessings and peace be upon him emphasize the same concept in different ways. Here are some of the his teachings in this regard:

On the authority of *Abu Malik al-Harith Ibn 'Asim al-Ash'ari* may Allah be pleased with him who relates that the messenger of Allah may Allah's blessings and peace be upon him said, "Cleanliness is half of faith. The utterance of 'All praise belongs to Allah' fills the scales of good actions. The utterance of 'Glory be to Allah and all praise belongs to Allah' fills the space between the heavens and the earth. And prayer is light; and charity is the test of faith; and endurance is a glow; and the *Qur'an* is a plea supporting or opposing you. Every person begins the morning ready to strike a bargain with his soul taking risk; he either ransoms it or he puts it into perdition." (*Muslim*)

It was reported on the authority of *Abu Sa'id Al-Khudry* may Allah be pleased with him that certain people of the *Ansar* begged of the messenger of Allah may Allah's blessings and peace be upon him and he gave them. Then they again begged of him and he gave them so all whatever he possessed, and was exhausted. Then the Prophet PBUH said, "What I have of good things, I'll not withhold from you. Who so would be abstemious, Allah will keep him abstemious. And who so would be independent, Allah will keep him independent. And who so would be patient, Allah will give him patience and no one is granted a gift better and more extensive than patience" (agreed upon).

On the authority of *Abu Yahia Suhaib Ibn Sinan* may Allah be pleased with him who relates that the messenger of Allah PBUH said, "How excellent is the case of a faithful servant; there is good for him in everything and this is not the case with any one except him. If prosperity attends him, he expresses gratitude to Allah and that is good for him; and if adversity falls on him, he endures it patiently and that is better for him." (*Muslim*)

Anas may Allah be pleased with him narrated that the messenger of Allah may Allah's blessings and peace be upon him was passing by a woman who was weeping near a grave and said, "Fear Allah and be patient."

She said, "Away from me! My calamity has not befallen on you." The woman was afterward told that he was the prophet PBUH; where upon she came to his door where she found no doorkeeper. She said, "O' prophet of Allah, I was unaware of you." The messenger of Allah PBUH said, "Patience should be exercised at the first stroke of grief" (agreed upon).

Anas may Allah be pleased with him said he heard the messenger of Allah PBUH declaring that Allah who is Glorious and Exalted said, "When I afflict my servant in his two dear things (i.e., his eyes), and he endures patiently, I shall compensate him for them with Paradise." (*Bukhari*)

Abu Hurairah (Allah be pleased with him) narrated that prophet Muhammad PBUH said, "The strong man is not one who wrestles, but the strong man is one who controls himself in a fit of rage" (agreed upon).

Khabab Ibn al-Arat (Allah be pleased with him) narrated: We lodged a complaint with the messenger of Allah (peace and blessings of Allah be upon him) regarding the persecution inflicted on us by the infidels. He was lying in the shade of the *Ka'bah*, having made a pillow of his sheet. We submitted, "Why do you not supplicate for our prevalence (over the opponents)." He replied, "From among those before you the man would be seized and held in a pit dug for him in the earth and he would be sawn into two from his head and his flesh would be torn away from his bones with an iron comb. But in spite of this he would not wean away from his faith. By Allah, He would bring this matter to its consummation till a rider will travel from *Sana'a* to *Hadramout* fearing nothing except Allah and fear of the wolf concerning his sheep but you are in hot haste." (*Bukhari*)

Importance of the concept

Patience is very important for all believers in general and for Muslim teens in particular, especially those of them living in a non-Muslim society. Anybody with a mission to achieve requires patience and endurance. That is why Allah advises even His messengers to equip themselves with patience. Your teen needs patience because of the challenges she will face when she tries to stick to certain principles and practices that may be in conflict with the mainstream norms of teen culture in North America. Patience is required for every believer to be able to practice her belief and stand strong in face of hardships and obstacles.

As described by the *Qur'an*, patience is required for us to be able to perform all our acts of pure worship in the proper format at the right time without feeling shy or hesitant to do them in front of others. Patience is required for all believers to stand firm in front of all the hardships they will face when they try to call in the way of Allah.

A believer needs patience to stand firm when she is faced with any of the tests in this life. After all, we know that life is one trial after another and one test after another. Believers will need patience to resist various temptations in this life, such as their desires and whims. In addition to all of this, your teen will need patience to ask the school administration to give her and the other Muslims in the school a quiet place to perform their prayers. Some school administration may be reluctant to honor such a request easily, and your teen will need patience to discuss with them and reach an arrangement.

Your teen also will need patience when she chooses to dress in a more modest and conservative way then those around her. Her clothes may completely conflict with the norms in her environment. When your teen abstains from talking about other gender, from free mixing with other gender, from going with her peers to a mixed party where alcohol is being consumed, patience will be needed. It will be needed in all these times and in so many other situations. In all the social relations your teen will establish, she will need patience. That is why it is very important to instill this great virtue in her. It is a valuable weapon that can be used on so many occasions and will prove to be of great help for your teens' well being.

How to instill it in your teen

With this special concept, there are a few more basic ways to infuse it in your teen in addition to the general ways we described in the previous chapters. These are:

1. Training your child/teen on practicing the concept itself. This usually comes through not giving your child everything she asks for all the time. A simple answer such as, "Can we discuss this later after I think about it for a while." Or "yes, we will do what you want, but we'll do it after we finish what we're doing right now" will give a chance to your teen to think about being patient.

2. Provide a model. When things happen that require exercising patience, you as parent should be the first to give the example. Your child will learn from you. Some situations where you have to illustrate this quality are when you're in a traffic jam, when you lose a loved one, or when your dinner is late. Rather than cursing the traffic jam, make *dua'a* or make *tasbeeh*.

3. Explain to them the great reward of exercising patience as was given by *Qur'an* in so many verses, such as verse 10 in *Surah Alzomor,* Allah says,

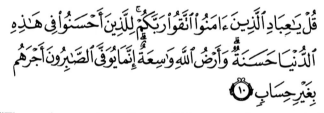

"Those who exercise patience will have countless rewards." (Q 39, V 10).

Also in *Surah Al-Baqarah,* verse 153 Allah says,

يَٰٓأَيُّهَا ٱلَّذِينَ ءَامَنُواْ ٱسْتَعِينُواْ بِٱلصَّبْرِ وَٱلصَّلَوٰةِ إِنَّ ٱللَّهَ مَعَ ٱلصَّٰبِرِينَ ۝

"Verily, Allah is with those who exercise patience." (Q 2, V 153)

4. Utilize the opportunity of the month of *Ramadan*. This month is a wonderful chance to teach your child/teen self control and patience. Being able to go for the whole day without food or drink is a great way to learn discipline.

Every one is individually accountable for what he or she does

Source

Allah SWT says in *Surah Al-Muddather,*

كُلُّ نَفْسٍ بِمَا كَسَبَتْ رَهِينَةٌ ۝

"Every soul will be held accountable for what it earns" (Q 74, V 38)

In *Surah Al-Toor* also Allah says,

وَٱلَّذِينَ ءَامَنُوا۟ وَٱتَّبَعَتْهُمْ ذُرِّيَّتُهُم بِإِيمَٰنٍ أَلْحَقْنَا بِهِمْ ذُرِّيَّتَهُمْ وَمَآ أَلَتْنَٰهُم مِّنْ عَمَلِهِم مِّن شَىْءٍ كُلُّ ٱمْرِئٍ بِمَا كَسَبَ رَهِينٌ ۝

"Every individual will be held accountable for what he/she earns" (Q 52, V 21)

In *Surah Mariam* Allah says,

وَكُلُّهُمْ ءَاتِيهِ يَوْمَ ٱلْقِيَٰمَةِ فَرْدًا ۝

"And all of them will be brought in front of Allah as individuals" (Q 19, V 95)

Also in *Surah Abbasa* Allah says, describing the situation on the Day of Judgment,

يَوْمَ يَفِرُّ ٱلْمَرْءُ مِنْ أَخِيهِ ۝ وَأُمِّهِ وَأَبِيهِ ۝ وَصَٰحِبَتِهِ وَبَنِيهِ ۝

"The day everyone will flee from his own brother, and from his mother and his father, from his companion and his children" (Q 80, V 34-36)

In *Surah Al Aana'am* also, Allah says,

$$وَلَقَدْ جِئْتُمُونَا فُرَادَىٰ$$
$$كَمَا خَلَقْنَاكُمْ أَوَّلَ مَرَّةٍ وَتَرَكْتُم مَّا خَوَّلْنَاكُمْ وَرَاءَ ظُهُورِكُمْ$$
$$وَمَا نَرَىٰ مَعَكُمْ شُفَعَاءَكُمُ الَّذِينَ زَعَمْتُمْ أَنَّهُمْ فِيكُمْ شُرَكَاءُ$$
$$لَقَد تَّقَطَّعَ بَيْنَكُمْ وَضَلَّ عَنكُم مَّا كُنتُمْ تَزْعُمُونَ ﴿٩٤﴾$$

"And behold, you come back to us bare and alone as we have created you for the first time. You have left behind you all (the favors) which We bestowed on you. We see not with you your intercessors whom you thought to be partners in your affairs. So now all relations between you have been cut off, and your (pet) fancies have left you in the lurch." (Q 6, V 94).

The teachings of our beloved prophet Muhammad PBUH emphasize this very same concept. It was reported after *Anas* may Allah be pleased with him that the messenger of Allah peace and blessings of Allah be upon him said, "Three things follow a deceased person to his grave. These are members of his family, his possessions, and his deeds. Two of them return and one stays with him. His family and wealth returns and only his deeds remain with him" (agreed upon).

All these verses of *Qur'an* and the teachings of the prophet PBUH indicate that we will all return back to Allah as individuals. We will not be able to take anything of our worldly belongings with us: no wealth, no family, no relatives, no friends – even the closest friend – will not accompany us to speak on our behalf or defend our position. Only our good deeds will go with us. Imagine, only you and your good deeds will stand in front of Allah on the day of judgment to receive the details of your account as the *Qur'an* says,

$$اقْرَأْ كِتَابَكَ كَفَىٰ بِنَفْسِكَ الْيَوْمَ عَلَيْكَ حَسِيبًا ﴿١٤﴾$$

"Read your own record, sufficient is your soul this day to make out an account against you." (Q 17, V 14).

Importance of this concept

This concept is particularly important for your teen. It will help him in selecting the right kinds of friends. It will help him in not wanting to follow the crowd just to fit in. He will think twice before selecting a friend who may have a negative influence on him.

How to instill it in your teen

1. Never apply a disciplinary measure on all your children at once for a mistake done by one of them. Make sure you are fair with every body when it comes to reward and punishment.

2. Try to use the stories of Qur'an to show that Allah punishes every one according to his own sin.

3. If your teen makes a mistake make sure he suffers the consequences of his mistake.

Select friends carefully

Source

In Qur'an, *Surah Al-Kahf,* Allah says,

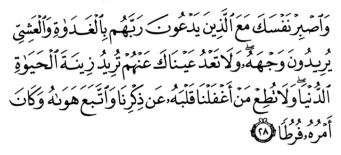

"Keep yourself content with those who call upon their Lord, morning and evening, seeking His pleasure, and do not let your eyes pass beyond them to seek the pomp and glitter of this world. Do not follow him whose heart We have caused to be heedless of our remembrance, and who follows his desires, and whose attitude is of excess." (Q 18, V 28)

It was reported by *Abu Hurairah* may Allah be pleased with him that Prophet Muhammad PBUH said, "A man follows the religion of his closest friend, so each one should consider whom he makes his friend." (*Muslim*)

In another narration, on the authority of *Abu Musa al-Ash'ari* (Allah be pleased with him) that he heard the messenger of Allah peace and blessings be upon him saying, "The similitude of good company and that of bad company is that of the owner of *musk* and of the one (iron smith) blowing bellows. The owner of the *musk* will either offer you some *musk* free of charge or you will buy it from him or smell its pleasant odor. As for the one who blows the bellows, he will either burn your clothes or you shall have to smell its repugnant smell" (agreed upon).

Importance of this concept

Here is how one of our daughters, (*Noha*, 18 years at the time of writing) sees the importance of this concept. "It is important to select the right friends for people of all ages, but especially for children, it's crucial to 'fit in' and feel a sense of belonging to a group of friends. This instills a sense of confidence in a child to try new things, to be active, to participate, and to grow in many ways. The type of friends a teen has is just as crucial. They dictate his behavior, what he says, what he is exposed to, and, often, what he views as right and wrong. With the wrong group of friends, many good children develop bad habits and bad attitudes that weren't otherwise there.

Every child dreams of belonging to the popular group. I know this first hand and can still remember how difficult it was to accept that they did not want me. My first experience with this came when I was seven and had just switched schools. Each child chose where he sat in the lunchroom, but had to stay at that seat all year. On my first day at my new school, I observed who the popular kids were, and without taking note of whether or not they were nice people, I sat next to them in the lunchroom. This ended up being a complete disaster, since the girls I had hoped to become friends with just teased and made fun of me for the rest of the year. Instead of looking forward to my recess period, I dreaded lunchtime everyday for the rest of the year. Fortunately, I learned a lesson from the experience. It was that the popular kids are not always the best kids to befriend, and even though it definitely wasn't fun, I was lucky to have made this discovery in second grade, before it could seriously affect my attitude.

As I've grown up, I have made an effort to choose my friends carefully. At the same time, I do not avoid befriending people who don't have the same opinions or attitudes as me. To a certain extent, I don't feel that there is anything wrong with getting to know people who aren't the same as me, as long as I am confident that they won't change me for the worse. Some parents feel that their children shouldn't talk to people who don't have the exact same values, but this can defeat the purpose of *da'wa*. Sometimes, people who are very different than us, or who live lifestyles that we don't approve of, might be affected by us positively if we take time to get to know them. I'm not saying that it's right to become their best friends or go to movies with them, but getting to know them at school or work is actually a good way to show them that Muslims are "normal" people that they can relate to and deal with."

How to instill it in your teen

Here is how *Noha* remembers what we did with her to stress the importance of this concept. "One of the ways that my parents emphasized the importance of choosing the right friends was to monitor who I spent time with. When I was younger, I would invite friends over to my house before I went to their houses so that my parents had a chance to see who I was spending time with. My parents didn't forbid me from getting to know people, they just requested that it be done in an environment where they would be aware of what was happening and how I interacted with my friends."

<u>Respect is what every respected person should get,</u> <u>especially parents and elders</u>

Source

The glorious *Qur'an* emphasizes showing respect to both parents in many places. In *Surah Israa'*, *verses 23 and 24* Allah says:

$$۞ وَقَضَىٰ رَبُّكَ أَلَّا تَعْبُدُوٓا۟ إِلَّآ إِيَّاهُ وَبِٱلْوَٰلِدَيْنِ إِحْسَٰنًا ۚ إِمَّا$$

$$يَبْلُغَنَّ عِندَكَ ٱلْكِبَرَ أَحَدُهُمَآ أَوْ كِلَاهُمَا فَلَا تَقُل لَّهُمَآ$$

$$أُفٍّ وَلَا تَنْهَرْهُمَا وَقُل لَّهُمَا قَوْلًا كَرِيمًا ٢٣ وَٱخْفِضْ$$

$$لَهُمَا جَنَاحَ ٱلذُّلِّ مِنَ ٱلرَّحْمَةِ وَقُل رَّبِّ ٱرْحَمْهُمَا كَمَا رَبَّيَانِى$$

$$صَغِيرًا ٢٤$$

"Thy lord has decreed that you worship none but Him, and that you be kind to parents. Whether one or both of them attain old age in their life say not to them a word of contempt, nor repel them but address them in terms of honor. And out of kindness, lower to them the wing of humility, and say, 'My Lord! Bestow on them Your mercy even as they nurtured me in childhood.'" (Q 17, V 23&24)

Also in *Surah Baqarah*, verse 83, Allah says,

وَإِذْ أَخَذْنَا مِيثَٰقَ بَنِىٓ إِسْرَٰٓءِيلَ لَا تَعْبُدُونَ إِلَّا ٱللَّهَ وَبِٱلْوَٰلِدَيْنِ
إِحْسَانًا وَذِى ٱلْقُرْبَىٰ وَٱلْيَتَٰمَىٰ وَٱلْمَسَٰكِينِ وَقُولُوا۟
لِلنَّاسِ حُسْنًا وَأَقِيمُوا۟ ٱلصَّلَوٰةَ وَءَاتُوا۟ ٱلزَّكَوٰةَ ثُمَّ
تَوَلَّيْتُمْ إِلَّا قَلِيلًا مِّنكُمْ وَأَنتُم مُّعْرِضُونَ ﴿٨٣﴾

"And remember We took a covenant from the children of Israel (to this effect): worship none but Allah; treat with kindness your parents and kindred, and orphans and those in need; speak fair to the people; be steadfast in prayer; and give *Zakat*." (Q 2 -V 83)

Also, the prophet PBUH has said, "He is not from us the one who doesn't have mercy on our young, and the one who doesn't respect our elders."

Importance of this concept

Children need to see respect demonstrated to parents and other elders in their everyday lives, but North American culture makes it very difficult for children to pick up this quality. In this society, children always hear comments like "why not", "it is not fair", and "I don't care" from their peers as well as from other adults. These types of comments don't promote respect. They are based on a very individualistic attitude. They reflect a self-centered approach where each person is only concerned with what he wants without considering anyone else. That is why it is important for parents to work hard to make sure the child understands what is respectful and what is not. If the child is left alone without parent's guidance in this area, he will grow up to be rude and disrespectful.

It is also important to instill this concept in your teen so that he knows how to get his rights in a respectful way through convincing others rather than fighting or shouting. This will also help him respect the rights of others.

Home life becomes much simpler and enjoyable when everybody exercises respect towards others. A respectful home will help greatly in creating the pleasant, positive, and healthy atmosphere necessary for the success of the training process for your teens. They will be more receptive to their parents' guidance and they will more likely accept it than reject it if they feel respected.

How to instill it in your teen

This can be easily done in many ways: always treat each other with respect so the child has a real life example, treat the child in a respectful way, and consistently instruct, train, and demand your child to do respectful things. For example, tell him to say "please" and "thank you" whenever he is asking for something or something is given to them. Even a situation so simple as thanking his mother for the food at the dinner table will give him an idea of how much his parents do for them.

Even when disagreeing, the children should be taught to do it with respect. For instance, say the parents take the children to the park to play. When it is time to go, the children ask, "Can we stay longer?" After the parents explain that it is time to go, the children insist that they still want to play. They begin to say, "It's not fair. Why do we have to go?" Parents should not tolerate this attitude.

If the children see that this disrespectful attitude is accepted, they will continue to behave in this manner. It is all right to let the children ask politely to stay longer, but they should remember to say please and to know where the limit is and when to stop asking.

Other important concepts that parents should try to instill in their teens include the following:

- Allah doesn't waste the reward of those who do good deeds
- The law of natural consequences
- Pride and arrogance are completely unaccepted
- A strong believer is better and more loved by Allah than a weak one
- Paradise and hellfire are not illusions

– Know Satan's ways and don't give him the pleasure of fooling you
– Don't go through life as a blind hearted person

In addition to the methods explained in the previous chapters and here with each concept, we have found, from our own experiences, that having the right setting while discussing these concepts is very important to the teen's reception. Among these good settings are youth camps and regular discussion groups. Following are few words about each:

A youth camp is a very useful tool to instill good values and important Islamic concepts in your teens. It provides them with an opportunity to live the experiences they are learning about in a nice, fun atmosphere, rather than just learning the theory through lectures. It also provides them with the opportunity to be close to nature and see the beauty of Allah's creation. These camps should be done frequently enough to keep your teen in touch with other teens of the same age and give them the opportunity to build brotherly and sisterly bonds. It can be done on a weekend basis or for a weeklong period during summer break. More than one camp yearly will certainly produce very good results. The camp program should be designed to cover a variety of subjects and activities. In a later section, entitled "Tools you need", we will provide you with the details on how to prepare for and run a successful youth camp, as well as sample of what a camp program should include and cover.

Regular discussion groups and small debates where teens could discuss openly, express their views, and get answers for questions that are preoccupying them and explanations for issues concerning them are another good forum for instilling such concepts. Some balanced, learned, and experienced members of the community should conduct these groups frequently. The leaders of these discussion groups must be patient, open-minded, tolerant and very approachable. They shouldn't be critical of the way the teens think and they should be careful and sensitive towards the teens' needs.

We also refer the reader to the chapter of 'Basic principles for tarbiya from Qur'an and Sunnah' in our book "Meeting the challenge of parenting in the west, an Islamic perspective". The principles listed in this chapter are applicable to teenagers as well as younger children. For this reason, we recommend that they should be observed while instilling these concepts. To refresh your memory, here they are in point form:

1. Understand your child
2. Link the child to Allah
3. Show mercy
4. Show Gentleness, Kindness, Leniency, and Love
5. Observe brevity in preaching
6. Never resort to force
7. Favoritism is not allowed
8. Every soul is accountable for what it earns
9. Good deeds erase bad ones
10. Emphasize and encourage
11. Do things step by step and consider the child's level
12. Express feelings and share happiness and pain
13. Be clear in communication
14. Be an active listener
15. Find suitable alternatives
16. Assist in skill development
17. Control anger
18. Help your child cooperate with you
19. Always fulfill a promise
20. Follow up on orders and be consistent
21. Teach them *Haya'*
22. Use examples from their environment
23. Use a holistic approach

Summary

We devoted this chapter for the discussion of some very important basic Islamic concepts that every parent is required to instill in his teen to help him/her have a strong, confident, rounded personality that wouldn't compromise his/her Islamic principles. For every concept, we indicated the source from *QUR'AN* and the teachings of Prophet Muhammad may Allah's peace and blessings be upon him, we discussed the importance of the concept in the life of the teen, and we provided certain suggestions as how you can instill the concept in the heart and mind of the teen. These concepts include Allah loves you, life is a test, our real home is in the hereafter, Allah is with you all the time, patience is a great virtue, Islam is a complete way of life, Select your friends carefully, and we are accountable for what we hear, what we see, and what we think about.

7. Case Studies

In this chapter we will provide you with some practical case studies that happen in many Muslim homes across North America. We have used some of these case studies in our parenting workshops and they proved to be illustrative and bring the point home to the parents. For you as a parent to benefit the most from these case studies, please follow the following instructions exactly:

1. Read each case study carefully.
2. Answer all the questions in writing and in detail.
3. Write down any other ideas that you may have which may have not been covered in the questions.
4. After you finish all case studies go to the next section and compare your answers with those in the section. Don't go to the next section except after you have finished all the cases.
5. It is beneficial to do this exercise together with your spouse.
6. While you are answering the questions try to remember the basic principles of tarbiya as well as the important concepts discussed and explained in the previous sections.

Get ready. Have a notebook and pen available and enjoy the exercises:

1. So much for building self-confidence

Alia is 14 years old. She lives with her parents and her brother *Sa'd* and sister *Saneiah*. One day, after she finished helping her mom in the kitchen to prepare for the guests they were expecting, she went up to her room to get dressed and brush her hair. She wanted to look nice when her mom's friends, and her own friends, *Layla* and *Sarah*, came over. When she came down, her mom looked over at her and said, "What are you wearing? That outfit doesn't look good at all. Go up and change into the purple dress I just bought for you." *Alia* tried to reply, but her mom went on without giving her a chance, "Hurry up before they come. And change your hair too. It looks awful like that." *Alia* tried to answer again, but her mom cut her off and said, "How many times do I have to tell you these things? I'm only trying to help you look nice."

    Alia went up to her room, sat on her bed and burst into tears.

Questions

1. Is this a common problem? Think of examples of your own.
2. Do you think a 14 year old has the same taste as her parents when it comes to clothes in a private setting and when it's not an issue of following the Islamic dress code?
3. What do you think of the way the mother expressed her opinion to her daughter? Is this positive or negative parental behavior?
4. How do you express your opinion to your children when you are faced with situations like this?
5. How do you think *Alia*'s mom's actions affected *Alia* regarding self-confidence and positive self-concept? How would this affect *Alia*'s ability to face peer pressure?
6. What would be your advice to *Alia*'s mom to make sure that her reaction is more positive?

2. School activities

Jamila is 14 years old and goes to high school. One day, while *Jamila* was in Drama class and they were doing warm-up games, the teacher chose a boy as *Jamila*'s partner. *Jamila* knew that there might be physical contact involved in the game, but she was too afraid to say anything to her teacher. She didn't want to embarrass herself in front of her classmates, so she participated and ended up having to link arms with her partner. *Jamila* felt bad about the incident all day, and discussed it with her mother when she got home. Her father overheard the conversation.

Questions

1. How do you think the parents reacted to this situation?
2. How do you think *Jamila* felt about herself after the incident?
3. What do you think the best way to handle the situation would be, as a parent?
4. Could *Jamila* have done anything to prevent the situation from happening?

3. Is there such a thing as "A Perfect Child"?

Safiya is a fifteen year old high school student. Since both her sisters are married and moved out when she was 11 years old, she feels lonely at home, living only with her parents. *Safiya* also doesn't feel close to her mom; she feels that no matter how hard she tries, she can never please her. *Safiya* feels that she has nothing in common with her parents.

One Saturday morning, *Safiya* asked her dad if she could go visit her friend *Hayat* for the morning. *Safiya*'s mom overheard her and answered, "no you can't. You have to stay and clean your room. Don't you realize how messy it is?"

Safiya said, "please mom, I'll do it later."

Her mom responded, "No, you shouldn't go out to enjoy yourself before you finish your chores." *Safiya* was very upset; she went to her room and slammed the door. The mom shouted, "what do you think you're doing *Safiya*? You are not going to visit *Hayat* even after you clean your room. Don't you have any manners!"

Safiya answered back, "Leave me alone, I don't care."

The next day, *Safiya* refused to sit at the dinner table with her parents. Instead, she stayed in her room talking on the phone with her friend *Alia*. This made her mom very upset. She told *Safiya*, "As long as you don't talk to your parents, you have no right to use the phone."

Safiya answered back, "this is too much, I can't live like this anymore."

The father interfered saying, "Come on ladies, let us stop this nonsense and talk to each other like a loving and caring family."

"Enough. Don't you see how you spoiled her," *Safiya*'s mom responded, "I'm not talking to her. She should learn what respect means first."

Questions

1. Do you think this is a common problem?
2. What do you think is the cause of the problem?
3. Do you think the mother is handling the situation in the right way? Why?
4. Do you think the father is spoiling *Safiya*? Is it better that he has a united front with the mother?
5. What do you think the best way to handle the situation would be, as a parent?
6. Can you relate to *Safiya*'s situation?

4. I pray to Allah. Do I need to do anything else?

Hassina is 15 years old. She lives with her parents and her brother *Ahmad* who is 13 years old and her sister *Zaynab* who is 11 years old. *Hassina* is a hard working ambitious grade 9 student. She has a good relationship with her family and she cares to please her parents. One day her mom noticed that *Hassina* was very upset and troubled. When she asked her what was wrong, *Hassina* burst into tears saying, "I got a B on my math exam!! I wanted to get an A+. I prayed so hard but my prayer didn't work!!" Her mother said, "Don't worry, next time insha' Allah you will get an A."

Two days later, while the family was having dinner together, *Ahmad* said, "My friend *Farid* finally came back to school today, but he looked really sad and distant. He's still feeling bad about his father's death. I tried to cheer him up but it didn't work. While we were talking, he seemed very angry about his dad's long illness and death. He told me, 'I prayed to Allah so much to cure my dad. I even took the Sheikh's advice to put my hand over my dad's chest while making the *dua'a*. I read the exact words the Sheikh taught me. But still my dad died. I don't understand why my prayers didn't work. Why?'"

Hassina said, "I don't understand either. Poor *Farid*."

Questions
1. How do you think *Hassina* feels?
2. How do you think her feelings are going to influence her attitude towards life and her commitment as a Muslim?
3. How do you think *Farid* feels?
4. How do you think his feelings are going to influence his attitude towards life and his commitment as a Muslim?
5. What would you suggest the parents do to help their children deal with this issue?

5. Mom, be careful of the impression that you are giving about Dad

Sarah is 15 years old. She lives with her parents and her two younger brothers. *Sarah* was late coming home from school on Friday, which got her mother very worried. While her mom was calling around trying to find out where she was, *Sarah* walked into the house with a friend of hers asking, "Can Tina have dinner with us tonight mom?"

Although the mother was upset, she answered, "Yes of course."

Sarah went to her room with her friend. Later on in the evening, *Sarah* asked her mom to drive her friend home.

One week later, *Sarah* called her mother from school saying, "I'm going to the mall with my friends after school. Don't worry if I'm late." The mother tried to tell *Sarah* to come straight home from school, but *Sarah* kept insisting and begging her mom to go until her mom let her.

When *Sarah* came home that evening, she showed her mom a blouse that she'd bought. Her mom looked at the blouse in a state of shock and said, "You know that you shouldn't wear such tight clothes, and where did you get the money for that anyway?"

Sarah answered, "What is wrong with the blouse? It's what's in style right now. All my friends at school are wearing it. I borrowed the money from *Farhat*. All my friends go out and do their own shopping, why can't I do the same thing?"

The mother said, "I don't know, but I know that your dad is going to be really upset."

Sarah threw the blouse on the chair saying, "What is this? I can't do anything on my own. Why is dad always upset?"

Questions

1. *Sarah* was late coming home from school to the extent where she got her mother worried. What do you think of her mother's reaction to the situation? What kind of message would this give to *Sarah*?

2. How would you describe *Sarah*'s mom's parenting style?

3. Why do you think *Sarah*'s mom is reacting this way towards *Sarah*'s behavior? Do you think her reaction indicates that she is confused or that she has a plan and a vision for her daughter's upbringing?

4. How do you think *Sarah* is going to view her dad from the way her mother is presenting him?

5. Fifteen year-olds love to spend lot of time with their friends going to movies and hanging around the mall. In your opinion, how can a parent deal with this using a balanced approach?

6. *Sarah* told her mom, " What is wrong with the blouse? It's what's in style right now. All my friends at school are wearing it." At what age you think a youth should know what is suitable and what is not in terms of

clothes? What can parents do to help their son or daughter develop the ability to make the right choice in spite of peer pressure in the areas of clothing and brand name buying?

7. Can the father do anything to help improve the situation? What do you suggest?

6. Please, Dad listen to me before it is too late

Faris is 13 years old and lives with his parents, his 12 year old sister *Hameedah* and five year old brother. At home, *Faris* is always in a grouchy mood, fighting with his siblings and rebelling against his mother. *Faris* always asks his mom to go outside and hang out with the boys on the street. Because his mom doesn't like the boys' attitude, she doesn't allow *Faris* to be with them. *Faris* gets upset, yells, shouts and demands to go out. His mom locks the door to keep him in. *Faris*'s mom has mentioned the situation to his dad several times. She asked him to take sometime off to spend with *Faris* and deal with the matter. The dad's answer has always been, "keep your son busy at home. Give him things to do; I'm too busy and you know that."

A year later, the mother received a note from *Faris*'s school informing her that *Faris* has been skipping school and asking that both parents come in for an interview. When *Faris*'s mom told his dad, he said, "I can't go. I have a meeting that day. You go and find out what kind of trouble he's in now."

At the interview, the teacher and the mother worked out a plan to monitor *Faris* closely in order to make sure *Faris* didn't skip school anymore. When the mother talked to *Faris*'s dad and asked him to get more involved with *Faris*, he called *Faris* over and said, "Listen son, you know how busy I am. Here, take these twenty dollars and be a good boy."

A couple of weeks later, *Faris*'s mom noticed that money has been disappearing from the family petty cash box. On the same day, *Hameedah* came home very disturbed. She rushed over to her mom saying, "I saw *Faris* standing with his friends and they were all smoking cigarettes. The mom hurried to the phone and called *Faris*'s dad who became very upset and said, "What a terrible boy! Why is he doing this to us? I'm killing myself working long hours to build a good future for him. Why can't he be good? What else can we do?"

Questions

1. In your opinion, is this a common problem?
2. What is your analysis of the situation *Faris* is in? What do you think the cause of the problem is?
3. How important is it for a 13 year old to have friends? *Faris* wants to go out and hang around with the neighborhood kids. Should parents allow that and under what conditions?
4. Do you think the mother solved the problem by locking the door and preventing *Faris* from going out, or does the problem go much deeper than this?
5. The father mentioned that he is working very hard to build a good future for *Faris*. Do you think that is all *Faris* needs from him?
6. What would you suggest *Faris*'s parents do to solve *Faris*'s steeling and smoking problems?
7. What would be your advice to *Faris*'s parents to help him get through this critical stage of his life?

7. He finds schools work Very Boring

Hamdy is 12 years old, and in grade seven. He lives with his parents and two sisters, *Suad* who is 13 years old, and *Safiya* who is 8 years old. *Hamdy*'s parents care very much about their children and are doing everything they can to make them happy.

When the children come home from school, *Safiya* and *Suad* rush make their prayers, then sit down and complete their homework right away. *Hamdy*, on the other hand, keeps fooling around until his mother calls on him to pray and to do his homework. *Hamdy* doesn't respond. The mother gets angry and calls again and finally sends him to his room to do his homework. Half an hour later, *Hamdy* comes down to the kitchen to drink a glass of water. He finds his sisters watching TV after they have completed their homework. He sits with them to watch TV and forgets about his homework. When his mother sees him, she gets very angry and yells at him, "*Hamdy*, go to your room and finish your homework right now!"

Hamdy answers back in a whiny voice, "why should I sit alone while *Suad* and *Safiya* are watching TV? I don't want to do homework. It is boring."

The next day, the same thing happens. *Hamdy* is sent to his room whining and protesting. Fifteen minutes later, his mother goes to his room to remind him to pray and finds him playing a card game instead of studying. She yells at him again and threatens to tell his dad. *Hamdy* answers back, "I don't want to do homework. It is boring."

Half an hour later, *Hamdy* comes out of his room and lies to his mom, showing her one page of math work and saying that he has completed his homework. Then he sits down to watch TV with his sisters.

The next day, his mother gets a call from *Hamdy*'s teacher requesting an interview with both parents. When she tells *Hamdy*'s father about the call, he says he has no time and asks the mom to go alone to meet the teacher. When the mother goes, she meets all of *Hamdy*'s teachers and they all tell her that *Hamdy* is very behind with his schoolwork. His homework is almost never completed. The mother discovers that he has been lying to her about finishing homework. The mother leaves the school very upset and disappointed. When the father comes home in the evening, she tells him about the interview. They are both very worried and don't know what to do.

Questions

1. In your opinion, is this a common problem? How serious is it?
2. What do you think the cause of the problem is?
3. What do you think the parents could have done to avoid this problem?
4. Do you think it is OK that *Hamdy* at 12 years of age still needs his parents to remind him to pray at each prayer time?
5. In your opinion, do you think it is too late to solve the problem?
6. If your answer for question 5 is no, what do you suggest *Hamdy*'s parents do to help *Hamdy* correct his attitude and behavior?
7. If you were to give one piece of advice to all parents to avoid having such a problem, what would that be?

8. Peer pressure and home expectation

Fatih is a grade seven student. He tries his best to live up to his parents' expectations. This takes a great deal of effort from him and often goes unnoticed. At school, *Fatih* is experiencing a lot of peer pressure and doesn't feel that he belongs; he doesn't enjoy sports, and doesn't belong to a group or have many friends. One day at school, the only friend he has asks him to go out with him during the lunch break to buy something from the store. *Fatih* goes along with his friend, who buys a pack of cigarettes and starts smoking. He offers *Fatih* a cigarette and keeps pressuring him to try it. *Fatih* has a hard time refusing, but he manages to say no. *Fatih* finds it hard to cope and needs to talk about it but he's very scared of mentioning what happened to his parents fearing that they'll become upset with him, and that his dad will get really mad.

Fatih goes home the same day with his report card. When his dad looks at it, he gets really upset. Without giving *Fatih* a chance to explain himself, he starts shouting at *Fatih* about two grades that don't meet his expectations. *Fatih* is very upset and finds it hard to meet his parents' expectations at home and deal with the peer pressure at school.

Questions
1. Do you feel that *Fatih* is in a difficult position? How would you feel if you were in his place?
2. As a grade 7 student, do you think it is important to feel like you belong to a group?
3. What do you suggest *Fatih*'s parents do to help him have high self-respect (high self-esteem), so he is in a stronger position when dealing with peer pressure?
4. Do you think *Fatih*'s dad is putting enough effort into keeping the channel of communication open between him and *Fatih*?
5. What would be your advice to *Fatih*'s dad to do to improve the situation?

9. Isolation is not the solution

Hasan is 15 year old boy. His mother loves him very much and takes good care of him. She has always tried to help him with everything. If Hasan needs to buy something from the store, his mom will drive him there and buy it for him, even though the store may be very close to his school and he could have stopped by on his way home and picked up what he needed. If *Hasan* has a project to research and has to check references in the library, she will take the trouble of driving him around and waiting for him to check the references.

One day, *Hasan* called his mom from school and asked her if he could go to the shopping center with his friends to buy some stationary needed for a project in the school. The mother was very hesitant, but finally she said, "OK. You can go with your friends, but don't be late."

After he hung up, she started questioning herself and felt that she made a mistake by allowing him to go with his friends to the mall. She took her car and started driving around from one mall to another searching for *Hasan*.

Hasan's mom finally found him leaving one of the shopping malls with three of his friends. She stopped the car right next to him and called him to get in right away. *Hasan* did as he was told, but he seemed really upset and would not talk to his mom all the way back to his home.

Questions

1. Do you think this is a common problem?
2. What do you think is causing the problem?
3. Do you think *Hasan*'s mom did the right thing by allowing him to go with his friends to the mall?
4. Do you think it is important for a 15 year old to be able to shop and buy things he needs without his mother's help?
5. What is your advice to *Hasan*'s mom?
6. Do you think *Hasan*'s mom's behavior may affect *Hasan*'s development?

10. The Internet dilemma

Imad is 16 years old. He is an average high school student. He lives with his parents and his older brother *Mohsen*. He spends a lot of time sitting at his computer. Whenever his parents invite him to go to a community activity, he declines their invitation and says, "I don't enjoy going there."

One night, *Imad*'s dad came home early in the evening, which rarely happens because he usually stays late at work. When the mother called everybody down for dinner, *Imad* answered, "I'll eat later, I'm busy right now."

The dad was hurt and said, "Here I am, coming home early to have dinner as a family, leaving tons of work behind, and your son is too busy for me!"

One night, *Imad*'s mom told him that *Ahmad* from the community youth group called to inform him that there will be a soccer game on the weekend and asked if he wanted to play. *Imad* nodded in agreement.

On Saturday, *Imad*'s mom went to his room to remind him about the game and found him on his computer. "Are you still sitting in front of your computer?" she asked, "Haven't you gotten tired of talking to a machine yet? You're going to be late for the game, hurry up and get ready."

"I'm not going," *Imad* replied, "I don't know anybody there."

"Go to the game *Imad*," his mom said, "you will meet other young people and get to know them."

Imad looked up and said, "You don't understand how it feels when you don't have any friends. Chat rooms are better. At least I have *Mona* to talk to. She understands me."

The mother was shocked and said, "What's the matter with you, *Imad*? Are you spending all this time in front of the computer talking to girl instead of going out and making real friends?"

"So what's wrong with that," *Imad* answered, "I don't even meet with her."

Questions

1. Judging from the case, do you think the way *Imad* spends his time will help him to have a balanced personality and enable him to build the social skills needed for a healthy life?

2. In your opinion, why doesn't *Imad* want to attend the soccer game or to participate in the community youth group activities?

3. What are the benefits and harms of spending a long time in front of the computer? Do you think there is a big difference between this and spending long hours watching TV?

4. *Imad* didn't rush down to have dinner with the family when his dad came home early. Why do you think he stayed upstairs? What do you think of the dad's reaction when *Imad* didn't come down?

5. *Imad* thought that he wasn't doing anything wrong by talking to *Mona* through the chat room. What do you think?

6. For a 16 year old, the need to be understood is very important. What could the family do to make sure that this need is fulfilled in a proper way?

7. Suggest some practical ways for the family to help *Imad* changes his computer habits.

11. Needs and wants (bad company)

Ghazi is a 19 year old university student. He lives with his mom and his 16 year old brother. Up until recently, his father, *Abbas*, used to live with them, but he was transferred to another city with work. Before the father moved, they used to spend the weekend together as a family. However, they were never part of the Muslim community at large. Now, *Ghazi's* father only comes to visit for few days once every three months.

Through university, *Ghazi* has met a group of students who like to go out together on Friday and Saturday nights for fun. At the beginning, they used to go out for dinner or coffee. One night, while they were at a coffee shop, *Morad* suggested that they go to a nightclub close by. *Tarek* and *Sayed* thought this was an interesting idea, but *Ghazi* said, "No. It's not a good place to go."

Morad answered, "Don't you see, we have needs and they need to be met."

Tarek suggested taking a vote to decide. They ended up going all together.

When *Ghazi* went home late that night, he found his mother worried and eager to know where he had been. *Ghazi* told his mother the whole story, but assured her that he would never do anything wrong, and that he'd only gone along this one time.

Ghazi started coming home late every weekend. His mom got worried, and when she asked him what was happening and brought up the nightclubs, he answered angrily, "What do you expect me to do? I'm under so much pressure. I still have at least three more years to go before I can get a job and get married. I'm 19 and I have needs."

"What are we going to do now?" his mom says, "Why can't you focus on your studies and I promise you, after 4 years you will have the best bride and the most expensive wedding party in the world."

"Three more years?" *Ghazi* says, "*Tarek*, *Morad* and *Sayed* all have girlfriends! And you want me to wait three years? That's impossible."

Questions

1. Teens like to spend time together away from their parents engaging in various activities and discovering new adventures. Different parents allow various degrees of freedom with their teens. In your opinion, what is considered healthy and reasonable?

2. To have a girlfriend or boyfriend is considered a normal part of non-Muslim western culture. Our teens are fully exposed to this. How can you help your son or daughter to standout and be different regarding this issue?

3. Although *Ghazi* knew that the nightclub was not a good place to go, he went along with his friends. Later on, he started doubting his views and even thinking differently. Is peer pressure real? What do you think?

4. How could you help your teen have better confidence in himself and his knowledge to resist peer pressure?

5. Suggest some practical solutions *Ghazi*'s parents could use to resolve the problem and help the situation.

12. Small problems grow bigger if not attended to properly

Tamer is 9 years old. He lives with his parents and his older sister and younger brother. *Tamer*'s parents have always had conflicts regarding his dad's lack of involvement with the children. *Tamer*'s mother is always complaining that his father does not do much with the children. She says that as soon as he comes home from work, he lies down on the couch and watches TV. On Saturdays, the dad goes out with his friends to play soccer, and often on Sundays they get together to socialize. On the rare occasion that the family goes out for picnic or other outings, the father is only there physically and doesn't show any interest or initiative in getting involved in the family activities. In turn, the mother keeps demanding that he do things with the kids and the tensions start to rise. *Tamer* is rather quiet and always complains that he is bored with his life.

A few years later, *Tamer* is 13 years old. He is always fighting with his mom to let him go out and spend time with John, his non-Muslim friend who goes to the same school. *Tamer* is also not doing well at school and doesn't keep up with his schoolwork. Both parents blame each other for *Tamer*'s deteriorating situation and are never able to agree on a course of action to correct it.

Several years later, *Tamer* is 16. His mother notices that he sleeps long hours and it is very hard to wake him up. He is loosing his appetite and he spends a lot of time by himself. *Tamer*'s parents take him to the doctor to check on his health. After an initial investigation, the doctor suggests running extra tests. After receiving the test results, the doctor informs *Tamer*'s parents that tests show that *Tamer* is on drugs. He suggests a course of treatment. *Tamer*'s parents are very upset at *Tamer* and they tell him to stop right away. He promises his parents that he will do that.

A few months later, *Tamer*'s parents receive a telephone call from the school requesting them to come in for a meeting with *Tamer*, as he has not been coming to the school for a week. At the meeting, *Tamer* tells everyone that he couldn't keep up with the school program. They all agree to come up with a special program for *Tamer* to follow which may be simpler and easier.

Later on the same year, *Tamer* can't follow the program and his parents discover that he has dropped out of school. They try to discuss the matter with him but it doesn't work. Everybody is really upset and pointing fingers at everybody else. *Tamer* can't take the pressure and he leaves home without telling his parents where he is going. Every now and then, *Tamer* will come home to see his mom and ask her for money to keep up with his expenses.

Tamer is now 20 years old. His parents have gotten him several jobs, but he has gotten himself fired every time. His parents are really sad about what happened with him. They want to help him but they don't know how.

Questions

1. What do you think *Tamer*'s future will look like if his mom and dad can't get their act together?

2. When *Tamer* was 9 years old, he started showing signs of problems. What did *Tamer* need then that he wasn't getting? What would you suggest the parents had done?

3. When *Tamer* was 13 years old, he showed even more signs of problems, but the parents were too distracted with blaming each other that they didn't help him. What would you suggest they had done instead?

4. At 16 years old, *Tamer* was on drugs!! His parents were shocked, sad and upset. They thought that it would never happen to them. Do you think any youth is immune to drugs?

5. What do you suggest *Tamer*'s parents could have done then to eradicate the drug problem?

6. At 20 years old, *Tamer* is a high school dropout, can't hold down a job, and takes drugs. *Tamer* is in deep trouble. Do you think all this could have been avoided?

7- Please give your analysis and suggestions for *Tamer*'s case.

8- Should *Tamer*'s parents give up on him, or there are other things that they can still do to help him? List your suggestions.

8. Anatomy of Case Studies

1. So much for building self confidence

1. Do you think a 14 year old has the same taste as her parents when it comes to clothes in a private setting and when it's not an issue of following the Islamic dress code? No, of course not. Each time and culture has its own tastes and what mother should be concerned with is to help *Alia* stay within the Islamic dress code. She should also allow her to develop her own taste according to her own time and culture

2. What do you think of how the mother expressed her opinion to her daughter? Is this positive or negative parental behavior? The mother's reaction definitely falls under the category of negative parental behavior. She expressed her opinion in a rude and forceful way. She didn't give her daughter a chance to respond to her comments.

3. How do you express your opinion to your children when you're are faced with situations like this? This is for you to answer.

4. How do you think *Alia*'s mom's actions affected *Alia* regarding self-confidence and positive self-concept? How would this affect *Alia*'s ability to face peer pressure? *Alia*'s mom reaction, where she undermined *Alia*'s opinion and taste and didn't give her a chance to make her own decisions, even on such a personal issue, will definitely cause damage. *Alia* will either have very low self-confidence, or will get stubborn and go against her parents' advice as a general rule. In both situations, it will leave her with very limited ability to face peer pressure.

5. What would be your advice to *Alia*'s mom to make sure that her reaction is more positive? *Alia*'s mom should have a clear vision with regards to what she wants to achieve in building *Alia*'s personality. Her vision should guide all her actions and reactions towards *Alia*. One important objective is to have *Alia* like herself just the way she is. This will help in building her self-confidence and thus, she will not try to imitate her peers just to feel accepted.

If the mother has a different opinion than *Alia* regarding the way she's dressing or doing her hair, she can suggest it in a gentle and loving way and let *Alia* decide whether to take or leave her mom's suggestion. Remember that *Alia* is 14 years old and that she is over-sensitive to how she looks and whether or not she's in style. *Alia*'s mom should show the same courtesy and gentleness toward her daughter as she would show a stranger she's inviting to Islam.

2. School activities

1. How do you think the parents reacted to this situation? The typical parents' reaction to such a situation, especially parents from Eastern backgrounds, would be to shout at their daughter for what she did and make a scene.

2. How do you think *Jamila* felt about herself after the incident? *Jamila* must have felt bad about herself after the incident. She knows that physical contact between different genders is not allowed; yet she wasn't able to say no. She also must have felt as though she was weak and that she couldn't face peer pressure and be different.

3. What do you think the best way to handle the situation would be, as a parent? As a parent, the best way to handle the situation would be to calmly discuss it with *Jamila*. *Jamila* has to realize that this was a mistake on her part and to understand that she shouldn't repeat it in the future. However, it may not be enough for her to only understand that this was wrong. She may need some support from her parents to get over the feeling of embarrassment she is experiencing for being different and to be able to say no in a polite way or suggest some alternatives to the teacher in situations like this. This support can be in the form of offering certain solutions to *Jamila* and making her part of the decision making process. It can also be with *Jamila*'s agreement –scheduling a meeting with the Drama teacher and discussing the issue in particular and Muslim children's requirements in general.

4. Could *Jamila* have done anything to prevent the situation from happening? If *Jamila* was a strong, supported, and encouraged child, she probably would have been able to think of some solution with her family's help. It looks like she was not getting enough support and encouragement from her parents to be able to say no in situations like this. As a result, she gave up and followed the crowd due to fear and embarrassment.

3. Is there such a thing as "A Perfect Child"?

It is very crucial for a teenager to feel accepted, understood and loved by her family. A Parent needs to educate herself about the psychological make-up of the teen. This will help her to understand why her teen is behaving the way she is. In this case, *Safiya*, being fifteen years old, wants to feel like she is in charge of her own life and can make her own decisions independently of her parents. Her mom, on the other hand, is still treating her like a child by ordering her around and not giving her a chance to be part of the decision making process. *Safiya* is also rebellious by the nature of her age, so if she believes that her mother is not being fair to her, she is going to protest and strike back. As this course of actions and reactions repeats itself over and over, *Safiya* will reach the conclusion that her parents don't understand her. As a result, she will keep things from them. She won't share her experiences or discuss things that are preoccupying her to try to get answers. She won't seek their advice regarding issues that are puzzling her. As the distance between *Safiya* and her parents grows, she will feel intimidated and uncomfortable at home and find a greater need to be with her friends so she can get over her loneliness. *Safiya* is living in a culture where teens generally have a lot of independence, make their own decisions away from parental supervision, and spend their time as they please. *Safiya*, like other Muslim youth, is aware of this and probably compares her situation to that of other teens in this culture. This fact should make Muslim parents more tactful when dealing with potential conflicts with their teens. We notice here that the mother's approach is not at all tactful, but actually very confrontational. This approach makes *Safiya* defensive every time her mom orders her around or yells at her. *Safiya* sees this as a personal attack, which leads her to focus on ways to fight back, causing her to behave inappropriately and show disrespect by slamming the door or answering rudely.

Safiya's parents have every right to expect *Safiya* to treat them with respect, however, the way to get it is through modeling respectful behavior themselves. When the mother takes *Safiya*'s feelings and needs into consideration, it is most likely that *Safiya* will answer nicely and not resort to disrespectful behavior. Now, let's answer the questions related to the case.

1. Do you think this is a common problem? Yes, this is definitely a common problem especially among families who live in the western culture and don't re-examine their traditional parenting techniques. Parents need to take Islamic standards and prophet's teachings as their point of reference over their own experience while growing up.

2. What do you think is causing the problem? The problem is a result of a lack of communication between *Safiya* and her mother. This was due to *Safiya*'s mother inability to recognize her daughter's needs and the nature of the stage she is going through.

3. Do you think the mother is handling the situation in the right way? Why? The mother is definitely not handling the situation in the right way. She is focusing on minor issues and creating big problems that are putting up strong barriers between her and her daughter.

4. Do you think the father is spoiling *Safiya*? Is it better that he has a united front with the mother? The father is in a very hard position. He recognizes that his wife's way is not working, but it is also obvious that the mother is not responding to his ideas about easing down with these minor issues and focusing on the important matters. As such, it looks like the father is taking his daughter's side. Although this is not a good situation, but it may be the only way for him to try to minimize the negative reaction of his teen towards the situation.

5. What do you think the best way to handle the situation would be, as a parent? The best way would be to give *Safiya* some freedom to make her choices and plan her time as long as it doesn't contradict Islamic ethics and values. Also, the parents can be flexible with the way she handles other issues such as room tidiness and use of the phone. This way, the teen will feel that her parents understand her and more likely than not, she will follow their instructions, even on less important issues.

6. Can you relate to *Safiya*'s situation? This is for you to answer.

4. I pray to Allah. Do I need to do anything else?

1. How do you think *Hassina* feels? *Hassina* may feel dejected, disappointed, disillusioned, confused, frustrated, sad and abandoned. She may also feel upset and let down. She can definitely sympathize with *Farid*, as she is concerned about why her prayers were not answered.

2. How do you think her feelings are going to influence her attitude towards life and her commitment as a Muslim? It is hard to predict if her attitude towards life will be affected. This event may not influence her

commitment to Islam if her parents respond properly to her questions and guide her in the right direction. However, if her parents fail to explain things and comfort her with respect to what took place, this may reduce her commitment to Islam and she may be in doubt of the legitimacy of supplication and prayers. In the extreme case, she may become rebellious and lose faith in *dua'a* as an effective tool for seeking help from Allah.

3. How do you think *Farid* feels? *Farid* would feel the same way as *Hassina*. In addition, he would also feel angry and betrayed, because his loss is also much bigger than *Hassina*'s, the Sheikh gave him advice and it didn't work.

4. How do you think his feelings are going to influence his attitude towards life and his commitment as a Muslim? As we explained in *Hassina*'s case, without parental intervention and a proper explanation, this incident may decrease his faith and made him lose interest in *dua'a*. He also may feel that he is not in control and he can't face the challenges of life, which may impact negatively on his self esteem.

5. What would you suggest the parents do to help their children deal with this issue? Parents have to be supportive and teach their children, in a loving way and over a period of time, that even if their prayers were not answered now, Allah SWT has wisdom and we should submit to Him. They should emphasize that even with *dua'a*, we still have to do our share in terms of working hard to get the best results needed. In *Hassina*'s case, may be the specific subject she was studying required more studies and drills. May be she thought that she had done enough, but she actually needed to do more.

Parents should also explain to their teens that Allah SWT answers prayers in three different ways as the prophet PBUH told us. These are:

– The prayer might be answered right away
– The prayer might be saved for the person and he will be rewarded extra on the Day of Judgment for his patience.
– Allah might protect the person and prevent a bigger calamity from befalling him with this prayer.

In addition, they have to teach their teens that death is a natural fact of life and that we all have to go through it. Even the most beloved person to us and to Allah, the Prophet Muhammad PBUH, has experienced death.

A close and healthy relation within the family would help parents do this job effectively in a loving and more acceptable way to their teens.

5. Mom, be careful of the impression that you are giving about Dad

In the case of *Sarah*'s dilemma, she has asked her mother why she can't wear the blouse she bought. Everybody is wearing the same type of blouse, all her friends are wearing it, so why can't she? *Sarah* is asking the question because she really needs an answer. It's natural for her to want to be like those around her. She is in a stage where seeking her peers' approval is very important to her. She is drawn psychologically and emotionally to imitating her peers in an effort to fit in.

The way she is asking the question really means that she wants to know, 'why can't I be like them? Am I any less important?'

The proper way to deal with the problem would be for the parents to DISCUSS, INDICATE, and TRAIN. Unfortunately, the majority of parents don't do this. Now, let us see how most parents would react to a problem such as this one, and how they would respond to their teens asking these kinds of questions. Generally parents could be divided into two groups:

1. Group one will include the parents who are afraid that their daughter will not listen to their advice and obey their instructions. Because of their insecurity, they will be easily frustrated and probably yell at the child, saying, "You can't do this because you are Muslim and Muslims are not allowed to do this. End of discussion." This is not a good or complete answer as it doesn't give the teen a convincing reason and it doesn't help to minimize the pressure the teen is experiencing. The teen will keep asking to do what she wants to do in the first place as long as she doesn't get a convincing answer. This might also lead her to think that being a Muslim is putting her at disadvantage compared to her peers. As such, she won't value her status as a Muslim, rather, she might seek a way to escape from it as she sees it as a limiting and restrictive religion, which ties her down with no apparent benefit.

2. As for the second group of parents, having witnessed that the child is under the pressure of wanting to fit in and be like her peers, and with continuous pressure from the teen on the parents, they may give in and let the teen have it her way, even though that would be un-Islamic. Parents usually do that to get away from the pressure. When they react this way, it means that they are not leading the upbringing and training process. On the contrary, they are reacting to the pressure that their teen puts them under. Parents must keep in mind that the teen is young and does not yet

have enough knowledge, experience or wisdom to know what will benefit her from what will harm her. Yes, although the teen might be acting like she is an adult and she may be as tall as her mom, she is not really in any position to lead the *Tarbiya* process. Parents should also realize that the teen is under a lot of pressure to fit in and feel that she belongs to her peer group. She is struggling with the urge to copy the lifestyle of the children in her peer group. At the same time, she is faced with the fact that her parents are trying to stop her. This is a real struggle for the teen.

The parent's duty is to help their teen to manage this struggle in a correct, healthy way. This means that they should empower her so that she feels good about who she is and doesn't need to copy others. Parents need to help her reach a stage where, although she may feel the pain of being different, she will not compromise her Islamic identity to get over this pain. Please refer to 'How to empower your teen' in chapter four.

Now to answer the questions.

1. *Sarah* was late coming home from school to the extent where she got her mother worried. What do you think of her mother's reaction to the situation? What kind of message would this give to *Sarah*? The mother's reaction to *Sarah* coming home late was inappropriate, as she didn't address the issue with *Sarah*. This sent the wrong message that what *Sarah* did was acceptable. The mother could have let *Sarah* and her friend settle down nicely, then asked *Sarah* to come and talk to her in private. Then she could have asked *Sarah* about the reason for being late and inviting her friend over without first checking with her mom. She could have let *Sarah* know that this behavior was unacceptable, however she would let it go this time to avoid embarrassing *Sarah* with her friend. It will be clear to *Sarah* that in the future, such behavior will not to be tolerated. If the mother had reacted in this way, it is likely that she would have put an end to *Sarah*'s careless behavior regarding following family rules.

2. How would you describe *Sarah*'s mom's parenting style? *Sarah*'s mom parenting style is haphazard and negative.

3. Why do you think *Sarah*'s mom is reacting this way towards *Sarah*'s behavior? Do you think her reaction indicates that she is confused or that she has a plan and a vision for her daughter's upbringing? The way *Sarah*'s mom has reacted indicates that she has no clear plan for what she

needs do with her daughter in an unplanned situation. She is confused and doesn't know how to get *Sarah* to behave the way she should. *Sarah*'s mom is reacting haphazardly to *Sarah*'s actions.

4. How do you think *Sarah* is going to view her dad from the way her mother is presenting him? Since the mother is portraying the dad as the source of all restrictions and limitations, it is only natural that *Sarah* will view her Dad as a mean, rigid and intolerant person. A parent should use every opportunity to explain the wisdom behind any required behavior and how it would help the person to reach long-term happiness. Irrespective of who is dealing with the teen in a specific incident, the rules should always be presented as family rules where both parents have the same opinion.

5. Fifteen year-olds love to spend lot of time with their friends going to movies and hanging around the mall. In your opinion, how can a parent deal with this using a balanced approach? Parents who understand the psychology of teens will accept the fact that their daughter would want to spend a lot of time with her friends. This will help them to workout a balanced approach. First they will acknowledge this need, then they will educate and train the teen about other responsibilities regarding her actions and the way she spends her time. A parent can use her daughter's question as an opportunity to explain, comfort and come to a common agreement of how to deal with the situation. *Sarah*'s mother may ask her, "Why do you want to go to the mall? What are you going to do there?" If the answer is, "I'll just hang around with my friends," The mother should indicate in a loving way that this would be a waste of time and that she will be accountable for it. Also, going to the mall for no real reason to buy something she doesn't really need will cause her to acquire sins, as the mall is full of unacceptable scenes. The mother could also mention the verse "Verily the hearing, and the sight, and the heart, of each of these will be questioned" (Q 17, V 36) as well as the saying of the prophet which indicates that no one will be able to move even one step on the Day of Judgment before being asked about four things; among which includes how he spent his life and his youthful years. The mother could also brainstorm with her daughter other places *Sarah* could go and other ways she could enjoy herself, such as going for a walk in the park or going hiking. After doing this, the mother needs to show her willingness to help organize and carry out such an activity. As for going to the movies, here

is a sample of how parents can handle the situation. First of all, they should ask their teen some questions regarding the movie. What is it about? What kind of message is it giving? Does it contain foul language or have bad scenes? If the teen answers that she doesn't know, she just wants to go with her friends, they can then ask her to do some research and find out the answers for these questions. At this point also, the parents should try to bring up the concept that everybody will be account-able for her actions as an individual on the Day of Judgment. Saying that she went because her friends went will not be a good enough reason. The parent might quote the verse of *Qur'an* "And everyone of them will come to Him alone on the day of resurrection." (Q 19, V 95) To achieve a balanced approach, whenever the teen researches a movie and finds it acceptable from the Islamic point of view, parents should provide the opportunity for her to watch the movie. Of course, this is not going to happen frequently because the teen will start to value her time and make sure she only spends it on useful activities. To summarize, parents should use each opportunity the teen is asking to do something to INDICATE, EDUCATE and TRAIN. As usual, this should be done in a loving way where the parents show empathy with the teen's situation and acknowledge her feelings and provide her with the needed support.

6. *Sarah* told her mom, "What is wrong with the blouse? It's what's in style right now. All my friends at school are wearing it." At what age you think a youth should know what is suitable and what is not in terms of clothes? What can parents do to help their son or daughter develop the ability to make the right choice in spite of peer pressure in the areas of clothing and brand name buying? *Sarah*'s comment to her mom regard-ing the blouse she bought indicates how much she wants to be in style and dress like all the other girls at school. Now is the right time for her to learn what the criteria that she should observe when choosing her own clothes are. Before *Sarah* can go out and buy her clothes on her own, her parents should discuss this matter with her at home. They should indicate the Islamic perspective about choosing clothes and make sure that she understands that whatever she chooses should meet the right conditions. The clothes should be loose and shouldn't be transparent or expose parts of her body. This will be a chance for parents to elaborate on the concept of accountability regarding spending money and that Allah SWT dislikes those who spend wastefully and considers them the companions of the devil, as indicated in *Surah Al-Israa'* verse number 27.

Parents also have to clarify to *Sarah* that we should not base our actions on what others are doing. Instead, we should always try to do what agrees with our system of beliefs. Our objective in this life is to work hard to go to Paradise. This requires us to accumulate as many good deeds as we can and base our actions on that and not on what everybody else is doing. *Sarah's* parents should also indicate what her allowed clothing budget is. Perhaps, *Sarah's* mom should go out shopping with her a few times to train her first, then allow her to go on her own after explaining the above concepts.

7. Can the father do anything to help improve the situation? What do you suggest? Yes, the father can play a more active role in his daughter's upbringing. He can spend sometime with her doing things she likes to do, which will help strengthen the bond and build up the trust between the two of them. He also can open the door for her to come, ask, and discuss about any issues that concern her. This will happen if the father makes a point of asking about his daughter when he comes home, talking to her and showing his love and care for her. The father should keep himself informed about any issues that take place between his daughter and her mother. He should also sit down with *Sarah's* mother, discuss the best way to deal with these issues, and agree on a certain course of action. Perhaps this will minimize the burden *Sarah's* mother feels and support her in reacting in the proper way when *Sarah* comes up with acts in an inappropriate manner.

* * * * *

The rest of the case studies in this chapter all share one common problem which has manifested itself in many different forms. This problem has become extremely prevalent among Muslim families in North America. Through out our travels and workshops, this is one of the things that we have noticed very frequently, unfortunately, too frequently. This problem is the issue of the father not being actively involved in his sons' lives.

6. Please Dad, listen to me before it is too late

There is a very sad situation, which is happening, in many Muslim communities living in the west. Many Muslim boys don't stay within the boundaries of Islam after they reach the age of 16 or so. This doesn't just happen in families where the parents neglect teaching their children about

Islam, but it also happens with parents who are very pious and have put a lot of effort into their kids' upbringing. Still, we find that more often than not, girls in such families grow up to be committed Muslims while the boys have gone and adopted the value system and social norms of mainstream culture.

One common factor between these families is the lack of the father's involvement in his children's lives.

The father, who in many cases is a very caring and committed Muslim, was too busy to play a noticeable role in the upbringing of his children. In such a case, because the child-father interaction was kept at a very low level, the children didn't feel an emotional bond with their dad. In a boy's case, where the need for paternal involvement is greater, the damage is also greater. The boy's need for the presence of a father figure in his life was never met. This need keeps growing but is never satisfied because of the lack of the father's involvement. The boy then starts to look for other role models as an alternative to satisfy his unfulfilled need. He finds these role models in popular figures, such as movie stars, actors on TV, and sports figures. He also starts to imitate whatever is popular among his peers, which, in many cases, is troubling behavior. Then, and only then, the dad starts noticing his son and paying attention in a big way. This leaves the youth with the impression that he can get the dad's attention through causing trouble. Because the teen is so hungry for his father's attention, he finds himself drawn to misbehave in order to get the attention he so badly needs.

Next, the child gets to be labeled in the family as the bad kid and the trouble-maker. Everybody starts to treat him on these basis and he becomes the focus of attention. Before long, he finds himself in a situation where his parents expect him to misbehave, so he does. As all this takes place, behaving in the wrong way becomes the teen's habit, and since it's always much easier to follow habits than to behave differently, it becomes a big challenge for the youth to go back to behaving properly. When parents start detecting signs of problems in a nine or ten year old boy, they should pay very close attention. The son is sending out a cry for help,

"Dad, please listen to me before it is too late.
Would you listen, dad? Please do!"

<u>Questions</u>

1. In your opinion, is this a common problem? Yes, the father not being involved in his son's life is a very common problem.

2. What is your analysis of the situation *Faris* is in? What do you think the cause of the problem is? *Faris* is in his early teen years, where it is very important for him to fit in with his peers and feel that he is part of a group. His desire to go hang out with the kids on his street is normal and perfectly justified from his point of view. On the other hand, his parents don't approve of those kids' attitude, but they are not providing an alternative way for *Faris* to get to know other kids. *Faris* is also in desperate need of interaction with his Dad, but his dad is not around and he doesn't acknowledge how much *Faris* needs his personal attention.

3. How important is it for a 13 year old to have friends? *Faris* wants to go out and hang around with the neighborhood kids. Should parents allow that and under what conditions? It is very important for a 13 year old to have friends and it is a natural part of their developmental stage. As mentioned above in question 2, it is normal for *Faris* to want to go out and hang around with kids who live on his street. However, it seems that the neighborhood kids are not going to have a good influence on *Faris'* character. His parents are probably worried about him picking up foul language, smoking, rudeness, etc. from those kids. In such a case, the parents should not allow him to go out, but they need to explain and discuss the matter with him in such a way that will make *Faris* be aware of the reasons he is not allowed to go out. This will also give *Faris* the opportunity to learn what the criteria for choosing his friends should be. For this discussion to be fruitful, please refer to chapter five. As for when they should allow him to go out and hang around with a group of kids on the street, the parents would have to do their research and make sure that the group is not involved in any unacceptable activities, that they don't use foul language and that they just play in the vicinity of the house. Although this may seem like a lot of work, the parents must do it. They have to research it and not simply take the easy way out and say, "No, you are not allowed to go."

4. Do you think the mother solved the problem by locking the door and preventing *Faris* from going out, or does the problem go much deeper than this? Physical restraint is not the solution, so the mother didn't help by locking the door. After all, *Faris* is exposed to the same

environment every day when he goes to school. The problem certainly goes much deeper than this. *Faris* needs to have the right tools to differentiate between what is right and what is wrong. This will help him to choose the right crowd to mix with and to be able to recognize wrongdoings and stay away from them. It is also clear from the case that if parents ignore the problem and don't deal with it in the proper way, it will keep growing and get worse.

5. The father mentioned that he is working very hard to build a good future for *Faris*. Do you think that this is all *Faris* needs from him? The father's comment indicates that he is only focusing his efforts on securing a good financial future for the family. However, there is much more to good family life than just financial security. *Faris* needs to be around his father in a situation where they interact and do things together so that he can learn from his father. He needs to feel that his father loves and cares about him. He needs his father to take the time to go to his school and work out a solution when *Faris* is in trouble.

6. What would you suggest *Faris*'s parents do to solve *Faris*'s stealing and smoking problems? Solving the stealing and smoking problem can not be dealt with at a superficial level as a Band-Aid solution that only treats the symptoms. The solution should address the real reasons behind the problem and deal with the situation at the level of the deeper causes. A great portion of the solution lies in implementing the ideas described in the answers of the previous questions. The parents need to educate themselves about the nature of the stage *Faris* is in and his needs as he goes through this stage: Parents need to acknowledge these needs, deal with *Faris* in a caring, understanding way, listen actively, brainstorm and discuss with him, as well as help him satisfy his need of having friends and spending time with them. In addition to this, the father's involvement in *Faris*'s life is a must. All of these things will take care of a great deal of the problem. The parents must deal with the stealing and smoking problem at hand as follows:

a. Parents can discuss the issue privately with *Faris* with the objective of reaching a mutual agreement about a plan of action to solve the problem.

b. Parents can write up a contract with *Faris* covering in detail all the required steps both *Faris* and his parents will achieve

c. Close follow up is a must

7. What would be your advice to *Faris*'s parents to help him get through this critical stage of his life?

a. To educate themselves about the nature of this stage and acknowledge *Faris*'s needs.

b. To examine their lifestyle and be willing to make the changes needed to meet their teens need, such as

i. Getting involved with community activities where *Faris* could meet other Muslim youth who have the same values

ii. Facilitating it for *Faris* to have companionship and friends through driving him over to his friend's house or hosting his friends at their home

iii. The father should free up some time to spend with the family, and specially with *Faris*, on a personal level where they spend quality time together

iv. Adopt proper techniques for informing and educating *Faris* about acceptable Islamic values to help him develop in the right direction. Techniques such as brainstorming, reasoning, discussing, and using what is best in conflict resolution as described in chapter five are very helpful.

7. He finds schools work Very Boring

1. In your opinion, is this a common problem? How serious is it? Yes, it is common problem. It is also serious, as *Hamdy*'s situation is getting worse and he has started to tell lies.

2. What do you think the cause of the problem is? There are several things that could have caused this problem, such as:

– *Hamdy* feels lonely as he has no brothers, no friends, and almost no interaction with his dad. His sisters are together and he feels left out.

– *Hamdy* feels bored with himself and his life which is a natural result of feeling lonely

– *Hamdy* has lost motivation to carry out responsibilities such as homework and prayer

– The mother has gotten into the habit of expecting *Hamdy* to misbehave, and *Hamdy* has gotten into the habit of expecting his mother to push him in order to carry out his duties

3. What do you think the parents could have done to avoid this problem? To avoid this problem, the parents should have sat down together and reflected on the situation as soon as they detected it. They should have defined exactly what they needed to do to help *Hamdy*. The

parents also could have used the school resources in terms of counseling if they felt it necessary.

4. Do you think it is OK that *Hamdy* at 12 years of age still needs his parents to remind him to pray at each prayer time? *Hamdy*, at 12 years old, should be able to keep up with his prayers without frequent reminders from parents. The parents should have followed the right approach according to the hadeeth of the prophet PBUH that indicates that parents must train their children for prayer at the age of 7 years old. By doing this, the child would be able to keep track of his prayers independently by the time he was twelve.

5. In your opinion, is it too late to solve the problem? No, I don't believe it is too late to solve the problem.

If your answer for question 5 is no, what do you suggest *Hamdy*'s parents do to help *Hamdy* correct his attitude and behavior? Both *Hamdy*'s parents have a role to play in order to correct his attitude and behavior. Here is what they should do:

– *Hamdy*'s parents must address the reasons that caused the problem in the first place, which is lonesomeness, loss of motivation, and boredom

– *Hamdy*'s parents need to be innovative and think of new, effective, and interesting ways to deal with the problem and do the unexpected

– They need to get *Hamdy* to realize that this is his problem and not his parents' problem. He is the one who should address the problem. If he doesn't keep up with his prayers and homework, he is the one who will suffer the consequences. His mom and dad are trying to help out of love and care, but he is the one in charge. Remind him with the verse, "Every person is a pledge for what he has earned" (Q 74, V 38) also remind him with the verse, "No one laden with burdens can bear another's burden" (Q 17, V 15)

– The parents can hold a meeting with *Hamdy*, express their concern and ask him some questions: What does he want to achieve out of life? What does he think is in his best interest? What does he suggest doing to correct the problem? They can then write an agreement or contract between all three of them. The contract should indicate exactly what each one should do to correct the situation. It will also indicate the consequences or reward of each action. It should also have a time line attached to it for completing various tasks. The date of the next meeting should also be specified. See a sample contract in chapter nine, "Tools you need"

– The father should spend some time with *Hamdy* interacting on a personal level. Go for a walk with him, go bike riding or go on a hiking trip together

– Help *Hamdy* have good friends who will have a positive influence on him and invite them over as a reward when he fulfills his duties

– Make it easier for *Hamdy* to follow rules at home by including him in his sisters' activities. The parents can have a family meeting with all the children where they explain that the family is all one unit and that they should all help each other, and encourage their children to carry on their activities as a group. So, when they come home, they will pray together, and if father is not around, *Hamdy* will lead the *Jama'ah* prayer. They will all try to sit down for dinner together as a family. They can also do their homework together, which might be some sort of encouragement for *Hamdy*. The parents can set a rule that there will be no TV until everyone finishes his homework. This way, *Hamdy* will not feel that he is the bad one and will avoid having low expectations of himself. He will also be motivated by being part of the group activities, which will likely help him not to feel bored and lonely

– The mother must stop having low expectations of *Hamdy*. Instead, she should greet him positively in the morning before he goes to school, indicating to him that she is confident that he will have a happy and productive day, agreeing on what he will do when he comes back from school. If the mother can keep up this positive attitude, it will really help *Hamdy* to put in the effort and also believe in himself. If *Hamdy* doesn't complete his work and perform his prayers, his mother should let him face the consequences agreed upon in the contract. Actions speak louder than words. Close follow up between parents and school is also needed to address the problem of telling lies.

– The father should take more interest in his son's life. He should make sure to be an active participant in family activities. Take themfor a trip, or travel all together as a family to attend an Islamic conference. Picnics as well as fun games or sports could also be useful

7. If you were to give one piece of advice to all parents to avoid having such a problem, what would that be? FATHERS MUST BE MORE INVOLVED IN THEIR SON'S LIFE.

8. Peer pressure and home expectation

1. Do you feel that *Fatih* is in a difficult position? How would you feel if you were in his place? Yes, *Fatih* is in a very difficult position and I would feel very bad and discouraged if I was in his place. I am trying my best with my schoolwork and also trying my best to cope with peer pressure and my parents don't seem to appreciate what I am going through. They don't even want to listen to me. What should I do? Whom should I speak to? Is there anybody around who I can share my feelings with or at least someone who can listen to what I have to say?

2. As a grade 7 student, do you think it is important to feel like you belong to a group? Of course it's important for a Grade 7 student to feel that he belongs to a group. The feeling of belonging is a natural need for every human being and is even more pressing for children and teenagers. When they are young, this is satisfied within the family. They feel they belong to this specific family. When they reach school age and start going to school their need to belong is still there; they don't want to feel like they are left out.

3. What do you suggest *Fatih*'s parents do to help him have high self respect (high self-esteem), so he is in a stronger position when dealing with peer pressure? High self-respect (self-esteem) can only be achieved when the child feels that he is loved and capable. The child has to feel that his parents love him for who he is. Parents shouldn't withdraw their love from the child for any reason or any mistake the child may commit. Yes, they should teach him that everything has consequences, but they should never withdraw their love from him. Being capable has to do with the various skills that the child should develop with the help of the parents. The parents have to provide the right environment and opportunity for *Fatih* to develop his skills. It is important to encourage *Fatih* for his achievements and emphasize his positive behavior such as trying his best in school, even if he doesn't meet the parent's expectations. As a matter of fact, parents should have realistic expectations for their child, appreciate the effort he is spending, and provide him with the necessary support. This will go a long way in helping raise the child's self-esteem. With a high self-esteem, the child will be in a much stronger position when dealing with peer pressure.

4. Do you think *Fatih*'s dad is putting enough effort into keeping the channel of communication open between *Fatih* and himself? On the

contrary, *Fatih*'s dad is shutting off the communication channel between *Fatih* and himself. He has certain expectations in his mind for *Fatih* as far as school achievement is concerned, and he is very upset when these expectations are not met.

5. What would be your advice to *Fatih*'s dad to do to improve the situation? To improve the situation, *Fatih*'s dad should do the following:

- Encourage and emphasize his child's achievements rather than criticize and be upset about *Fatih*'s report card

- Support *Fatih* by being close to him and doing things with him. This way the channel of communication will be open and *Fatih* won't feel that it is difficult to talk with his dad

- Have realistic expectations for his son. This will go a long way in improving the situation. Every child has certain potentials; the most important thing is that *Fatih* tries his best. The results should be left to Allah and as parents we should show our appreciation to the effort exerted by the child, even if the results are not what we had hoped for. If our expectations are realistic, the child should be able to meet them without feeling the guilt that he is not satisfying his parents. It is important for the child to feel the approval of his parents for his efforts and achievements

- Sharing some quality time with *Fatih* will help both the father and the son to be closer and help in improving the communication between them. The child will open up and share his feelings and problems with his father if he feels that the father is concerned with his affairs and loves him for who he is, not for the high grades he gets. This quality time could be spent going camping together, attending a ball game, working on a community project together, or by the father volunteering some of his time to *Fatih*'s school programs. Even cutting the lawn or preparing a fun meal together would be quality time for *Fatih*.

To help open the channel of communication, the father has to earn *Fatih*'s trust back so he'll start loosening up and feeling at ease to communicate with his father again. One very effective way of doing this is for the father to take interest in activities that *Fatih* loves. If *Fatih* loves watching basketball games, the father should try to get himself interested in watching some games with *Fatih*. He can use *Fatih* as his mentor in learning about the game while watching with him. This will kill two birds with one stone, first it will provide an opportunity for both to spend some quality time together; and secondly, it will help improve *Fatih*'s self esteem by feeling that he is teaching his father something he knows.

9. Isolation is not the solution

1. Do you think this is a common problem? This is not necessarily a very common problem, but it certainly happens with a portion of the Muslim families living in North America.

2. What do you think is causing the problem? This problem is caused by the mother being insecure and worried about how *Hasan* is going to handle himself when he is outside and she can't keep an eye on him. The mother wants to keep him under her supervision as much as she can.

3. Do you think *Hasan*'s mom did the right thing by allowing him to go with his friends to the mall? Yes, she was right about allowing him to go to the mall with his friends. In this case, *Hasan* needed to buy some material for his project, and it was just easier and made more sense to go to the mall straight from school rather than going home first and then going out again with his mom.

4. Do you think it is important for a 15 year old to be able to shop and buy things he needs without his mother's help? A 15 year old is looking for independence and ready to be able to look after his personal needs without his mom's help. Buying stationary for a school project is a simple task that he should be capable of doing alone.

5. Do you think *Hasan*'s mom's behavior may affect his development? Although *Hasan*'s mom's intentions are in the right spot, her actions are not going to lead him to develop in a healthy way. *Hasan* needs to learn how to handle himself in the different kinds of environments he is exposed to, so that whether or not his mom can see him, he will do the right thing. *Hasan*'s mom is trying to protect him from wrongdoings by isolating him as much as she can. Isolation can't be the solution, as she can't isolate him fully from the society and it is not healthy for his development to do so. After all, *Hasan* lives in this society. He still needs to go to school and in the future he should be able to hold down a job and conduct himself properly.

6. What is your advice to *Hasan*'s mom? Instead of being over protective, she should focus her efforts on empowering him with the tools he needs in order to be able to conduct himself properly. *Hasan*'s parents

should help him in selecting the right friends through educating him about the qualities of the friends he should spend time with. As discussed in previous chapters, a good, healthy family atmosphere and an open channel of communication are key factors in helping *Hasan* to acquire these tools. The presence of *Hasan*'s father in his life as a loving and caring person with whom *Hasan* has a good chance to interact is very important. Through this interaction, *Hasan* can share his daily experiences with his parents and they can give him guidance in reflecting on these experiences. This way, *Hasan* will learn the Islamic perspective on how to deal with daily events in his life and learn about which qualities to look for in the friends he hangs out with. *Hasan* will then be ready to have more room to practice what he has learned and his parents should allow him to go out and spend time with his friends under certain conditions; these conditions include knowing where they are going and when they are going to be back, as well as the type of activity they will be doing. *Hasan*'s parents should always pay close attention to him when he tells them what went on while he was with his friends. They can then give him the needed advice or answer his questions accordingly to help him make the right judgments.

10. The internet dilemma

1. Judging from the case, do you think the way *Imad* spends his time will help him to have a balanced personality and enable him to build the social skills needed for a healthy life? *Imad* is isolating himself from interacting with real people by refusing to attend youth activities and family get-togethers. He spends the majority of his time in a chat room, which will not help him to develop the social skills needed in real life situation. For a person to have a balanced personality, he needs to develop in many different aspects: spiritually, emotionally, psychologically, intellectually and physically. He needs to have the appropriate amount of interaction in all these areas. *Imad* is only concentrating on one aspect of his personality, his need to socialize, and he is doing it in a very limited way by spending so much time in chat rooms. To truly develop the social aspect of his personality, *Imad* must socialize in real life settings. This means going out, meeting people, and taking the risk of rejection when trying to make friends. Since *Imad* was too afraid to take this risk, he spent time in front of his computer instead, however, he still

needed to fulfill his need to communicate and so once he discovered the chat rooms, he delved right in. This kind of socialization is very limited and will not teach *Imad* about how to deal with people.

2. In your opinion, why doesn't *Imad* want to attend the soccer game or to participate in the community youth group activities? It is likely that when *Imad* goes to such activities, he finds out that most of the youth there already know each other and have already formed their groups of friends. This makes it hard for him since he is new to the group. Unless the group really makes him feel welcome, it will be difficult for him to take the initiative and join in. It is also possible that *Imad* is not confident in his athletic ability. If he feels that he is not good at sports then he won't want to meet people while playing sports. He will likely feel self-conscious and worried that people won't want him on their team because he will only bring them down.

3. What are the benefits and harms of spending a long time in front of the computer? Do you think there is a big difference between this and spending long hours watching TV? Spending a long time in front of computer for reasons other than studying or conducting useful research is not advisable. Though there are some benefits such as becoming very skilled and efficient at maneuvering through the Internet, the drawbacks far outweigh the benefits. Firstly, all the time *Imad* spends in front of the computer is taking away from time he could spend in other, more useful activities. In short, it is waste of time. Another drawback is that the Internet is laden with moral garbage and it is very easy to run into all sorts of harmful things on the Internet. The more time he spends on the computer, the more likely he is to view the harmful and negative things. Of course, the computer screen also emits rays that are harmful to the eyes. Another potential drawback to spending long hours in front of the computer is that he can become socially isolated and accept this as a natural way to live. This is just to name a few possibilities and is by no mean an exhaustive list of the effects of time spent on the Internet. As for the difference between sitting in front of the computer or watching TV, the main difference is that some activities on the computer require the user to not be as passive as he would be if he had been watching TV, but parents should be aware that much of what was available on TV has become available through the internet now. Music videos, songs, lyrics, interviews with rock stars and actors can all be watched, heard, and read

on the Internet. Furthermore, these are all more convenient through the computer than the TV because the user can access them these at his own convenience and is not restricted by the time that they are available, as he would be with TV.

4. *Imad* didn't rush down to have dinner with the family when his dad came home early. Why do you think he stayed upstairs? What do you think of the dad's reaction when *Imad* didn't come down? Because the father is rarely home, the relationship between him and *Imad* is not strong at all. If *Imad* doesn't have a strong bond with his father, it's normal that he wouldn't rush down to greet him. Since the father doesn't go out of his way to spend time with his teenage son, the son doesn't go out of his way to spend time with the father either. Why would *Imad* make time for his father if his father doesn't make time for him? The dad's reaction was also very negative. Though the father may not mean it, the phrase that he used when describing *Imad* to his mother, saying, "your son is too busy for me!" has plenty of harmful implications. First of all, when he refers to *Imad* as the mother's son this implies a sense of disowning towards his own son. It is very hurtful for any child to hear his parents refer to him as somebody else's son, even if that person is his other parent. The other implication of this reference is that *Imad*'s father is blaming the mother entirely for *Imad*'s behavior and is not taking any responsibility for *Imad*'s actions himself.

5. *Imad* thought that he wasn't doing anything wrong by talking to *Mona* through the chat room. What do you think? Although the chat room is not a physical room and people are not physically in one place, that doesn't make it a good place to communicate without worries or regulations. There are Islamic rules and regulations that should be followed whenever there is a need for communication between the two genders. Chat rooms, e-mail messages, and private messaging over the internet are all modern ways of communication which should follow the same Islamic regulations that are appropriate for the intended purpose. So *Imad*'s idea that nothing is wrong with him spending hours talking to *Mona* over the Internet is clearly wrong. He shouldn't do that, as they have no legitimate reason to spend that time together.

6. For a 16 year old, the need to be understood is very important. What could the family do to make sure that this need is fulfilled in a proper way? The family has a big role to play in order to help a 16 year

old feel that he can relate to others and be understood. First, both parents, especially the same gender parent, should take an interest in the teen's life and devote some time to interacting and listening to him. Parents should listen to his feelings, his concerns, what is troubling him, as well as his interests. When the parent is able to listen and show empathy without jumping to conclusions and passing judgments, he learns a lot about his teen and can usually figure out what is troubling him. Through dialogue, discussion, and compromise, both the parents and the teen can reach a mutual understanding regarding issues and concerns. When teen feels that he can relate to his parents and that they understand his situation, he will come to them with his problems and he will take their advice with lots of consideration instead of going to others who may lead him to do something harmful or foolish.

7. Suggest some practical ways for the family to help *Imad* changes his computer habits.

To help *Imad* have the right habits when using the computer:

a. Place the computer in an area of common use in the home and not in a closed room. For example, it could be placed in the family room or in a general study room.

b. Help the teen to have the proper Islamic knowledge regarding personal responsibilities for one's use of his own senses such as eyes, ears and mind. You can quote the verse from *Surah Al-Israa'*, "Verily the hearing, and the sight, and the heart, of each of those ones will be questioned" (Q 17, V 36).

c. Help the teen to have proper Islamic knowledge and practices regarding how he spends his time and teach him to take responsibility for his personal growth. You can quote the saying of the prophet PBUH, "Be keen to gain what would benefit you and seek help from Allah".

d. Help the teen to have proper Islamic knowledge and practices regarding regulations related to opposite-gender interaction.

It is advisable that parents educate themselves regarding these issues. Through constructive interaction, dialogues, discussions, and asking their teen to do some research on the topic at hand, they can all come up with the proper way to deal with any issue. Here is a reminder that the *TAQWA* of Allah is a must for parents to open the doors of knowledge and wisdom to their children as indicated in *Surah Al-Baqarah,*

" ... So have *TAQWA* towards Allah and Allah teaches you"
(Q 2, V 282)

11. Needs and wants (Bad company)

1. Teens like to spend time together away from their parents engaging in various activities and discovering new adventures. Different parents allow various degrees of freedom with their teens. In your opinion, what is considered healthy and reasonable? The nature of this adolescent stage for a 19 year old is to seek independence in his actions, enjoy discovering new things, and experience new adventures by going to new places he didn't used to go with his parents. The parents' role is to allow enough room for the teen to fulfill these needs and, at the same time, guide his activities so that these needs are fulfilled in a healthy and Islamic way.

2. To have a girlfriend or boyfriend is considered a normal part of non-Muslim western culture. Our teens are fully exposed to this. How can you help your son or daughter to standout and be different regarding this issue? *Ghazi*, who is nineteen years old, lives in a culture that considers somebody who has no girlfriend as abnormal. The pressure to have a girlfriend is everywhere, starting from the internal pressure associated with his age group to the way he sees girls dressed on the street, in university, and on TV. Parents should not underestimate these pressures. To be able to handle standing out from those around him and to be able to resist these pressures requires a lot of strength on *Ghazi*'s part. This will not happen spontaneously if *Ghazi* is left without the means to build up his strength. The first step is to educate *Ghazi* fully about the Islamic view on this matter so that he knows the Islamic limits regarding mixing with the other gender and understands what's halal and what's haram about all the different areas related to his feelings with this issue. The parents should tell *Ghazi* what the consequences are of obeying or disobeying Allah's orders in such matters. This will help *Ghazi* to make the appropriate decision and take the right direction when he is faced with

outside pressure from this society. *Ghazi* also needs an alternative where he can channel his energy. This could be fulfilled through being part of a group of young men of his age who have the same understanding regarding following Islamic principles. The group could focus its energy on sports and social and spiritual activities, such as going for biking trips, hiking, picnics, lunch out at a restaurant, group fasting and getting together for iftar, group nightly prayers, and youth camps. Parents can help by taking the steps needed to get their son or daughter involved in such a group and to keep up with what the group is doing. Parents need to make their teens join these groups during their early teen years and not to wait until the teens are older and are reluctant to join. If parents cannot find such a group available in their community, they should take initiative to form one. The group could have as few as two to three members or as many members as there are in the community. Parents should also help by being ready to offer their services for any organization of group activities such as driving, preparing food, participating in camping trips, hosting youths at home, providing supervision whenever needed, etc.

3. Although *Ghazi* knew that the nightclub was not a good place to go, he went along with his friends. Later on, he started doubting his views and even thinking differently. Is peer pressure real? What do you think? We saw, through *Ghazi*'s case, how his views started shifting from one side to the other, and it all happened from getting exposed to new ideas and going along with his friend's views. This is a very clear indication that peer pressure is real. The prophet, peace be upon him, told us that, "your religion is that of your friend, so be careful who you select as a friend." He also gave us the example of good company and bad company, illustrating to us that a person is greatly affected by his companion's views and ideas. On the authority of *Abu Musa al-Ash'ari* (Allah be pleased with him) that he heard the messenger of Allah (peace and blessings be upon him) saying, "The similitude of good company and that of bad company is that of the owner of musk and of the one (iron smith) blowing bellows. The owner of the musk will either offer you some free of charge or you will buy it from him or you will smell its pleasant odor. As for the one who blows the bellows is concerned, he will either burn your clothes or you shall have to smell its repugnant smell" (agreed upon). So PEER PRESSURE IS REAL.

4. How could you help your teen have better confidence in himself and his knowledge to resist peer pressure? To help the teen to have strong confidence in himself so he can bear being different, please refer to chapter four. As for how to help the teen to have confidence in his knowledge, please refer to chapter five.

5. Suggest some practical solutions *Ghazi*'s parents could use to resolve the problem and help the situation. Practical solutions *Ghazi*'s parents could use to help the situation:

a. Parents may consider reuniting the whole family in one household where the father will have a chance to have continuous interaction with *Ghazi*.

b. If this is not possible, the dad needs to keep in close touch with *Ghazi*, he could call frequently and speak to *Ghazi* on a personal level. He could also email messages to his son on a regular basis. While in town, he should make sure to invite *Ghazi*'s friends over for breakfast or take them out for lunch where they have a chance to converse and share views.

c. Both parents should make sure that the home environment is an Islamic one so that they provide their children with an opportunity to learn from good models. This means observing the prayer times, not renting and watching unacceptable videos and movies, etc.

d. Parents should elevate their level of knowledge and commitment to Islam to be able to teach their children and answer their questions in the proper and convincing way regarding all these matters. They can also advise *Ghazi* to do frequent voluntary fasting and night prayer.

e. Parents should also use the tool of *dua'a* to ask Allah's help in finding a way out of their difficulties for them and protect and keep their youth on the straight path.

f. Consider early marriage, even if it is not going to be done the traditional way. The marriage could take place during university years and the young couple could stay with parents in the same home where the parents can partially support them. With this suggestion, necessary steps must be taken to ensure the success of this marriage.

12. Small problems grow bigger if not attended to properly

A nine year old is a preteen who is approaching the difficult years of adolescence. He needs to be prepared to properly face the challenges associated with the teen years, when most teens his age will start smoking, maybe using drugs, having girlfriends, joining gangs, and doing other activities which we may not approve as Muslims. This means that he needs his parents to be interactively involved in his life. This is the right time for the father to start taking special interest in his son's affairs and spend time with him on a personal level. They can do things together like bike ride, go to the park for a nice walk, and play sports. *Tamer*'s father can take some of these opportunities with his son to talk to him about his expectation for him in a hopeful and trustful way. In short, it is very important to keep a close relationship and follow up with his son. This way, the channels of communication between the dad and his son are kept open, which will help the boy to be receptive to his father's instructions and guidance. When the dad ignores devoting time and energy in his son's affairs at this age, more likely than not, a chain of problems will be set off. As the boy grows, the problems will grow and get deeper and deeper. Children need to see a good role model in their life. Boys need a good male figure, which in this society, should be provided by the father, especially due to the absence of extended family and the absence of good external role models.

During the early teen stage, boys like to be part of a group and enjoy group activities. At this stage, parents should take all the necessary steps to make their son part of a group that is on the right track. Parents who fail to do that, in most of the cases, lose their son to the wrong crowd as he struggles to satisfy his needs. A teen can't be expected to just sit at home and only do homework. He has lots of energy, and an active, busy lifestyle is the best answer to channel this energy in the right direction. This is where involvement with community youth groups, youth camps and projects are proven to be of great value.

When problems arise in this stage, and parents try to solve the problem in an assertive and serious manner, the problems can be corrected with some effort. However, if parents don't take the problem seriously and aren't ready to reorganize their priorities and sacrifice some of their conveniences in order to give the time and energy needed to take care of the problem, the situation deteriorates until it reaches a stage where correcting the problem may be very difficult. Again, this emphasizes the importance of early start and trying to solve the problems at the earliest stage.

1. What do you think *Tamer*'s future will look like if his parent's don't get their act together? The state *Tamer* is in right now, he is at a great risk of joining gangs and going into a life of crime. He has very low self-esteem, no confidence in himself or his abilities, can't hold a job, and is not on good terms with his family. The continued failure of his parents to deal with his problem has put him in this situation. It will not be easy to correct the situation now. It may require some drastic measures to be taken on the parents' part to see any glimpse of hope in a brighter future for *Tamer*.

2. When *Tamer* was 9 years old, he started showing signs of problems. What did *Tamer* need then that he was not getting? What do you suggest the parents could have done? As indicated in the analysis, at 9 years old, *Tamer* needed to be prepared for the challenges he would face as a teen by spending more time with his parents, especially his dad. However, his dad was busy playing soccer and socializing with his own friends. Rather that doing this, his dad should have provided Tamer with the quality time needed to build an open channel of communication and stay on good terms to protect *Tamer* from deviating.

3. When *Tamer* was 13 years old, he showed even more signs of problems, but the parents were too busy pointing fingers to notice. What do you suggest they had done instead? *Tamer* needed his dad's attention but he didn't get it when he was a preteen. At 13, the problem had become more complicated because his schoolwork had gotten affected.The answer to his problem still lay in getting his father's attention. However at this age, he would be more reluctant to open up. The parents should have stopped pointing fingers at each other and tried to work together with *Tamer* to come up with a course of action that would have taken care of fixing the problem

4. At 16 years old, *Tamer* was on drugs! His parents were shocked, sad and upset. They thought that this would never happen to them. Do you think any youth is immune to drugs? The risk of drug taking among teens in North American society is real according to the statistics given in chapter two. Easy access to drugs and peer pressure to try them constitute part of the problem. As for immunity, the only way is to build up the teen's internal strength by having strong and healthy family bonds, an active lifestyle where the teen is involved with lots of positive activities,

a strong personality, and self confidence with the ability to differentiate between right and wrong. Please see chapter four for how to build a strong and confident personality.

5. What do you suggest *Tamer*'s parents could have done when he was 16 to eradicate the drug problem? The drug problem should have been a wake up call for *Tamer*'s parents. They should have realized that the problem had become dangerous and serious. The parents should have followed the recommended course of action by the doctor in a more serious way, rather than just asking *Tamer* to stop right away. They should have also consulted counselors at drug treatment centers and implemented the steps they recommended. They should have exhausted all possible means to turn his case around such as:

a. Move to another neighborhood or to a completely different city where there is a better school environment

b. Get *Tamer* involved in Muslim community activities where he is kept very busy in positive and rewarding projects or experiences

c. Start working on the long overdue relationship between *Tamer* and his father

d. Take him to Muslim conferences and conventions, where he may see and listen to some of the good Muslim role models who excelled in their areas, like some of the dedicated Muslim NBA stars

6. *Tamer*, at 20 years old is a high school dropout, can't hold down a job, and takes drugs. He is in deep trouble. Do you think all this could have been avoided? Yes, all the troubles that *Tamer* has now could have been avoided with the will of Allah, if his parents had made their children a priority in their life and had taken the appropriate steps needed as soon as they detected the first signs of a problem.

7. Please give your analysis and suggestions for *Tamer*'s case.

Should *Tamer*'s parents give up on him, or there are other things that they still can do to help him? List your suggestions. Again, parents should never give up on their own children. However, this case has gone too far and nobody can force a solution on *Tamer* at his age. At 20 years old, *Tamer* is an adult who has full legal rights and he can't be forced to take any course of action against his will. All that his parents can do now is keep the channel of communication open with *Tamer* and

– Let him know that he is welcome to come back and live at home as long as he follows and respects the family rules such as

1. Curfew time
2. Making good use of his time (studying or holding a job)
3. Showing courtesy and respect to his parents

– Consider convincing him to move with them to a new environment

After all, parents should never give up on their children.

9. Tools You Need and Ideas You Can Use

In this chapter we will provide you with some useful tools and ideas you can use to ensure the presence of a strong support system for your teen while living in this society. These tools will, *insha' Allah,* cover a wide spectrum. They will range from detailed guidelines on how to prepare youth camps to samples of letters for different occasions as well as how to prepare and organize certain activities to support your teen.

Youth Camps

As indicated in chapter six, youth camps are very useful in helping parents instill the needed positive concepts in the minds and hearts of their children. Here are some guidelines for organizing youth camps and an outline of a camp program:

– The program should always start with *Fajr* prayer every day.

– After *Fajr* prayer teens shouldn't go back to bed. The time between Fajr and sunrise should be spent in repeating certain *dua'as* (morning supplications as reported by the prophet PBUH). The camp director should assign a different teen to lead the *dua'a* each day. Try to make it interesting through doing this outside, if weather permits, and also do it in a chanting way. Another way to make it interesting could be by doing it while marching around the campgrounds and repeating the *dua'as.*

– Watch the sunrise together as a group. The director could ask one or more of the campers to express his feelings at this moment. The camp director should take advantage of this moment to elaborate on the beauty of creation and the greatness of Allah in a very brief and simple way.

– After watching sunrise, the teens should go back to their cabins, clean and tidy them, wash up, and get ready for breakfast.

– Teens should be divided into groups to do various tasks; one group can prepare breakfast; a second group can set the tables; a third group can serve breakfast; and a fourth group can clean up after breakfast.

– Before every meal, one of the teens should read the *dua'a* for eating food.

– The time between breakfast and lunch should be divided into two periods, one for a short educational session structured in an interactive way rather than as a lecture. This could be a group discussion or a debate. It's better to divide the campers into smaller groups for this session. The second period could be allocated to some sort of sports activity, such as swimming, hiking, volleyball, etc.

– During this time, one group should be assigned the task of preparing for lunch. This task assignment should be rotated everyday so everyone has a chance to participate in the activities.

– Again, lunch should start with the *dua'a* and various groups should perform the various tasks

– After lunch, *Zuhr* (noon) and *Asr* (after noon) prayer should be combined. This is an opportunity to teach teens about *fiqh* rules of prayer during travel.

– After prayer, a short (not more than 5 minutes) spiritual reminder while everybody is still sitting always has a great impact. Various campers should rotate in delivering this reminder.

– It may be a good idea to allow time for a short nap after lunch and prayer.

– The afternoon should be divided into two periods, one period for crafts activities and the other for sports such as soccer, basketball, etc. Make sure you end the afternoon period early enough before sunset to allow campers to wash up and get involved in the evening supplications (*Athkar Al-Misaa'*). One camper, or the camp director, should lead everyone else in these supplications.

– Depending on the location of the camp and how long the day is, dinner can be served either before sunset or after *Maghrib* and *Isha* prayer. Again, *Maghrib* and *Isha* prayers should be combined, and the dinner should start with *dua'a* as always

– The night period can either be a time for social hour, or you can start a campfire. The social hour should contain skits, games, quizzes and fun competitions. The campfire is a good opportunity for all campers to listen to a good story about the life of the prophet PBUH, or the life of one of the companions, may Allah be pleased with them all. This time can also be used to teach campers how to find the direction of the *Qiblah* using the stars. While doing this, you should link the learning process with some verses of *Qur'an* such as

> "And makes signposts and by the stars, men guide themselves" (Q 16, V16)

– At bedtime, all campers should learn the *dua'a* to be said before going to sleep.

Following are some general rules and guidelines to be observed while running, or preparing for, a youth camp:

– The camp schedule should be structured around prayer times. If, for any reason, the time of an activity overlaps with the beginning of a prayer time, the activity should stop temporarily and the call for the prayer (*Athan*) should be given while everybody is listening and repeating after the person who is making the call for prayer. After the call for the prayer is over, the activity should continue and prayer should be performed as soon as time permits.

– Campers should be divided into smaller groups according to age. Each group should not include more than 8 campers.

– Every group should have a counselor to lead the group and serve as the link to camp organizers.

– Counselors should receive enough training before the beginning of the camp. The training should cover the objectives of the camp, general rules, basics of conflict management and resolution, and basic Islamic knowledge.

– Counselors should be selected from attendants of previous camps who exhibited good behavior, dependability, reliability, dedication to the cause of Islam, the ability to work in groups, and leadership qualities.

– Boys sleeping quarters should be completely separate from girls sleeping quarters.

– Camp should be structured in a way that doesn't permit or encourage free mixing between the different genders.

– Make sure there are enough adults supervising the camp.

– Safety is of utmost importance. Make sure you have a trained nurse or medical official available on permanent basis.

– Before starting any games, explain the rules and encourage fair and clean competition. Emphasize the fact that exerting effort and building team spirit are the two primary objectives of the game and that results are secondary. Winning is not everything. Learning how to cooperate and good sportsmanship should be greatly stressed. Here is a story I received through my e-mail which I think appropriate to mention:

"A few years ago, at the Seattle Special Olympics, nine contestants, all physically or mentally disabled, assembled at the starting line for the 100-yard dash. At the gun, they all started out, not exactly in a dash, but with a relish to run the race to the finish and win. All, that is, except one little boy who stumbled on the asphalt, tumbled over a couple of times, and began to cry. The other eight heard the boy cry. They slowed down and looked back. Then they all turned around and went back, every one of them.

One girl with Down's Syndrome bent down and kissed him and said, "This will make it better." Then all nine linked arms and walked together to the finish line. Everyone in the stadium stood, and the cheering went on for several minutes. People who were there are still telling the story. Why? Because deep down we know this one thing: What matters in this life is more than winning for ourselves. What matters in this life is helping others win, even if it means slowing down and changing our course."

– Observe and exercise safety in all water related activities, such as swimming, boating, canoeing, etc. Make sure you have enough lifeguards and that every participant is wearing her life vest properly.

– Make sure to provide enough time for feedback from campers and have all campers complete a camp evaluation at the end of the camp.

– Compile all feedback received in a record to use when you plan for the next camp to avoid repeating the same mistakes. Ensure to communicate a summary of the camp evaluation to all campers with a "Thank you" note.

– Keep records of all campers and communicate with them on a regular basis to inform them of new coming activities in the same town or in close by cities.

– Make sure that activities in the camp program cover a variety of topics and subjects to help campers develop rounded personalities. Activities should cover Islamic and general knowledge such as basic beliefs, the biography of Prophet Muhammad PBUH, fiqh, sayings and teachings of the Prophet Muhammad PBUH, etc.

– Activities should also cover physical education, sports, arts, scouting, management, and organizational skills as well as planning for community projects.

– Ensure that the program teaches campers various Islamic manners and *Adab* such as communication manners, eating manners, sleeping manners, dressing manners, attending classes and learning manners, etc.

Some parents may complain that they have no experience with youth camps and the way they should be run. This is not an excuse. In every community, there are usually a few community members who can run camps and have good experience in dealing with teens. Most of the time, those individuals are over loaded with various other responsibilities. Parents should not expect those individuals to carry out everything that is needed to get the youth camp going. The least that parents should do is to carry the load of the legwork and physical preparation for these camps. They should form committees to plan and implement all the needed physical arrangements before and during the camp such as

– Selecting the camp ground location
– Renting the camp site
– Making all the required announcements and taking care of the publicity
– Printing registration forms and taking care of the registration process
– Driving teens to the camp site
– Preparing food during the camp
– Volunteering for camp security and safety
– Etc.

Parents' cooperation in the above aspects will make it mush easier for those key individuals who know how to interact with teens to run and conduct the camps in the best possible way. It is impossible for those individuals to take care of all the physical arrangements and conduct the camp at the same time. Parents should make the youth camps their own project and seek the help of those individuals in areas of their expertise.

The same principle should apply to discussion groups, although the physical arrangement needed is not as demanding as it is in the case of youth camps.

A Behavioral Contract

It is advised as part of the solution for some cases to make a contract with the teen as a way to change the teen's undesired behavior. A behavioral contract is a written agreement between the teen and his parents that outlines which behaviors the teen will perform and what rewards or consequences the parents will provide. Behavioral contracts are proven to be particularly useful with teenagers, older youths, and adults.

This procedure is very useful for a teen whose behavior is not under control and is often a source of fighting and disharmony. If the contract is used properly, it will bring good results, *insha' Allah*. Parents are urged to use contracts as an alternative to shouting, arguing, and fighting. Listening, using reason, dialogue, discussion, and negotiation are all part of the process of writing a contract. This gives the teen a lot of comfort and makes him feel that he has some input in the matter, which in turn makes his cooperation more likely.

The ultimate goal of the parent is to help their son exhibit self-control, be conscientious of Allah SWT, and behave responsibly. A behavioral contract gives parents a tool to use in situations where the teen's behavior is out of control and eventually leads the teen to self-control. The use of the contract goes through three stages.

Stage one: The parents impose a certain amount of external control in arriving at a contract. However, the teen still feels that he has some input and the parents must allow proper negotiation.

Stage two: Both the teen and the parents share control and responsibility. This happens gradually and over a period of time. The teen now has better communication with his parents and his behavior has improved.

Stage three: The teen begins to manage his own behavior. Natural and social reinforcers maintain the behavior and the contract fades. The teen is in the habit of good behavior and believes in its benefits. He also feels the appreciation of his parents.

When to Use a Behavioral Contract

Behavioral contracts can be used to help solve problems such as some of the ones mentioned in the case study section. An example is the case entitled "is there such a thing as a perfect child?" We find that *Safiya*'s mom has become increasingly aggravated by her 15 year old because *Safiya*'s bedroom is always messy. *Safiya*'s mom had found it increasingly difficult to get *Safiya* to make her bed and to put dirty clothes in the hamper and keep clean clothes in her drawers and closet. *Safiya*, on the other hand, resents her mother's constant nagging, stopping her from visiting her friends and conversing over the phone. Their conflict had resulted in several shouting matches and caused a lot of tension between them.

This is a perfect situation for *Safiya*'s mom to negotiate a written agreement with *Safiya*; such an agreement might say: If *Safiya* makes her bed five days a week and keeps her clothes in their proper place, her mother will agree not to nag her about it more than three times a week. *Safiya* can go to visit her friends on Saturday or Sunday morning and *Safiya* can also get 15 minutes of extra telephone time for every day that her room is clean.

It is more likely that both *Safiya* and her mother will be more satisfied. *Safiya* will be pleased to know that she can count on visiting her friends, and her mom will no longer feel that she needs to nag. Their shouting matches will become much less frequent, resulting in less conflicts and a better overall relationship.

<u>Conditions That will Ensure the Success of the Contract</u>

1. Be willing to negotiate. Both the teen and the parents should dialogue and discuss openly and listen to each other's concerns.

2. The set goal must be reachable and within the person's ability. Higher goals can be negotiated in a new contract after the person has successfully completed the previous one. Settle first for modest gain or gain in one area only, then pursue further improvement in subsequent contracts.

3. The reward should be worthwhile for the teen and she needs to feel that she is being treated fairly. This can be achieved when both the teen and the parents are involved in selecting the behaviors and rewards.

4. It is very important to provide support for the teen and to show approval for any progress made toward fulfilling the contract. Tell your teen you know he can do it and express your trust in him. Do whatever you can to help your teen succeed. Encourage him for any improvements. This helps in bridging the time between doing the behavior and receiving the reward.

5. Provide frequent small rewards that immediately follow the desirable behavior. Design your contract so as to provide small rewards along the way while waiting for the big reward. An extra fifteen minutes of phone time each day for *Safiya* was her daily reward for every day she tidied her

room. The long term reward was the opportunity to visit her friends on the weekends. A father who promises his son to buy him a skateboard as a reward can follow this technique by giving his son five dollars to save each week until they've saved enough money to buy the skateboard. In this way, the son accumulates tangible evidence that he is making progress.

Questions and Potential Problems
A. What to do if the contract doesn't work
– If it becomes clear at any time that the contract is not working, it is necessary to renegotiate. It is always better to do that than to let the contract fail. It may be necessary to change the amount or the kind of behavior requirements, or to change the reward.
B. What to do when the teen has a major problem
– Although it is better to start gradually by changing a behavior that is more manageable, sometimes you can't do that if you're pressured to deal with a major problem. When parents are faced with serious problems such as skipping school or smoking, they have to deal with them immediately. In such cases, to ensure success, insha' Allah, the contract should be done for a relatively short period of time so the teen is more likely to fulfill it and receive the reward. After succeeding in the first contract, another one can be negotiated for an equal or perhaps greater length.
C. What to do when the teen and his parents disagree about the way the contract has been fulfilled
– If this happens, parents should compromise first, then sit down with the teen and clarify things using more specific terms.
D. What to do when the teen partially fulfills the contract
– If the teen fails to fully fulfill the contract, he should not receive the reward. Some teens may need to feel the loss of not receiving a reward before they will take the contract seriously. If the parents have been providing too many privileges, the teen may be taking things for granted. It may be necessary to stop the privileges and then start providing them one by one as a reward for the contracted behavior.

Now that you have a good idea of what a behavioral contract is like, you are ready to use it as a tool to help your teen behave more responsibly, be conscientious of his duties and the purpose of his creation, be mindful of Allah SWT, and have more communication and better relationship with his parents.

Steps to Write a Contract

Step one: Sit down with your child and tell him that you have some concerns that you need to discuss with him. Agree to meet at a suitable time for both of you. Tell your teen how much you care about him. Talk about memories together and talk about the things you appreciate about him. After that, mention the issue of concern and tell him how it's your role as a parent to help him reach his best potential and that you value this responsibility and have to answer to Allah SWT. This meeting should be full of caring and loving feelings and not of blaming and condemning.

Tell your teen that you really need his help to deliver your responsibility regarding the trust that Allah has given to you, which is to raise him up to be a good Muslim, a righteous, responsible person. Tell him that it's a big trust and tell him how it makes you shiver when you think of the risk of failing. Ask your teen about issues that bother him too. Listen attentively and do not cut him off or be judgmental of what he says. Show empathy to his feelings.

Explain the behavioral contract to him as a tool to help both of you reach an agreement regarding his and your concerns.

Step two: Discuss what consequence or reward you will provide if he performs the desired behavior.

Negotiation and discussion in steps one and two are very important for the success of the contract. Both you and your teen should have an opportunity to be heard and feel that you have negotiated a good contract that is fair to both of you.

Step three: Write the contract. Fill in the youth's name in after "who" and the desired behavior after "what". State the goal in positive terms and be specific. Fill in the exact time after "when". Fill in the period and frequency after "how much". Include any exceptions or special conditions here.

Fill in your own name after "who" on the consequences side. Fill in the reward you will provide, or the behavior you will engage in if it is an exchange of behaviors, after "what". Write down when you will provide the reward after "when". Write down any specifications needed to clarify the conditions of the reward under "how much". Through discussions with the teen, decide about how you will keep track of his performance. Make a form for keeping a record at the bottom of the contract or attached to it.

Step four: Go over the contract one more time for revision. If you are both satisfied. Sign and date it.

Step five: Post the contract in a mutually agreed upon place. It is better if the contract is posted in a more public spot like the kitchen.

Step six: Follow up on recording the behavior. Provide feedback, support, and positive reinforcement. Be sure to deliver your reward on time.

Generic Parents Teen Contract	
Teen (Behavior)	**Parent's Reward**
Who: Name of teen	**Who**: Name of parent
What: Task to be performed	**What**: Reward of consequences
When: Time for performance	**When:** Time for reward
How much: Frequency and specifications	**How much**: Frequency and specifications
Signed ——— Date———	Signed——— Date———

Mon	Tue	Wed	Thu	Fri

Mon	Tue	Wed	Thu	Fri

Here is a sample of the contract between *Safiya* and Her Mom

Generic Parents Teen Contract	
Teen (Behavior)	**Parent's Reward**
Who: *Safiya*	**Who**: *Safiya*'s Mom
What: Makes her bed. Keeps her clothes in proper place.	**What**: Not to nag *Safiya* (>3times/week). Allow Safia to visit a friend. Allow 15m of extra phone calls.
When: Every day	**When**: Every day
How much: 5 times a week	**How much**: " Visit" every weekend. " Phone use" everyday *Safiya* tidies her room.
Signed *Safiya* Date 01/01/2001	Signed *Safiya's Mom* Date 01/01/2001

Mon	Tue	Wed	Thu	Fri

Mon	Tue	Wed	Thu	Fri

Other Ideas
Pre *Ramadan* Lunch
This was a lunch done by the high school children for the school staff on the occasion of the coming of *Ramadan*. Here, our daughter *Hoda* talks about a good idea she had to make the school staff at her high school more aware about *Ramadan*.

"It was in my last year of high school that we finally had enough practicing Muslims at my school to have a Muslim Student's Club. We were eight Muslims who regularly came to *Jum'ah* prayer held every week in a room branching off from the library. There were three brothers and five sisters (including my sister *Sumaiya* and I) and this was the largest number of Muslims that my high school had ever seen. There was a feeling of power and unity because we were all regular attendees and on top of that there were two more sisters who belonged to the club but were not very regular.

We had actually registered as a club only to make it easier to secure a room for *Jum'ah* prayer every week. Now that we had a club though, I couldn't shake the idea that we could organize some sort of activity, but I wasn't sure what we should do, so I just let the idea mull a little in my head.

One day when I was at home, someone brought up that *Ramadan* was coming up. The mention of this brought many memories to mind. I had been in the public school system the majority of my life and had had all sorts of experiences with regards to *Ramadan*. There was the time one of my peers was determined to catch me off guard and make me break my fast. She had offered me all sorts of food hoping that I would forget and eat something during the days of *Ramadan*. Then there were the pitying looks and comments that I received from teachers; some teachers glanced worriedly at me and asked me if I was okay and others asked me when the fasting month would be over in pitying tones. Many people didn't know the rules and weren't familiar with exactly how we fasted. One teacher thought that we fasted through the entire month, without breaking our fast each evening, and was very worried about me. Others were positive that we were allowed to drink water through the fasting. Through my interactions with my teachers over the years, I realized that though most of them knew that *Ramadan* was a month of fasting for Muslims, they didn't know much about how or why.

With that realization, in my last year of high school it hit me: this was my last chance to let them know. How many people could I really inform about this? There were many teachers in the school, but I only came in contact with a small number. I wanted to let all the teachers know what *Ramadan* was really about. If the ones I knew were asking me questions, then chances are that many of the teachers I didn't know had questions as well. The best way, I thought, would be to have a luncheon where we would serve different kinds of traditional foods to the staff and give a brief talk about *Ramadan*. The only problem was that it would be strange to have a luncheon in *Ramadan* since we wouldn't be able to eat at all. So, I thought, it must be a Pre-*Ramadan* Luncheon.

Excited about my idea, I told my parents and sisters and asked them what they thought. I needed a more definite and concrete plan. Together we mapped out the steps that had to be taken to turn Pre-*Ramadan* Luncheon into a reality.

I made an appointment with the principal and told him about our idea and he agreed. My mother and I sat down and brainstormed a list of ladies in our community from whom we could request a traditional dish. I called up each of the Muslim sisters on our list and explained our project. *Masha' Allah,* they were very helpful. Meanwhile, with the Muslim Club, we were busy at school holding meetings and trying to break down all the steps needed to pull off the luncheon. Colorful flyers were made and hung in the staff room and office. Invitations were made and distributed into the teachers' mailboxes and taken to the custodial staff's office. I approached the cafeteria staff and requested the partial use of their kitchen and oven to heat and serve the food on the day of the luncheon. This was a little problematic because we needed to be in their kitchen at lunch time and that was quite a hectic time for the cafeteria staff themselves. *Alhamdulillah,* we overcame that problem through patience, *dua'a* and compromise.

When we started dividing up the tasks for the day of the actual luncheon we found that there was plenty to do; decorating and setting up the room, receiving, preparing, and setting up the food, welcoming and hosting the staff, and cleaning up. Our little club didn't have enough people to do all that stuff so we decided that we would ask dependable friends who were free at the times we needed assistance to help us out.

Since, of course, we couldn't skip class for this, those of us who could afford to miss class explained the project to our teachers and asked for their permission to be excused from class on the day of the luncheon. Between the people who obtained permission to leave class and those who naturally had free time during those periods, we figured out exactly who was responsible for what.

There was still one major detail that needed some attention: who would be the speaker at the luncheon? When the club discussed this at a meeting, we came up with two ideas: either a person from the club could address the staff (and the choices had been narrowed down to me) or we could invite a speaker from outside the school from among the university brothers who came to give the *Jum'ah khutba* every week at our school. After doing *shura* (consultation) with my parents, I was convinced that it would be a better idea for the club to have one of the students in the school present than to invite a guest speaker. If a student from the school presented, that would leave a positive impression on the staff that we were able to tell them about our religion ourselves. If a guest speaker came to present, that might leave the staff with the impression that we (the Muslim students in the school) were just followers and we were just doing whatever our community and our families told us to do without choosing or understanding. If we were the ones standing up and presenting to them, they were more likely to understand that this was our conviction, our belief, and our choice. This was very important to take into consideration, seeing as the whole point of having this luncheon was to correct misconceptions about Islam, so we certainly didn't want to do anything that might give the wrong impression and perpetuate more misconceptions to the school staff.

With that decided, I wrote out my speech and ran it by my family for suggestions and constructive criticism. There were two parts to my speech. First, I spoke about the basic technicalities of *Ramadan*, what it is, and what the exact rules of fasting are. Then I spoke about the personal benefits that I've experienced through my practice of fasting in *Ramadan*, such as the self-control and perseverance that it gives me, and the empathy with those less fortunate than myself. The speech was brief and personal and not too technical or historical. It was prepared that way on purpose in order to cater to the audience. If my memory serves me correctly, the speech was about five minutes long.

As the day grew near, I realized the true magnitude of the task we had taken on. I, in effect, was the coordinator between the community and the club. In terms of the club, everything was under control, but, in terms of the community, I didn't really have a clear plan of action formulated in my head as to how things would work out. I had taken down each sister's address and asked all of them to please have the food ready for that morning, but who was going to drive? How would I get the food from the sisters' houses to the school?

I was overwhelmed by the thought. With two days left until the luncheon, my parents came to the rescue. The three of us sat down together and worked things out. I was in over my head and my parents and two kind sisters in the community came to the rescue. My father, my mother, and a graciously helpful sister from the community named *Ghada Turk* and a club member's kind mother named *Amy Setiadi* took care of the transportation, *Jazahum Allahu kheiran* for all their work. They picked up the food from various different neighborhoods and delivered it to the school. I know that it was a difficult day for my father to go into the office late and that he had plenty to do. I'm sure that it wasn't convenient for sister *Ghada*, Sister Amy, and my mother either, especially on account of the short notice due to the lack of planning on my part. *Masha' Allah*, they were all so willing to make personal sacrifices and help out for the sake of Allah even though it was not their fault that I had put myself in this position. The helpful, tireless, and positive attitude taught me a lesson that day that, God willing, I think I will never forget.

After the food had all arrived, my mother and sister Amy stayed to help out with all the preparing, serving, and cleaning up. *Alhamdulillah,* the luncheon went very well. There was plenty of food and a big turnout. In fact when Mr. Wyatt, our principal, came into the staff room and saw how much work we had put into the event, he turned around and went straight back to the office and made an announcement over the P.A. system reminding all the staff that the Pre-*Ramadan* luncheon was going on right now and encouraging them to come attend it.

The speech was well received and everybody enjoyed the variety of traditional dishes. Pictures were taken and the event was documented in the yearbook. That night over the dinner table at home, my mom, *Sumaiya*, and I told the rest of our family how it went. *Alhamdulillah,* we all felt very positive about it.

During the next couple of weeks, we received many comments from our teachers telling us how much they enjoyed it. One of *Sumaiya's* teachers told her she felt it was a great idea and really appreciated learning about our religion. She told *Sumaiya* that she felt she didn't know enough about other religions and that she didn't understand why some did things the way we did. She said that she needed and appreciated the information. All the members of the club said that their teachers were very appreciative of the luncheon and one teacher in particular was already making plans for next year's luncheon!

Alhamdulillah. It took plenty of planning and organizing, but a small Muslim club was able, with plenty of help from the cafeteria staff, our friends, family, and community, to pull off the Pre-*Ramadan* Luncheon to inform the school staff about *Ramadan* and open the door for further discussions. I would like to thank everybody who helped out and made this event possible, thank my parents for raising me in such a way that made it possible for me to envision such an event, and thank Allah for all His help in this matter and all others."

Here is a copy of the personal invitations put in each teacher's office mailbox and of the luncheon program:

The Muslim students of
Nepean High School
cordially invite you to experience
the celebration of....

The coming of *Ramadan*

Lunch hour
Monday, December 7th
Staff Room

• *Try many of our*
traditional foods
• *Find out what Ramadan*
is really about

We look forward to seeing you there.

The Muslim Students of Nepean

Welcome You To

The Ramadan Celebration
~ Luncheon ~

12:11 Arrival and lunch
12:30 An address about Ramadan

* Enjoy *

****

Christmas Presents

Here is another idea *Hoda* had to deal with gift exchange around Christmas time.

"In grade nine each of the girls in my group of friends brought me little presents, tokens of our friendship, at Christmas time, just like they brought to all their other friends. It was clear to me from a very young age that I did not celebrate Christmas and I had no problem with that. I never went to Christmas parties when I was invited and I never did Christmas crafts in school. This was different though. The girls were bringing me little presents. I wasn't going to reject their presents. It was really sweet of them to do this, but it made me feel bad. Everybody was giving me presents and I wasn't getting anything for them.

At the same time, there was no way that I could get them presents, because it would be as if I was celebrating Christmas too. This was frustrating and I shared my frustration with my family. We discussed the issue until finally we came up with a solution that wouldn't compromise my values and at the same time wouldn't make me feel so bad about not giving my friends presents. I would wait until *Eid* rolled around and then

I would give them all little present bags and an explanation for why they were getting presents. This way I felt that I could accept their presents and be part of the group and still celebrate my own holiday and not have to take part in Christmas. So, a week before *Eid* (even though it was several months after Christmas) I stopped by the mall on my way back from school and bought all sorts of different kinds of chocolates. I wasn't going to be at school on *Eid*, so I had to give it to them before then. So the night before my last day at school before *Eid*, my sister and I sat in my room with the chocolates, the wrapping paper, the ribbons, the notes, and the scissors and had ourselves a little wrapping party until all the packages were done and I had a package for each of my friends.

The notes read as follows:

Hey,

As you probably already know, I've been fasting everyday from dawn until dusk for the past month. That's because it was the month of Ramadan. Well from the fast, I've gained appreciation for the food that I usually take for granted and compassion for those who don't have as much to eat. This weekend Ramadan will end and I will have a great big celebration called Eid-Ul-Fitr which just means the celebration of breaking one's fast. Just wanted to share my happiness with you on this special holiday.

Love Hoda

Alhamdulillah, this way, I felt good because I still gave them presents and didn't need to participate in any Christmas activities and, at the same time, my friends learned a little bit about Islam (not much, but at least they were exposed to it.) *Alhamdulillah,* I felt this solution really helped me out."

The rest of the material in this chapter draws heavily on the valuable information provided on Sound Vision web page.

School visits to talk about Islamic events

– Parents talking to their children's principals, teachers and classmates in public schools about *Ramadan* is of immense importance.

By doing so, Muslim children feel less awkward identifying themselves as Muslims, since someone in a position of authority has discussed what they do. As a result, the children often feel more confident and secure.

Muslim children need to feel the importance of their own celebrations and holidays, especially since we are living in a non-Muslim environment where kids don't see fancy lights and decorations, commercial hoopla or consistent reminders of the "holiday season" during *Ramadan.*

Of course, talking to your child's class about *Ramadan* is a great way to make *Da'wa* to non-Muslim kids and Muslim kids as well, in particular those who may come from non-practicing Muslim families.

There are a couple of tips to keep in mind when approaching the school or your child's teachers about presenting, as well as some tips for how to present the information to your child's class.

Tip #1: Start early

Calling your child's teacher in the middle of Ramadan and asking to do a presentation on the topic is too late. Less than a month before Ramadan is the best time to bring up the issue, especially if Christmas is coming up around the same time and holidays are on the minds of most people, teachers and students included.

Starting early also helps you think about and gather the right materials to make a good presentation.

Tip #2: Get permission from your child's teacher

While parents do have a lot of clout in the school system, this does not allow them to show up unexpectedly one day at their son or daughter's class to do a presentation on Ramadan. Send a letter (a sample is available at a later part of this chapter or see http://www.soundvision.com) giving a general indication that you want something done about Ramadan. Then wait for the teacher to call. If he or she does not do so within a week, call them and tell them you are following up on the letter you sent earlier.

Tip #3: Select the right period in which to do the presentation

Does your child study Social Studies? Or does she have a period once a week for Moral and Religious education? If so, suggest to the teacher that you would like to do the presentation during this period, or you can ask the teacher if he has ideas about which time would be best to come in and do the presentation.

Tip #4: Be polite but firm
Speaking nicely to people, including non-Muslims, is part of our deen. We should remember that the purpose of this exercise is to not just educate the students, but the teachers as well. Being polite and courteous will not detract from your desire to present. It will serve to build bridges and communication, and could lead to further contact to do presentations on other Islam-related topics and more teacher-parent cooperation in the future, *Insha' Allah*.

Tip #5: Ask the teacher what areas to cover and how long the presentation should be
This helps to adjust your presentation to the age level of the students, as well as connect it to what they are already learning. This doesn't mean you can't bring in other information, but knowing what to cover from the teacher helps you put down what has to be covered, and from there you can develop more points on these, or related topics. Asking how long the presentation should be can also help you decide how much you can include in your presentation.

Tip #6: Read, prepare, read, and prepare again
Now that you've gotten the permission, you don't just sit back and wait for the night before the presentation to put it together. Remember, if you want to appeal to the students, especially younger ones, you are going to need more than just a talk. Visuals are a great help. You can get a *Ramadan* banner (see *Sound Vision*'s *Ramadan* packet at http://www.soundvision.com) pictures of Muslims fasting, show part of a video aimed at children about Ramadan (see Adam's World's *Ramadan Mubarak* video at http://www.soundvision.com). To get the right material, you will have to find out where to get it from, and ordering it might take a couple of weeks. Preparing is important, even though you may have fasted all of your life and think you know all about *Ramadan*. Get a children's Islamic book and read what it says about *Ramadan*. Or an article written by a teenager about *Ramadan*. This will also help you understand what points to emphasize in your presentation.

Reading up will also clarify any incorrect cultural norms that may have seeped into the practices of *Ramadan* that you may not have been aware of. Talk to a knowledgeable Muslim for advice as well.

Tip #7: Talk to your son or daughter about the presentation
Who would know better the mindset of the kids in the class than your son or daughter? Consult your children about what to include, what the kids like, and what kinds of things they are interested in. Not only will this improve your presentation, *Insha' Allah,* but it will also make your son or daughter feel important and more confident as an individual, and as a Muslim.

Tip #8: A few days before the presentation
Call the teacher to check the date and time of the schedule. This will serve to remind him or her about your visit and prepare the class accordingly. It will also help you get the exact time and date.

Tip #9: Write presentation points on note cards
Reading off papers about *Ramadan* will not hold the interest of many people, young or old. Instead, writing brief notes on note cards that you can look at so you don't miss any topics will help you avoid straying from the subject while allowing you to make eye contact with your audience and maintain a conversational style of presentation.

Tip #10: Practice your presentation in front of your son or daughter
Practicing helps you identify what can be improved, changed, or omitted. Practicing in front of your daughter will give you the opportunity to present before one of the kids in the class who can really give you the best advice. It will also help you time your presentation, so you can make it shorter or longer.

Tip #11: Dress for success
This does not mean pulling out the Armani suit or the most expensive dress you have. It just means looking as a Muslim should – clean, respectable, professional and Islamically covered. Clothes don't always "make the man" but they do affect others' perception of you.

Tip #12: Arrive early
Teachers and students are busy people. They have a certain curriculum to cover. The fact that they've squeezed in your presentation is somewhat of a privilege. Don't take advantage of this by wasting their time and

coming late. Anyway, Muslims should be on time as a principle. Coming early can also help you set up the audio-visual material.

Tip #13: Make *dua'a*...

Before your presentation, ask Allah to help you convey this message sincerely, properly and clearly. And say *Bismillah*.

Tip #14: Speak calmly and clearly

It's important not to race through the presentation, nor to talk too slowly. A clear, conversational style, but emphasis on the major points or terms you want the students to understand, can help convey the message properly.

Tip #15: When answering questions

If you don't know something, say so. Then check up on it and get back to the teacher. Ask him or her to convey the response.

Tip #16: Thank Allah...

For this opportunity He blessed you with and your ability to go through with it.

Tip #17: Send a thank you note to the teacher and class...

Thanking them for their time and attention, as well as their cooperation.

Eid celebrations

Eid prayers are a great opportunity to talk about Islam and get media coverage for it. One way of doing this is by putting together and sending out a press release to media outlets in your town or city. Here is a sample you can easily put together to invite the media to *Eid* prayers arranged by your local mosque.

FOR IMMEDIATE RELEASE – March 9, 2000

OVER 300,000 CHICAGO MUSLIMS CELEBRATE NEXT WEEK

WHO: Muslims in Chicago, Illinois and the U.S.
WHAT: Will be celebrating the Islamic holiday of

Eid-ul-Adha with over 1 billion Muslims worldwide. (There are about 6 million Muslims in the U.S. including converts from the African-American, Latin-American and Caucasian-American communities. Many of these converts are women).

HOW: With congregational prayers in halls and stadiums across the city and states, social gatherings and food and meat distribution to the needy.

WHEN: Thursday March 17 at 9:00 a.m.

WHERE: Smith Stadium (1600 Drummond street, Downtown Chicago, corner Oxford)

WHY: *Eid ul-Adha* is how Muslims commemorate Prophet Abraham's willingness to sacrifice his son Ishmael at God's command.

CONTACT: To arrange media coverage of this occasion, please contact *Ali* Smith, media relations coordinator of the Sunnah mosque in downtown Chicago:

Telephone: (123) 456-7890
Cell: (123) 321-9876
Mosque: (123) 567-8901
E-mail: eidmediacommittee@hotmail.com

PLEASE KEEP IN MIND:
– While *Eid* prayer will be held on March 17, festivities will take place between March 16 and 19. As well, please note that every year, *Eid-ul-Adha* coincides with *Hajj*, a pilgrimage Muslims must make to Makkah, Saudi Arabia, which is a religious obligation. This year, the peak day for *Hajj* will be March 15 (which is the ninth day of the Islamic month in which *Hajj* is performed, known in Arabic as *Thul Hijjah*).
– Since this is a prayer service, media professionals who will be

attending, both men and women, are asked to dress modestly (i.e. no short shorts or skirts, tank tops, etc.). Women reporters, photographers and/or camera women may be asked to cover their hair with a scarf while at the prayer service.

Saying No to Your Child's School Christmas Party: Advice and a Sample Letter

During the month of December, Christmas fever starts. Soon the cartoon specials will begin, (the shopping began in early November) and soon your teen's class party, as well as Christmas parties at your office, will start. Class Christmas parties are not marked by things like alcohol, which you would find at many parties for adults. However, parents should remember that class Christmas parties are being held during the day, when your son or daughter may be fasting. In this case it would be a good idea to keep them away from the party, which usually features delicious junk food that can make fasting harder for your children.

We discussed *Ramadan* in schools earlier. For instance, 17 tips were provided on how to present Ramadan to your child's class. Also, if you visit the Sound Vision website, you can find a sample letter to the principal about *Ramadan*, a sample letter to your child's homeroom teacher about *Ramadan*, a fact sheet on *Ramadan* for teachers, and also a sample student *Ramadan* presentation.

But if you or your child hasn't been able to speak about Ramadan to her teacher and class, the class Christmas party provides the perfect opportunity for this kind of *da'wa* (and remember, in *Ramadan*, you receive more rewards for good deeds than during the rest of the year).

To support you further, here is a sample letter drafted by Sound Vision that you can use to get her out of the Christmas party and into *Da'wa* mode, *Insha' Allah*.

SAMPLE LETTERS TO TEACHERS

Tuesday December 14, 1999
Dear Ms. Jenkins:

Greetings of peace. I am the mother of *Hafsa Nafees*, who is in your fourth grade class.

Hafsa has benefited greatly from your help as a teacher so far this year, and I hope she continues to do so under your supervision.

I would like to bring to your attention the issue of your class Christmas party scheduled for December 14.

December is traditionally associated with Christmas. But this year, the month is special for Muslims like Hafsa and our family as well. We are taking part in the month of *Ramadan*.

Ramadan is the ninth month of the Islamic lunar calendar. It is notable for its emphasis on seeking closeness to God through fasting, prayer and charity. This year, *Ramadan* begins on November 17.

During *Ramadan*, Muslims abstain from food, drink and sex between dawn and sunset each day. Although fasting is not required of Muslims until they reach puberty, many Muslim children may fast as well.

They often do this to experience *Ramadan* with their parents and older siblings. *Hafsa* is an example of this.

Hafsa's class Christmas party will be taking place at lunchtime, which is when she will be fasting. After discussing it with *Hafsa* and her father, we all decided that it would not be a good idea for *Hafsa* to attend the party, therefore, she will be absent from school that day.

Please note that this is not meant to exclude her from activities with her peers, since she will continue in other class exercises as usual. Rather, because *Hafsa* is fasting, her participation in a party at this time with food and drink will make it difficult for her.

Perhaps one way for *Hafsa* to share and participate with her classmates this month is by doing a presentation on *Ramadan*.

In it, she can explain what it is like to fast, and the importance of this month for Muslims.

I have included a short article which explains *Ramadan* and fasting in further detail for your interest (print out the article). If you would like to discuss this issue further, please don't hesitate to contact me at

(123) 555-7890 in the daytime or at home (123) 555-3456 after 7 p.m.

Thank you for your attention and cooperation.

Sincerely,
Mrs. *Aneesah Ghazi*

Saying No to Hallowe'en
Here is another sample letter to teachers referring to Hallowe'en.

Thursday October 12, 2000

Dear Ms. Griffin:

Greetings of peace. I am the mother of *Ali Syed*, who is in your fourth grade class.

Ali has benefited greatly from your teaching so far this year, and I hope he continues to do so.
I would like to bring to your attention the issue of Hallowe'en and *Ali*'s involvement in class activities relating to the occasion.

As you have organized a class Hallowe'en party for Tuesday October 31, I would like to inform you that *Ali* will not attend this activity. He will be absent the day it is held.

This is not meant to exclude him from activities with his peers, since he will continue in other class exercises as usual. Rather, due to the nature of Hallowe'en, its origins and its connection to non-Islamic beliefs and practices, *Ali*'s participation will compromise his beliefs and principles as a Muslim.

I would like to meet with you to discuss and seek your advice on further issues surrounding class celebrations and holidays, so that *Ali* and students of other religious backgrounds can fully participate in your class while maintaining their beliefs and principles.

I would appreciate it if you would kindly contact me so that we may set up a meeting this week or next week to further discuss this matter. You may call me at (123) 555-7890 in the daytime or (123) 555-3456 in the evenings.

 I look forward to hearing from you. Thank you for your time and attention.

Sincerely,

Memuna Al-Khabyyr

10. Positive Teen Experiences

In this chapter, we will present you with some positive teen experiences. These real life experiences are illustrated to you through our daughters' writing. They were lived and felt by them. At the time they took place, some of them represented a burden. They had to struggle with them and experienced difficulties. It was mainly because of our teen's complete faith in Allah SWT and their clear understanding and conviction of the concepts we presented in chapter six that they were able to turn these experiences into positive ones. In some cases, they were even able to further the cause of Islam and *Da'wa* in North American society through sticking to their beliefs without compromise and presenting themselves as Muslims on all occasions.

Now, we leave you with *Hoda* to present a couple of these experiences:

1. Allah Does Not Waste The Rewards of Those who Do Good Deeds

It was a cold February morning, the first day back at school after exams and everyone in the class looked sleepy. It was hard getting up and getting ready to be at school by 8:20 a.m. again after having a week of sleeping in, but I was looking forward to this class, Families in Canadian Society. After taking a grade eleven parenting class, I had only done maths, sciences, and languages for a while, and I missed learning about real life topics. I had heard from many people that this was a great course. Mrs. Johnson had been teaching Canadian Families (Can Fam) for as long as I could remember and all my friends loved both her and the class. This year, a new teacher had taken over the course but he had taken her materials from her and he seemed like a nice guy.

He stood at the front of the classroom telling us his expectations for us and our behavior. He was stressing that we had to be respectful of other people and their opinions. "Now some of the things that other cultures take part in might seem strange to you and me, but we have to remember not to be judgmental. I mean, maybe some to of the things we do seem bizarre to them, right? Remember, we're here to learn about different families, different values, and different lifestyles. It is not our place to judge other people's lifestyles. Who knows? Maybe their ways are better than ours."

I was impressed; he seemed enthusiastic and understanding, but despite his positive attitude, I was still concerned.

Throughout the rest of the class time, he had each one of us ask him questions about the course and about himself. He was friendly and casual. The fact that he was so approachable made me relax a little because there was something important I had to talk with him about.

After class, I went up to his desk and waited my turn. I let the other students who wanted to speak to him go first. Then, as the class emptied, he turned to me and smiled . "Hi," he said.

"Hello Mr. Brown," I responded, smiling back. "I, ummm . . . I had friends in your Can Fam class last semester and they would come and ask me about some of the issues that were brought up in class. I found that a lot of the information that they were being taught in class about Islam was actually not true. Sometimes newspapers and stuff, they give the wrong impression about Islam so I just thought, you know, I would tell you now, because I'll probably be needing to make comments and stuff, if something like that comes up in class. I hope you don't mind." I realized that throughout my little explanation, both my heartbeat and my speech had quickened. Now I was standing nervously, holding my breath and waiting for his response.

"Oh really," he looked concerned. "I'm sorry that that was happening, and I am so glad that you're here with us. This is wonderful; now you can shed some light on the myths . . . oh, yes, that would be great. Just catch my eye and let us know. I mean, it's so good to have someone here who really knows what it's all about. Oh that would be great . . . yeah, wonderful."

His response was such a relief to me. It's always good when the teacher is on the same side as you; it makes the task a whole lot easier. "Thank you," I smiled, turning to leave the room.

"Oh," Mr. Brown called. "Before you go – what's your name?"

"*Hoda Beshir*," I said and watched as he put a little mark down next to my name on his class list. I walked into the hallway smiling and content. Mr. Brown had put my worries to rest. He recognized me as the authority about Islam in his classroom and wasn't going to give me a hard time when I tried to correct him. *Alhamdulillah.*

That evening I told my mom about the little talk that I had had with Mr. Brown and we both smiled contentedly about his attitude. I was glad that I didn't have a semester of battling ahead of me. Clearing up misconceptions about Islam is a lot easier when the teacher values your opinions.

As the year went on, I found out that this was not going to be as easy as I thought. Time and time again, Mr. Brown made belittling comments about Islam and humiliating remarks about Muslims, and specifically about Muslim women. Time and time again, my hand shot up and I defended my beliefs to the class and to the teacher only to have my comments undermined the moment Mr. Brown started summing up what I'd said. The teacher who I thought had accepted me as an authority on Islam actually seemed to think very lowly of my expertise on the religion that I had lived by my entire life. Every time I corrected a statement that misrepresented Islam, he defended it. He acted as if the people who wrote the articles were the utmost authority and that my opinion couldn't refute theirs.

Sometimes when I wouldn't give up my position that Islamic law was being misrepresented, he would say, "Well *Hoda*, you see, maybe because you've lived in Canada for so long, you've adopted some ways that are different from the traditional Islam." He often did this, hinting that I was the exception to the Islamic rules and that I was presenting not the rules but the exceptions.

The teacher who had seemed so sensitive and conscientious of not making fun or judging others began to show his politically incorrect side. He let comments slip out of his mouth about how "weird" or "crazy" other cultures were. He rolled his eyes, raised his eyebrows, and made faces when we talked about different traditions that were unfamiliar to him. After he was finished rudely expressing his disapproval, he would reprimand himself sarcastically in front of the class: "Oh, bad bad teacher! You're not supposed to judge people! Baaaaad teacher! Baaaad!"

My class was mostly Caucasian Canadian kids, but even so, they were unimpressed with his ways. Still, I felt that I was alone in my fight.

He always brought up the most controversial topics and pinned Islam's name to them, and I always put up my hand knowing full well that my comment would be rejected; my knowledge would be pushed aside and made out to look worthless by Mr. Brown's response. Still, I put up my hand and presented the other side, because at least that way, the thirty students in the room would know that there was another point of view, that what he was saying may not be true. It wasn't easy though. I was humiliated and upset enough by the comments he made initially. By putting my hand up to argue with him, I brought the attention of every student in the classroom to my bright red face and invited him to pick on me.

If I had stayed quiet, he would have been insulting Islam, but when I spoke up and defended Islam, I put myself into the group that he was insulting. I brought attention to myself so that all my fellow students could look over and notice me and say, "she's one of those. She's one of those people that he's talking about."

But still, I could not just stay quiet; Islam was an essential part of me, and I was a part of the Muslim *Ummah*. No matter how bad it felt to be the center of attention in a controversial discussion arguing against the teacher, I knew that it would feel much worse to sit silently as my teacher spread lies and provoked hatred toward Islam.

So the year dragged on, with me being forced awake at 8:30 in the morning only to listen to Mr. Brown talk about arranged marriages in which the bride and groom are not allowed to see or speak to each other until after the marriage, and somehow relate these traditions to Islam.

I was fed up with the class, tired of always being on guard, of putting up my hand and explaining politely only to be undermined by Mr. Brown as soon as I was finished. Then, one day, Mr. Brown announced that we should pick the topics for our independent study projects. The independent study project (IDS) – twenty minutes when the class was mine to address, when I could present whatever I pleased to everybody in the room. What a great opportunity for me to present my side of the argument without having to argue.

My mind was made up and I told some of my friends about my decision. Fatma and Aethne, two friends who had heard plenty of my complaints about the comments my teacher was always making, both thought it was a great idea.

As the time drew nearer, my teacher's opinions grew stronger in my head and suddenly; I started having doubts that this was the right thing to do. I told my friend Sue, "Two things that are very important to me are at stake. You know how important my religion is to me and I don't want to compromise any part of that. At the same time, I really want to get a high grade in this course. I don't think that it's such a good idea for me to mix the two together. I mean, maybe I should keep them separate from each other so that I don't have to compromise either one."

Sue was supportive and understanding to my situation. I was stuck between a rock and a hard place. I, of course, could not tell lies about my religion and with Mr. Brown's bias, what would he think of the truth? Up to this point, I had decided that the purpose of my IDS was to clear up all the misconceptions that he had given in class. Now I realized that he could get offended and upset and he was the one grading both my paper and my presentation. They were worth a big chunk of my mark: between the essay and the presentation, that was 20% of my mark right there.

I decided that it would be a better idea to keep the two matters separate. I didn't want to risk either one. I wasn't comfortable with my decision though. I felt bad. I mean, Allah has given me so many blessings. He gave me a supportive family, a house, a peaceful life, a healthy body, a working brain. His blessings to me were endless. And now that I had found myself with an opportunity to give back, to do something purely for the sake of Allah, I was backing down because I couldn't handle the idea of losing some marks for it. So, even though, outwardly I had made my decision to choose a topic unrelated to Islam for my IDS, on the inside there was a battle going on and though I tried to suppress it, I still felt its traces.

One day when I was sitting studying during my spare period, Fatma and Aethne asked me about how Can Fam class was going. I poured out what was on my mind. I told them about my conflict of interest.

"So, I don't think that I'm going to be doing my IDS about Islam anymore, even though I really wanted to . . ."

"No way," Fatma said. "That's horrible. You really wanted to though, and I mean you have to listen to all the stuff he says. You should be able to say the real stuff, you know? . . . Man, *Hoda*, you should go for it."

"I know and I want to," I replied. "But I'm worried about him. I mean, he's obviously not going to be very happy with what I say. He could give me a really bad mark."

"Well," said Aethne. "Why don't you just ask him. If he agrees with the topic, then he'll be fine with whole thing."

"Okay," I said hesitantly. "But guys – I don't know."

"I'll come with you to ask if you want me to," said Aethne.

"He could use it against me that I'm presenting about my own religion," say that I'm biased or that I didn't have to do research or something like that."

"So let's go ask him, *Hoda*," Aethne suggested again.

"Okay," I stood up and so did she. We went up the stairs and into his office where I told him that I was thinking of doing my IDS on Muslims and asked him if he had any problem with that since I was Muslim.

"No, not at all," Mr. Brown assured me. "I think that's a great idea. Just remember to do your research just like everybody else and you'll be fine."

"Alright, thank you Sir." As soon as I was out the door an excited squeal escaped my mouth. My grin stretched across my face and I gave Aethne a hug.

"Thank you so much, Aeth. This is great."

Well it was decided: I would do my IDS on Muslim women because I felt that he had misrepresented the treatment and rights of women in Islam.

The challenges didn't stop there; the resources of our class research time in the library were dismal. The school library had only one good book about Islam and when I searched magazine and newspaper articles, I found that their information was even worse than Mr. Brown's. So, that night I went home and searched the bookshelves that my parents had stocked with goodies. There, I found what I was looking for, plenty of books and pamphlets discussing women's issues in Islam.

At school, we drew the dates for our presentations out of a hat. There were two people presenting every day, but I got the last day of presentations and I was alone.

I wanted to make my presentation fun and interesting. I didn't want to sound like I was looking for pity and I didn't want to sound like a preacher who was telling the class what to do. So I read and wrote and asked my parents endless questions and received tremendous support from everyone. Baba (my dad) photocopied whatever I needed and made me slides as a backup in case my slide show didn't work on the computer at school for any reason. *Amirah*, my older sister, patiently taught me how to make and run a slide show. Mama (my mom) brainstormed the different visual aids and props that I could use to make my presentation more interesting, and then rummaged through the basement and the various closets to find them all. *Sumaiya* helped me with my poster and listened to my rehearsals again and again, and *Noha* stayed up with me the night before to write Q-cards, make up questions for the game, edit my essay, and put the finishing touches on my presentation.

Not only was my family supportive, but so were the sisters from the community. A French Canadian sister named Lyne, who had converted to Islam many years earlier, agreed to let me interview her for my project. Another Muslim sister, Sally, who knew how to videotape, agreed to come with me to Lyne's house and tape the interview and edit the tape until it was in the form in which I could use it for my presentation. Both were very generous with their time and effort, *jazahum Allahu kheiran.*

Needless to say, all the support and help that I got pumped up my confidence and excitement. When I walked into class the morning of April 30th, I was ready to go.

The presentation worked out great. First I took the class through my slide show about women in Islam, which had three main topics, with the purpose of cleaning up common misconceptions about Muslim women. I started off the slide show with this verse from the *Qur'an*:

> The believers, men and women, are protectors, one of
> another: they enjoin what is just and forbid what is evil:
> they observe regular prayers, practice regular charity and
> obey God and His apostle . . ." (*Qur'an* 9:71)

Then, I explained that this showed the equality of men and women in Islam, and that Islam views women as capable people.

The first topic I presented was a little background about the etiquette of interaction between men and women in Islam. Then I presented the what and why of the ever-misunderstood *hijab*. Then to end the slide show, I walked the class through the process of an Islamic marriage. After the slide show was finished, I approached the wall at the front of the classroom where I had hung up numerous different examples of clothes that would fulfill the requirements of *hijab*. So I had a display of different skirts, shirts, blouses, dresses, extremely baggy pants (like those from Pakistan), *jilbabs* and different kinds of scarves of different colors.

The point was to show them that Muslim women still have a choice in how they dress, we can still express our identity and our personality is not suppressed; we just have to meet certain requirements while dressing.

While talking about the clothes, I passed out some Islamic magazines that I had opened and marked on pages that showed active Muslim women participating in different activities.

Then I showed the class the video of my interview with Lyne. Lyne answered questions like how her life had changed since she embraced Islam, whether she had any regrets, how her family had reacted, and what the best thing about embracing Islam had been for her. Weeks earlier I had asked several of my non-Muslim friends what questions they would want to ask a woman who converted to Islam. These questions gave me an idea of what my class, the audience of my video, would be interested in. The class looked very interested in the video as I watched their reactions to Lyne's answers.

After the video, it was time for the interactive part of my presentation. I divided the class into two teams and introduced the rules of the trivia game about the information in my presentation. I promised the winning team prizes and I also promised that if any one individual answered most of the questions for his/ her team, that one person would get a special prize (the purpose of that was to prevent any one person form answering everything for their team.)

The game was going great. I was getting super class participation. Then finally I got what I was waiting for: Mr. Brown put up his hand to answer a question for his team. I read out the question: "True or false: Muslim women have to wear *hijab* as soon as they turn fifteen years old."

"True," Mr. Brown answered confidently. Before I could tell him that the answer was wrong, the rest of the class did. The students from the other team booed him and the students on his own team yelled at him for losing the point and the entire class yelled out the right answer at me. The game went on until I finished all the questions. At the end, if my memory serves me correctly, the teams were tied. Both teams wanted to break the tie so I thought up of a tie-breaker question and one team won. I gave the winning team's members two tasteations each (a tasteation is a kind of candy) and the members of the other team received one tasteation each. *Alhamdulillah*, nobody received the individual prize, but, for the record, it was a big pack of Twizzlers (red licorice.)

Now it was time for questions. We only had about ten minutes until class was over and my classmates had many questions. I took questions as I passed out prizes and collected my materials and visual aids. People kept asking really intelligent and open-minded, truly curious questions. I was thrilled. I was even more thrilled when I saw Mr. Brown's hand go up.

"Yes, Mr. Brown," I called.

"What does the Qur'an say about homosexuality?" he asked.

My heart fell; I couldn't believe that he just asked me that. I was making such a great impression on the class and, in light of homosexuality's recent popularity jump, my answer wasn't going to be too welcome.

Thoughts raced through my mind. Obviously I couldn't change the answer, but the way I phrased it would be really important. Finally, I remembered a phrase that I had heard my mom advise somebody to use. "Like all other major religions, Islam doesn't approve of that lifestyle." Then I took the next question as the bell rang to end the class.

There was only one thing that upset me about my presentation: the number of people in class. Our class had around 28 students enrolled, but there were only 16 students in class that day. Apparently, there had been a dance or a party the night before and so people were hung over and sleeping in. Still, I had reached 16 people with real information about Islam, *Alhamdulillah*.

I was thrilled with my presentation and the class participation. My happiness only increased the next day when I found out that I got 29 out of 30 for my presentation. The mark that I lost was because I went over the time limit, which I had done intentionally. I knew that no other students were presenting that day and the more time I had, the more myths I could tear down. What a small price to pay: one mark for 56 extra minutes to spread the truth about Islam.

All over the marking sheet, there were comments from my teacher about both my presentation and Islam. The one that really caught my eye said something to the meaning of, "A really interesting and informative presentation on a widely misunderstood religion."

From that day on, my classmates approached me much more often with questions about Islam and its different rules and reasons. My *hijab* was seen as a liberator and not an oppressor over me; two of my friends were discussing how they were going to do their hair, what they were going to wear, etc. and they turned to me and said, "*Hoda*, you're so lucky that you're not always worrying about that. Oh, believe me, you're in the best position."

Mr. Brown's undermining comments, though they subsided a little, did not disappear. I realized then that my teacher was not intentionally spreading lies about Islam. He just passed on whatever he was told through popular media. I also realized that next year, he would be making the same comments to God knows how many classes. This semester, I could defend my religion and show my classmates that what he said was opinion not fact, but for the coming years, his insults to Islam would go unanswered and that thought troubled me a great deal.

I decided to go speak to the head of the department, who also used to teach Canadian Families the year before, Mrs. Johnson. I asked her if I could speak to her and she let me into her office. I voiced my concerns, telling her about the misconceptions that were being taught about my religion. I didn't realize just how upset I was until that moment. I couldn't hold back the tears as I told her how personally insulting and demeaning it was to sit and listen to such things being said about me day in and day out. I told her that I was worried about the years to come when I would not be there to show the other side.

She was very understanding. She told me that she wasn't the expert on Islam; I was. She asked me for a copy of my sister *Noha*'s essay about marriage in Islam (I had mentioned it during our meeting). I had also told her that my parents had given the school a copy of their book "Parenting in the West: An Islamic Perspective" so that it would be in the library for student use but I had only seen it on Mr. Brown's shelf in his office.

"Well, I didn't even know about the book," she commented.

I'll take care of that. First, I'd like to read it and then I'll make sure that it goes to the library." She also assured me that she would speak to Mr. Brown and invited me to come see her with any other concerns that I might have in the future.

At the end of the year I no longer felt that Can Fam class had been a waste of time. On the contrary, I felt it had been an opportunity for me to teach others about Islam and to learn how to stand up for what I believed in.

* * *

The gym buzzed with chatter and excitement. It was October of the following school year and we were all back with our high school comrades for our commencement ceremony. I stood in line to get my card and when it was my turn I looked up to see Mr. Brown.

"Well well *Hoda*, congratulations. Some special achievements tonight."

"Thanks sir," I said, wondering why he was smiling so slyly.

I soon found out. Called up to receive my diploma, I was told to stay on stage a little longer because there were some other things they needed to give me.

"The recipient of the subject award for the Ontario Academic Credit of Families in Canadian Society," the voice boomed throughout the auditorium. Mrs. Smith held the certificate out to me, a genuine smile gracing her face.

"Congratulations *Hoda*, I am really proud of you. I had to be the one to give you the award. Even though Mr. Chelser said 'It's my job. I'm giving out the social sciences awards this year.' I told him, 'I know; I know you are, Mr. Chelser, but you've got to let me give this one. I've got to do it." With that we embraced. Standing there on stage listening to the applause, my father's words echoed in my head. When I had told him that I felt helpless and hopeless, that there was too much damage in this world and that despite everything I do I can't correct it, he always had the same response. He told me that a Muslim should never feel hopeless because we should have trust in Allah. He told me that we are not responsible for the results; we must do our best and the rest is up to Allah. And, he told me that Allah does not waste the rewards of those who do good deeds.

A Letter to my teacher

My seventh grade homeroom and French teacher was a tall, kind lady. My best friend Sue and I were both good students, so she liked us and we got along with her quite well. We were always joking with her and had lots of fun just being silly around her.

Sometimes when Sue and I wouldn't want to sit in the loud crowded cafeteria, she would let us sit in her office and eat our lunch while she was in the staff room. That way we could sometimes avoid going outside on the bitter cold days of Ottawa's winter. One day Sue and I walked through the hallway hoping we would find Ms. Harrington in her room. If we had missed her then we had missed our chance to stay warm through the lunch hour. We poked our heads into the doorway and we both sighed in relief.

"Hi Ms. Harrington," I said. "Can we have lunch here . . . Please?"

"Oh, okay you two," Ms. Harrington rolled her eyes and shook her head. "Now I'm not staying here much longer. I'm going to pick some things up from my office and then I'll head down to the staff room. I'll lock the classroom door and the office door and when you leave just pull the doors shut. Oh, and don't let anyone in."

"Of course we won't Ms. Harrington!" I said as we followed her into the office.

Ms. Harrington shuffled through the papers on her desk while Sue and I settled down for lunch.

"Whoa!" Sue exclaimed. "You don't need all these drinks Ms. Harrington! You should give us one." I followed Sue's gaze and saw that Ms. Harrington had three juice boxes and two Coke cans next to her desk.

"Oh, you two," Ms. Harrington shook her head at us.

"Come on Ms. Harrington," Sue coaxed. "We don't have a drink and you have five! It wouldn't hurt you to give us one of them." (My friend is a little forward.)

"Oh alright," Ms. Harrington gave in. "But I'm only doing this because I feel so sorry for you – starving yourself for that month like that. God, I can't imagine..." Ms. Harrington was out the door before I could say anything. The comment had taken me totally by surprise. I shrugged it off and went on joking through lunch with Sue as usual.

The next year, for grade eight, Ms. Harrington was my homeroom and French teacher again. One day during *Ramadan*, Ms. Harrington stood by the door at the end of the day, as we headed out of class toward our lockers. "Oh poor you," she shook her head sympathetically as I walked by her. "You look so tired and so hungry!" Ms. Harrington meant well, but she didn't know that her pity was not necessary or even appreciated.

I told my mom about her reaction to my fasting and, together, we decided that I should write her a letter. A letter would be better than talking to her, because then I wouldn't be put on the spot confronting my teacher face to face. It was the easiest way of bringing things out into the open.

For the next few days I worked on my letter to Ms. Harrington. It was long and detailed. I wrote about how I chose to fast because it's part of my religion and so I don't want her to feel sorry for me. I wrote to her about all the positive things that fasting through *Ramadan* taught me: empathy for the poor, dedication, persistence, self-control, and self-discipline. I pointed out to her in the letter that these were the same qualities that made me a good student and a hard worker, two things that she appreciated in me.

I gave her the letter at the beginning of the day and anxiously awaited a reaction. I think it was two days later when I was packing up at my locker at the end of the day that I got one.

"*Hoda,*" Ms. Harrington called. I approached her and she said to me, "Thank you so much for your letter. I didn't know how I was supposed to act. It made things a lot clearer."

Well, that incident made it clear to me that instead of complaining or sulking when somebody treats Islam in a negative way, we should step up and do something. We should take responsibility to tell them our side of the story and who knows how they'll feel then.

Strong, supported teens that have conviction about their deen can always find alternatives to satisfy their social needs without stepping out of the boundaries of Islam. On a few occasions, our teens came across situations where they had to think hard for themselves, and with the help of their parents, they were able to find a solution for their needs. Here are some examples; again related to us by *Hoda* for certain experiences during her high school years:

"Throughout my high school career there were many things that I could not participate in due to my religious belief. *Alhamdulillah*, I hold my belief high above anything else and I did not want to compromise it for anything. At the same time, I wished that I could spend more time with my friends. It wasn't that I wanted to participate in their activities (since these activities included drinking, being out really late, and hanging out with guys), but it was more that I wished they would do other activities, namely *halal* activities, so that I could go out and enjoy myself with them.

Well, these *halal* activities weren't exactly popping into my friends' heads all the time and I found that the older we grew, the less likely any of the activities they planned were *halal*. After we reached a certain age, it seemed that all the gatherings now had to include either guys or alcohol.

My religious beliefs were very obvious to my friends since I spoke openly and discussed my views and values with them and told them that these were based on my religion. Every time that they were getting together and I couldn't make it because religious reasons I would tell them just that and they all knew what my rules were and why I couldn't do what they were doing. One friend of mine, a very sweet and considerate person named Andrea, noticed that I did not go to the Christmas party. When she asked me about it and I explained that I did not celebrate Christmas because I didn't believe in Christianity as such, she found my answer very curious. You see, Andrea was not Christian, in fact she did not adhere to any religion, but she celebrated Christmas because it was the culture around her and not out of any religious belief. Anyway, that was the beginning of many discussions for Andrea and I; to her, the concept of religion was so foreign and to me it was so inherent and this made for a very interesting mix of ideas and thoughts.

One day during Ramadan in grade 12 (my second last year of high school), I was telling Andrea about *Ramadan* and about *Eid Al Fitr*.

"*Hoda*," Andrea said. "We should have a party for *Eid Al Fitr*."

The idea was marvelous. We both got very excited and immediately started planning. Upon Andrea's suggestion, we decided it would be a semi-formal event so that everyone would dress up. A semiformal potluck was what we would have, *insha' Allah*. We planned games and I was going to present a short address to explain *Ramadan*, it's purposes, and, of course, *Eid Al Fitr*. Well, now it came down to making up the guest list, making the invitations and coordinating all the food. The guest list was easy to make up, my parents put no limit on how many girls I could have over and so I invited all my friends from school which I think was about 22 girls.

Now as for the invitations, they weren't quite so simple. I didn't want my friends to think that they were coming to just another party, because then things might have gone bad. I was concerned about a few things: the topic of conversations, clothes, and the food content. Food content was by far the easiest thing to take care of. Everybody knows that different religions have different dietary restrictions; society recognizes and respects that fully. The clothes and the conversation issues, I felt, were much more delicate. If the conversation switched to an inappropriate topic, I didn't want to ruin the party by intervening right then and embarrassing my friends and asking them not to talk about that particular topic. At the same time, I couldn't very well just let them continue talking about inappropriate things. I discussed my concerns with my family and we tried to think of different ways to tackle the issue. In the end, we decided that people must know ahead of time what the limits were, and that they could then choose for themselves whether or not they could adhere to those limits. The phrasing of the invitation was thought through many times and the finished copy looked just like the invitation below:

Sue, you are invited to
Hoda's Potluck *Eid* Party
On Saturday, January 31,1998
from 6:00 pm -10:00 pm
At 178 Keyworth Ave.
RSVP by January 12, 1998

ISLAMIC PARTY ETIQUETTES

*It is expected that you refrain from swearing,
discussing people of the opposite sex, and mentioning
private body parts (using profane or obscene language)
*It is expected that you follow a certain dress code.
This is a semi-formal event, but low-necks and short
(above the knee) clothes aren't acceptable.
*Due to Islamic eating etiquette, please refrain from
using any pig products in the dish you bring.
Pig products include: ham, bacon, pork, lard, gelatin
and can be found in yogurt, marshmallows, etc.
Please read all product ingredients carefully.
*There will be no alcoholic beverages or sauces served
due to Islamic eating regulations.
If you do not feel that you can enjoy the party within
these rules, please feel free to regret your attendance.
To confirm or regret, please call 728-7010.

My sisters and I cut out the computer invitations decoratively and glued them onto greeting cards and then I distributed them to all my friends. *Subhan Allah,* a month before the time of the party, two of my friends were refraining from swearing at all as practice for the night of the party. *Alhamdulillah,* all in all about 19 of my friends were able to come and we had a really great time. Mostly everybody respected the rules, except for two people and they did so very quietly (whispering to each other about the inappropriate topic that they wished to discuss). I saw them and they saw me looking over, but they just lowered their voices more. The food was great, the company was great, and the general atmosphere was so decent! I really enjoyed myself and my friends later told me that the little talk I gave about *Ramadan* and *Eid* was informative and interesting and that they also had fun at the party. The only unfortunate thing is that Andrea had to be out of town on that weekend and so she couldn't attend the party, but we had our own personal little *Eid* party the next weekend so that we could catch up on her trip and my party."

*   *   *   *   *   *

"It was springtime in our last year of high school. Graduation was fast approaching and we were all starting to become nostalgic. This was the conclusion of five years of ups and downs, of roller coasters of workloads, emotions, and friendships. The hallways, the lockers, the classrooms, the teachers, and the students, they all seemed to hold a special significance now that I thought I would not see them anymore. It was difficult to look forward to graduation night, but it was also difficult not to.

There was still one last event that everybody was preparing for, the final farewell; it was the grad. The parents, the teachers, and all the students were invited. It would be held at a hotel and there would be dinner, dancing, a few key addresses, and, of course, alcohol. I, like all my peers, wanted to see my classmates together for one last time, wanted that last chance to mingle with my peers, to share those conversations, those memories, those plans and dreams that we had all acquired through the years, but I did not want to be where alcohol was being consumed. So for months I stood still in the whirlwind of grad talk. What was each of my friends going to wear? Who was sitting at which table? How were they going to get to the grad? Who was going in which car? I thought and lamented about my decision not to go. Somehow, I wished that I could justify this event to myself, wished that I could find a way to be able to go and feel fine about what I was doing. The days flew by and the talk kept spinning around me. It didn't make sense. I had spent five years with these teachers and peers. It couldn't all just end like this. . . with nothing, no concluding moments. I tried to find a solution. I asked the grad coordinators if they knew when the alcohol would be served. I thought maybe I could go for the beginning and then leave before the drinking started. I discovered that it couldn't be done. The parents were supposed to arrive at the hall before the students and surely on a celebratory night like this one, the parents would be toasting to their children's success.

Well, I couldn't sit around and feel sorry for myself any longer. Just because grad dinner wasn't going to be my moment of conclusion, that didn't mean that I couldn't have a moment of conclusion of my own. Well, that was it then; it was decided. With my parent's permission, I invited all my friends out for a farewell day (and I think there were at least 20 girls who came). We met at 11:30 and had lunch at my favorite restaurant and then we went out for a walk by the Rideau Canal through the beautiful greenery. It was a really wonderful day. I got a chance to see all my friends and we shared our dreams and worries and memories. There it was, such a simple solution. I had my moment of conclusion and I didn't have to compromise my values for it."

* * * * * *

Hoda concludes with some advice to teens:

"Throughout my experiences in high school, I have learned that my social needs will not always be met by those around me. Things are not going to be perfectly presented to meet my needs and values, and that is a blessing from Allah. Through this, I have learned to be innovative and take the initiative in order to make up my own activities that will fill in the gaps. *Alhamdulillah,* this way, not only were my needs fulfilled, but through taking an active role in fulfilling them, I acquired many skills about how to tackle problems and organize solutions. My advice is that you should never be afraid of doing something new, inventing something yourself if the thing that suits you isn't readily available. Even if you think that there is no solution to a problem or an emotion that you are feeling, don't despair. Remember that three heads are better than one; include your parents and ask for their advice. You may think that they can't understand your feelings, but they just might surprise you with stories from their childhood where they may have been in the same position that you are in now. Our parents have a wealth of experience, which may cause them to notice details that often pass us by. If it wasn't for the help from my family, I don't think that I could have pulled off many of the alternatives that I needed to have available, and I am positive that I definitely would not have pulled them off so smoothly. *Alhamdulillah*, I thank Allah first and foremost, and my parents for all their understanding and advice, and my sisters for all their willingness to help me in any task I need help with, no matter how big or small it is."

Here are some positive experiences that *Sumaiya* went through and would like to relate to us:

1) The magic of a smile

"The prophet (PBUH) has advised us to smile frequently. In one hadeeth, he said, "And your smile in the face of your brother is considered a charity." However, it can be hard to always smile, especially if you're tired and you've had a long day. But *Subhan Allah*, it's amazing how one smile really can make a difference in someone's life. We hear all the touching stories, poems and emails about how smiling can make or break someone's day and it is so true. It is really something to think that contracting some of your face muscles can have such outstanding effects. One day, when I was working at the coffee shop, a customer asked to speak to me personally. She said to me, "I come here often and I noticed that you're always so happy and smiling, so I was wondering why you wear that thing on your head."

By "that thing on your head," she was referring to my *hijab*. It just didn't make any sense to her that somebody wearing a *hijab* could always be happy, let alone ever be happy. I mean, what would they be happy about? They're abused and oppressed, right?

"Well," I explained, "have you ever heard of the religion of Islam?"

"No," she replied, so I decided to start off by giving her some facts. "Islam is one of the three major religions of the world, it's also the fastest growing religion in the world." And then I went on to explain the significance of the *hijab*. "We wear this, the *hijab*, because we believe that people should be judged based on their actions and not their appearance. We believe that its what's inside that counts and no matter what your skin color, eye color or hair color is, or whether you have a big nose or a small nose, wide eyes or small eyes, a round face or a square face, it doesn't matter. God judges everyone based on their character and he wants us to do the same."

The women seemed totally shocked. "Wow," she said, "that's not what I thought at all."

"Really, why did you think we wore it?" I asked. The women looked ashamed.

She hesitated before she continued, "Well, I thought you wore that because some man forced you to and because you were ashamed of the way you looked." But it was actually just the opposite. I had chosen to wear the *hijab* myself and my body was too precious to be on public display.

Well that day I made some discoveries. I had always wondered what ran through people's minds when they saw me or any other women wearing a *hijab*. Did they wonder why I wore the *hijab*? Or did they believe the media and assume my father or husband forced me into it? Or maybe they just didn't care. Now I knew, at least, what some people thought. But I also knew that by following the actions of the prophet (PBUH), we could shatter the stereotypes haunting Islam and inform people about what Islam is really about. So, how do we begin? With a smile!

They look and peer with a sideways stare
And wonder why I cover my hair
They question, ask and sometimes mock
But deep inside they yearn to talk
They want to discuss and understand
The true religion of Islam
They want to unveil the hidden treasure
And discover how it can bring them pleasure
And when they argue and debate
It may seem as though Islam they hate
But in the truth they are desperately searching
For something pure to stop their hurting
It's funny how "advanced" they are

Yet how they're always at the bar
They live in mansions with a ranch and horses
But can't control their increase in divorces
Their paychecks come with six digits or more
And they go to their parties and clubs galore
They're full of style and full of pride
So tell me please why they commit suicide
Their walls are decorated with five degrees
And they make sure you notice their Ph. D.'s
They've got their Jacuzzis, laptops and microwaves
But still there is something else they crave
What could be missing in such a life
2.5 children, a dog and a wife
They've got it all what could it be
They're satisfied financially
But what about their hearts and minds
They're set on a course with roads that wind
There is no meaning in their life
No passion, belief, just moral strife
Could there be a reason for this life, a purpose
Because without one life is worthless
Guidance love and honesty
Are all human necessities
And though their tummies and banks are full
Their souls and spirits are dead and cold
And so they slowly realize
Those material things can't compromise
Can't compromise for a religion
Which provides to all a clear vision
Islam has answers to every question
And leads us in the right direction
Equality and justice Islam demands
Our feelings and hardships it understands
So the next time you think someone's hassling you
And you're tempted to tell them to stop bothering you
Remember that it is everyone's duty
To share Islam's message and phenomenal beauty

2. My work experience

As I was doing some odds and ends at work, I noticed a customer who had already been served, waiting for me to look in her direction. When I did, she motioned me over and asked me seriously, "Are you allowed to work?"

As funny or fake as the question may sound, this women was asking it in all honesty. When she looked at me, she saw a walking contradiction: a Muslim girl, wearing the *hijab*, working? To her, that made no sense.

"Yes," I replied, and to prove my point that I wasn't an exception I told her that my mother was the principal at a private school, my sister was a software engineer with a computer company and that I had many Muslim friends that were women--and worked. My point, however, was not to embarrass the women but simply to inform her that Muslim women were not oppressed and that there was nothing in the religion that says that they are not allowed to work.

Then the women asked, "So you're allowed to go to school too, like, even University?" *Subhan Allah*, I thought, the poor woman had been fed so many lies and stereotypes by the media. I explained to her that education and knowledge were very highly regarded in Islam for both men and women and that all my sisters and Muslim friends went to University. She looked very pleased to hear this, as she had read that Muslim women were not allowed to work or go to University. I explained to her that, unfortunately, the media portrayed Muslim women in a very negative light and that most of the information was incorrect or inaccurate. The women agreed wholeheartedly and said that she'd even noticed a lot of Muslim women wearing *hijab* in the engineering department at the University of Ottawa and that this had confused her a little. She thanked me for clearing up that misconception and I thanked Allah SWT for having given me the opportunity.

When I had first decided that I wanted to work, I worried about how people would react to me because I was wearing the *hijab*. Other Muslim friends who had part time jobs told me that customers would often talk to them slowly and in a loud voice because they assumed they couldn't speak English. Generally I had heard mostly bad stories, but still I wanted to try it for myself. When I discussed getting a part time job with my mother and father they thought I wanted it for the money, so my mother said she'd pay me if I did extra work around the house. But for me, it had nothing to do with the money. I wanted to prove to myself that I could get a job on my own while wearing the hijab. By 'on my own' I mean without the help of a family member or relative. I was in grade 11 when I became very serious about getting a part time job and by grade 11 almost all my friends were doing the same. Everywhere I turned, people had a part time job, even people I thought didn't have the qualifications for it. That just proved to me that, really, anyone can get hired if they put their mind to it, so I put my mind to it.

I started revising and updating my resume, I asked one of my teachers to edit it for me and help in the formatting, and then I went out and started distributing it to places I knew I would be comfortable working at. This was a very important factor. I made sure to avoid places like restaurants or any other businesses that would be open late or that serve alcohol. I stuck to libraries, coffee shops, card stores, pharmacies, clothing stores, that type of thing. The way I saw it, getting a job was something halal that my peers and I would have in common. When you're a religious Muslim in a non-Muslim society, as you grow older, the gap between you and your peers at school gets bigger and bigger. This is because there are so many things that they do that you can't participate in because they're *haram*. A part time job, however, was one of the rare exceptions. It filled that gap up just a little.

As well, I saw a part time job as a great opportunity for *da'wa*. Not only do my boss and co-workers know a whole lot more about Islam now, but regular customers also ask me questions about Islam all the time. They'll discuss an article they read in the paper about Islam and I'll have a chance to clear up all the misconceptions they've heard. Even if customers don't ask me questions about Islam, they see a Muslim women smiling and working (two things Muslim women supposedly can't do). Working really is a whole new experience. You learn to deal with a boss, co-workers, happy customers, and not so happy customers. It's different from school because at school, you're mostly dealing with people of your own age group. It's not as professional. At work you've got to deal with many of the same problems you deal with at school but at a much more professional level because now you represent a company. As Muslims, we represent Islam. So in a way, work helps with that. It gets you in the habit of remembering that you don't just represent yourself as an individual, but your company and more importantly, your religion.

Work can affect your Islam in a positive way but if you don't take certain steps in a new job, it can affect your Islam in a negative way too. For example, when I was called back for my second interview, and I could tell that it was getting to the serious point, I made sure to mention my prayer schedule and requirements. I let my boss know that I would need to pray anywhere from 1-3 prayers a shift depending on the shift I got, and that I would need a quiet room for about seven minutes for each prayer. This is something that absolutely must be discussed when taking on a job because your prayer should not be sacrificed for a job. *Alhamdulillah*, my boss was very understanding, though not at first, to the prayer issue. But let's say I had gotten a boss that was not so happy with the idea and didn't hire me. In that case, I would thank Allah because you probably wouldn't want a boss like that anyway. From what I've seen, most bosses are totally fine with the prayer issue, but it is important that you mention it and make sure there's a place you can pray. I think parental support plays a big role in this job issue. My parents main concern was that I wouldn't be able to keep up with schoolwork. So we made a deal that if my grades suffered due to work (and not any other reason) I would quit my job. My personal outlook was that, with work, I would be forced to use my time more wisely and cut down on other non-productive things like television. Really, I think that's what happened. I had always had the time to work about two shifts a week but instead of working, I was wasting it. So, work made me maximize the use of my time. The other thing is that I don't work too much. I actually work less than normal. I spoke to my manager about giving me as few shifts as possible (since it's not about the money for me). So I only work about two shifts a week, one of which is on the weekend, which gives me time to do other things and keep up with school-work.

The important thing is that my parents had justified reasons (such as keeping up with school) for questioning whether or not I should work. They didn't say I couldn't work because I was a girl or because I was Muslim. Since I was able to keep up with school and work, my parents honored their side of the deal and let me work. But, they didn't stop at that, they supported me. They'd pick me up from work when I was closing or they'd drive me there when I was running late. All these things showed me that my parents didn't mind my working as long as I could handle it.

My parents' support was important to me. I don't think teenagers should ever intend to upset or disagree with their parents. But all too often, parents and their teenagers are in two very different worlds, two different continents and they can't seem to build a bridge and crossover to the other person's side. My parents support meant that when customers would ask me questions like whether or not I was allowed to work, I could answer truthfully without any resentment. I could tell them in all honesty that I was allowed to work and that my parents and I didn't spend countless nights shouting or fighting over my job. We discussed it rationally, they took my request seriously, and they supported me in my decision because it wasn't *haram* or harmful to my Islam. My parents also encouraged me to make an *istikhara* (decision making) prayer, so that whatever happened, we knew it was the will of Allah SWT. For me, working really was a positive experience, it taught me many things and it taught others many things about me as well. It really is important that parents keep an open mind to their children's requests, for if my parents had ignored or dismissed my request of getting a job, I would not had many of the experiences that have made me a stronger Muslim.

3) OSAID Conference

When I was in grade 10, I got involved with an organization at school called OSAID. This stands for Ontario Students Against Impaired Driving. One of my teachers, who happened to be the teacher advisor for OSAID, recommended it to me. She thought I might be interested because I had written my independent study project on the negative effects of alcoholism. The organization was quite small when I first joined and it was looking for someone to attend a three day conference in Toronto. Now, considering I lived in Ottawa, which is about a five hour drive from Toronto, that would mean that my teacher and I would drive to this conference and spend three nights in a hotel. This idea might not have gone over too well with a lot of Muslim parents, considering it was an event organized and run by non-Muslims, but *Alhamdulillah*, my parents did not rule the possibility out right away, even though we generally didn't attend school trips that included sleeping over. I think an exception was made because this is not a school trip per say, but it was a national conference that supported a good cause.

When I came home that day and told my parents about the

conference, they were actually very open to the idea of my participation in this conference, even if it was not an event run by Muslims. My parents told me that because I had earned their trust and shown them in previous situations that I knew how to conduct myself Islamically when I was away from home, they would be all right with it. They had no problem with the idea, but of course we would have to make sure that the trip wouldn't put me in a situation where Islamic rules would be violated.

I talked with my teacher about my restrictions. We inquired about the traveling arrangements and she assured us that she would drive me up along with two other ladies and that there would be no boys in the car. We also inquired about the accommodations and made sure that I would be rooming with girls and no guys would come to our room. I told my teacher that I could not have any pig products in my diet and that I would need a place to pray five times a day. I also told her that I would not be able to attend certain events and participate in some activities such as dances. *Alhamdulillah*, my teacher was very understanding and talked to the coordinators of the conference about my needs and restrictions. So, after making sure that everything was taken care of, I packed my bags and we headed off to Toronto.

Alhamdulillah, I'm glad I decided to go. I definitely had my doubts at first about whether or not I should go on this trip, but it really was a great experience in the end. It was a great opportunity for *da'wa*. My teacher and I, as well as two other female participants talked about Islam during our ride to Toronto. I was able to clear up a lot of misconceptions and inaccurate information they'd heard about Islam. My teacher confessed to me that before we'd gotten to know each other, she thought Muslim women were oppressed and confined to their homes. After she got to know me, whenever she'd see something about a Muslim woman on TV, she would question the accuracy of what she saw, as it was clearly contrary to the example she knew. While in her class, I had participated regularly, presented my point of views confidently and didn't give in to peer pressure or societal norms. My teacher told me that now when she watches a program about how Muslim women are forced into marriage and not allowed to attend University, she thinks of me and of how she could never see me submitting to such ways.

I made a lot of friends at that conference and I was able to show them, by example, what Islam is really about. I explained to numerous people why we wear hijab and many of them were very impressed with the reasoning behind it. Through the duration of the conference there were three different dances. During these times I would stay in my hotel room and either read some *Qur'an* (which I had brought along with me) or do some homework. My three roommates were very understanding when I explained to them that I woke up at dawn everyday to pray. So, I would set the alarm for 4:00 every morning and wake up for *fajr*. All these things gave my roommates an awareness of Islam and they were interested to learn more about it.

Participating in the conference was a positive experience, as I had the opportunity to show that Muslims care about our society and that we have something positive to contribute to societal events, issues and affairs. I ended up making some good friends at that conference that I still keep in contact with today.

Here is how a strong confident teen could turn a negative comment into a positive experience and an opportunity to write something that could be used for *da'wa*. This piece is written by *Sumaiya* as a response to one incident in her physical education class. It was published in the American Muslim magazine.

Misunderstood

Baldy, Baldy
climbing the apparatus in gym class
the words stung my ears
it baffled me
as to how at 13
one still felt the need
to insult others
in order to feel good
for I was not bald
nor did I have a scalp disease
nor was I oppressed
I was simply communicating
communicating that I have a right
to be treated based on my actions ·
and not based on my appearance.

The following story was written by a friend of *Hoda*'s named Aethne Hinchliffe. This was after they had been close friends for four years. In the last year of high school, Aethne chose to do her Independent Study Project in her English Writing class about women who converted to Islam. As part of that project, she wrote the following story. It was wonderful to see that, in a society that portrays Muslims as oppressive, aggressive, and completely ignorant, Aethne's description of Muslims was completely the opposite. This really sent our daughter a strong message that when she lives Islam as it should be lived, those around her will learn it and come to see how positive it actually is.

Dear Diary,
Tues., Sept. 6, 98.

Mom was angry today. I came home from school and she was yelling. My brother, Nicholas, was standing in the kitchen. The first thing I heard when I came in the house was, "You'd better smarten up Nicholas! If I ever hear that again, I'll take you right out of school." Nicholas held his skateboard to his side. The shorts he wore hung down below his knees. My mother hates that style. I'm not crazy about it either. Mom finished up by saying, "Out. Just get out of the kitchen. Go do homework, or whatever. I don't care. just go." So he did. He lay his skateboard down on the black and white tiled floor, placed his left foot on the board and pushed himself out of the kitchen and down the hall. Mom sighed, too tired to yell at him about scratching the floor. She turned and saw me standing in the dining-room doorway. "And you," she said. "You, you, you. I think that by now you're old enough to make your own bed Michaela."

"Yeah, I'm sorry," I responded.

I've spent the rest of tonight in my room doing homework, besides having dinner with

Mom and Nicholas. Dad is visiting Grandpa Crouse in Vancouver, and will be home in a week.

Dear Diary,
Thurs., Sept. 8, 98.

In my first entry I meant to explain how I got this journal, but I guess I forgot. My birthday was last week and Grandma Swinamer asked Mom what she thought a beautiful thirteen year old girl would want on her fourteenth birthday. Mom suggested school supplies or a lunch bag. That's Mom, always sensible. Well, in the end Grandma ended up giving me a diary and when she said to me, "Oh Michaela, I'm so proud of you. You're growing up to be such a beautiful girl, and I know that every girl your age just starting high school needs a diary," I wasn't too enthusiastic, but of course I had to pretend. I smiled wide, trying to look as sincere as possible. This is what always happens. Grandma Swinamer asks advice from Mom. Mom recommends something sensible, and Grandma buys something completely insensible, as Mom would say.

Today I was eating lunch outside and I saw Nicholas in the smoking section. I walked over to say hi to him, and saw that he was holding a cigarette. He didn't even look guilty for a second. "I'm holding it for Jessica," he said turning toward his friend. Jessica Gillroy is Maddie Gillroy's older sister. Maddie Gillroy is a friend of mine. Jessica's in grade twelve. Nicholas and Jessie know one another from the rowing team. I don't understand how Jess is such a good rower, when her lungs are probably damaged. "Oh Nicky, she doesn't know you smoke? I thought Mummy was mad at you last night for smoking," her tone was sarcastic. Nicholas glared at her, dropped his cigarette to the pavement, placed his black Airwalk over top and pressed down, his toes to the ground, his heal swivelling back and forth.

I'm not quite sure how to feel. I mean, my brother was smoking. As far as I know he's never touched a cigarette in his life, but he is my brother, so who knows what he hides from me.

Papers are cluttered all over my desk. Mom is downstairs cooking stir fry. The smell is floating up the stairs, so it's difficult to concentrate on my math, especially because it's my worst subject. I remember Mom saying that Grandma Swinamer is coming for dinner tonight. Grandma Swinamer comes for dinner just about once a week. After dinner Mom and Grandma sit talking for about an hour, sipping tea. They even sit drinking tea on hot summer evenings, when all I can imagine is going swimming.

The phone just rang. It was a girl's voice asking for Nicholas. I wasn't sure if he was home, so I called to Mom, and she told me he's at the library.

I got back on the phone. "Nicholas is at the library," I said.

The girl shrieked, "the library?" Then, "Okay, can you please tell him to call Jessica?"

I hadn't recognized her voice. "Oh, hi Jess."

"Michaela, hi," she said. "So can you give him the message?"

I had barely begun to answer before she cut me off, "Thanks." Click. The dial tone rang in my ear.

I'd better stop writing, because I just heard Grandma come in. Now Mom is calling me, probably to set the table.

* * *

Dinner is over now, and I feel so full. Grandma and Mom are at the table still. Mom is angry because Nicholas didn't come home for dinner. I know that she's worried too, but right now she's more angry than worried. I really have to stop to get finished with my math.

* * *

Nicholas just came home. I was getting ready for bed, and I was in the bathroom brushing my teeth. The front door opened, and foot steps came running down the hall. As I said, Mom was angry, and she began to yell, "Nicholas, the library does not close at 10:00! You know that it closes at 9:00. There is no excuse for this."

"Mom, I was at the library, I can show you my-"

"I don't want to hear it. Get upstairs now!" I listened without breathing as Nicholas went up the stairs, his door slamming a few seconds later.

I'm lying in bed now and I can hear Mom talking to Nicholas. The only words I can make out are 'cigarettes', ' curfew' and 'what next?'. Now it's close to 11:00. Boy I've written a lot today! Goodnight.

Dear Diary,
Fri., Sept. 9, 98.

I got to English this morning, and sat where I always sit, beside David Newell, and in front of Adrienne Schnare. I have been friends with Adrienne since the beginning of grade eight. I had to change schools after grade seven. At first I was a bit startled by Adrienne's upfront attitude. I remember my first day of grade eight, I walked into the schoolyard, and there she stood by the gate. She jutted a pale, slim hand out and she said, "Hello, I'm Adrienne Schnare. I'm the grade eight-school president. Are you new?"

I was so taken aback that I said, "No, I'm not new." I stuck my head in the air, and walked off. Despite that, we still became friends. Now, a year later, Adrienne still makes fun of me for that. This morning Adrienne sat kicking lightly at the back of my seat.

There were still about five minutes before the bell, and only a few other people were in class. The class doesn't begin to fill up until about two minutes before nine. Ms. Meisner strolled in at about three minutes to the bell, behind her a girl, who must have been a new student. Of the students who were seated, the class became silent. Everyone was looking at the girl. Covering her head, she was wearing a white scarf. Her clothes covered her whole body, except for her face and her hands. She was wearing sandals. Ms. Meisner spoke to her, "*Aisha*, you can sit here, in front of Michaela." We didn't have another chance to gape wide eyed at the new student, because the bell had rung. Ms. Meisner instructed us to begin reading *To Kill a Mockingbird*.

At the end of the period I noticed *Aisha* leave the class, and wander off to her next class. She must have been pretty noticeable in the halls. We've never had anybody who wears that thing on her head here at Chester Municipal High School. I have seen people like that in Halifax, but I can't remember what it's for. Maybe someone in her family died or something. I'll have to ask Mom!

Dear Diary,
Sat., Sept. 10, 98.
Last night I ended up staying home, even though Moira and Maddie were going to see a movie. I was tired, and just didn't feel like going out.

I won't write too much today because I have soccer practice in an hour, and my hands are a bit sore. I've written a lot lately.

At dinner last night, Nicholas was there, and the first thing he said was, "So who's that *Little White Riding Hood* in your class?"

"What?" I was confused for a second, and then I realized, "oh, her. Yeah, she's new. Her name's *Aisha*."

"What's this? Who?" Mom asked.

"Mom, it's not that interesting. It's a new girl at school. Her name's *Aisha*. She wears some thing over her head. Not a bandana, but some kind of white scarf thing. What's it for?"

"Well, by your very accurate description," she said laughing,

"I assume this young lady is Muslim. It's a religion. I worked with a family once who was Muslim. They were very kind. I remember they made me a loaf of banana bread, thanking me for all my help." Mom finished explaining.

Whoa! I guess I lost track of time. I've got to go.

Dear Diary,

Mon., Sept. 12, 98.

On my way to school today, as I was walking up the hill, past the tennis courts I saw *Aisha* up ahead of me. I felt strange, but I ran up the hill to catch her anyway. She seemed a bit startled at first, but then she smiled. "Hi, I'm *Aisha El-Haddi*."

"Oh, hi. I'm Michaela Crouse."

We walked on in silence, but it wasn't uncomfortable. Then *Aisha* spoke, "your school seems very ignorant. The students have been very rude." She went on to tell me what had happened in French. "This girl, I think she's in our English class, she sits behind you. Anyway, M. Goreham asked me a question, and I answered it, and all the girl did was laugh. I have trouble with French, but I want to learn it, and try to do well. No one is going to hold me back by making me feel badly about myself."

By then we were at school, so the conversation ended. She went to her locker and I went to mine.

Dear Diary,

Thurs., Sept. 15, 98.

I've been having a pretty busy week. Dad got home yesterday. I thought I'd be happy to have him back, but I'm not. I forget what a pain it is. He won't be working until October, so he has more time to get angry at Nicholas and me. Mostly it's for little things, like wearing our shoes in the house, or not scraping our plates. But still, nag, nag, nag. That's all he does.

I've been thinking about *Aisha* a lot. I told her she's welcome to sit with us at lunch, but she hasn't yet. I don't think she likes Adrienne, because all Adrienne does is giggle. I'm starting to get sick of it myself. *Aisha* and I have sort of made a habit of walking to school together. We meet at the tennis courts, and walk the rest of the way. I look forward to walking with her. She told me that her family moved here from Toronto, because her grandmother lives in Halifax, and is very ill. They chose to live here, away from Halifax, because they've been living in Toronto for ten years, and they wanted a break from the city.

I think Dad's calling me. Oops! I forgot to put the wash in. I better go.

Dear Diary,

Fri., Sept. 16, 98.

Today at school *Aisha* asked me if I want to have lunch at her place on Saturday. I said yes. That means I won't go to soccer. I'm sure Mom and Dad will understand.

* * *

It looks as though Dad doesn't understand. I just went down to ask Mom and Dad about missing practice. It's Friday, so I really thought Dad would be in a good mood. Apparently not. He said, "You want to miss soccer? How much do I pay to have you in that stupid sport? If you don't like it then quit."

Mom said, "Okay Brad, calm down. It's just one time, come on. Anyway, she's making new friends.

Dad didn't respond.

Mom came up as I was pulling myself under the covers and told me that Nicholas' teacher had called. Nicholas is failing math. Don't take anything Dad says right now too personally.

Dear Diary,

Sat., Sept. 17, 98.

I just got back from *Aisha*'s house from lunch. It was great. *Aisha*'s family is so nice. She has a younger brother just seven years old, named *Hakeem*. He was so well behaved at the table. Talking to him, it seems as though he's about nine or ten.

I learned so much this afternoon. *Aisha*'s mother also wears a scarf. The funny thing is I rang the bell at 11:59. I was so nervous that I knew the exact time. A girl, whom I did not recognize, answered the door. "Hi Michaela." It was *Aisha*. She was not wearing her scarf. I shrieked, "*Aisha*, I didn't know who you were." She explained to me that she doesn't have to wear her scarf in the house with just her mother, father and brother. I wanted to know why she didn't wear the scarf with me there, and she said because I'm a girl.

Dear Diary,

Mon., Sept. 19, 98.

I talked to Adrienne for the first time since Friday, and that was pretty brief. She said she was going home because she wasn't feeling well. Today when I talked to her we were in the gym change room. We had gym last period. Everyone else was gone. "You're getting to be pretty good friends with that girl *Aisha*, or whatever."

"Um, yeah, we're friends," I felt defensive, and I'm not sure why.

"Well, whatever, she's weird. Why does she wear that stupid thing on her head anyway?" Adrienne sounded a bit jealous.

"For her religion. Islam," I sighed.

"What the heck's that? Anyway, I don't care. Michaela, we're supposed to be best friends. You never call me anymore. I have to go." She walked out of the change room.

That's when I understood Adrienne isn't mad, but upset. I can't believe how quickly she went from jealous and angry sounding, to sad, to not caring. I feel bad. Adrienne isn't good at expressing her emotions.

I'm interested in finding out more about *Aisha*'s religion. I asked her today if she has any books she can lend me. She said she does, and she'll bring them tomorrow. I'm happy about that, but the books might cut my journal time short.

Dear Diary,

Wed., Sept. 21, 98.

Aisha lent me books. I started to read one last night. It's simple, and easy to follow. I'm beginning to learn much more about Islam. Some things I learned today are they pray five times a day and Muslims practice modesty. *Aisha* said I should feel free to ask her any questions I want. I definitely will.

Dear Diary,

Fri., Sept. 23, 98.

Nicholas is going to a party tonight. The party is at his friend Matt's house, for his birthday. Mom told him to be home by 12:15. Mom took fifteen minutes off his curfew. If he's late this time, no going out for a month. He still smokes. I haven't told Mom and Dad.

Aisha is coming over for dinner to meet Mom. Dad is at a business dinner. We're having lasagne, *Aisha*'s favourite.

* * *

Mom thinks *Aisha* is a very sweet young lady and she is happy we've become friends.

* * *

I just woke up. The phone was ringing. I have to write, even though it's 3:43 a.m. Bridgewater Children's Hospital just called. Nicholas is there. That's all they said. No details over the phone. Now I'm very scared. Mom just pulled the Jeep out of the driveway. Dad came back upstairs just now, and saw me writing and told me to go to bed for heaven's sake. Turn off the lights. He does not understand that I'm not a child. I'm scared. I can't just go to bed when my brother is in the hospital. Dad is downstairs now. I can hear him puttering around in the kitchen.

Dear Diary,
Sat., Sept. 24, 98.

My Mom must have come home sometime in the night, because Mom and Dad are arguing. I think they're in the kitchen.

"But the curfew should have been earlier," Dad said.

"Brad, don't you dare blame this on me. You're his parent too."

"Oh God Bronwyn, I know that. But 12:30 is too late. How in the world did he get beer? He's sixteen!"

"He's a teenager, they find their ways," Mom was crying now. "Let's just stop fighting. We'll wake Michaela."

"I'm sorry, sweety. Okay, ssshhhh."

Mom called me for breakfast soon after the argument. I still can't believe what I blurted out. I was on my third pancake, and Mom sat down with the paper.

"I want to be Muslim," I said.

"What?" Mom peered at me.

"*Aisha*'s religion," I added.

"I know who's religion it is," she spoke precisely.

"Mom, I believe in it. I don't believe that Jesus is the Son of God."

"No," that was all she said.

Right after saying those actual words I felt really shocked. Maybe I didn't realize how I feel until then.

Tonight I have to sleep at Adrienne's house. Mom and Dad are going to see Nicholas in Bridgewater. I can't go until the weekend! I hate being a kid. It's not fair. They haven't even told me anything, and they don't know that I heard them arguing.

Dear Diary,
Mon., Sept. 26,98.

When I slept at Adrienne's Saturday night she wasn't even home. She'd gone to a movie with Moira. When I used to stay at Adrienne's I would sleep on a mattress on the floor in her room. This time I slept in the guest bedroom.

I didn't write yesterday. Instead I spent the day sulking. I walked up to the tennis court and smashed a ball against the backboard. After, I lay down in the grass and fell asleep. I walked home close to dinner.

Dear Diary,
Sat., Oct. 1, 98.

I told *Aisha* that I want to be Muslim. She said I should think about it longer, but I don't want to. No one can guess how I feel, not even *Aisha*.

I remember thinking that *Aisha*'s scarf at first looked to me like a pillowcase. Mom keeps pillowcases in the linen closet. I pulled one out, and tied if around my head. In the mirror it looked to me like the real thing.

The real thing or not, Mom was far from pleased. I came to the dinner table wearing it. She stared at me. "I will not have you wearing that Michaela. First of all it is disrespectful. You are not Muslim. And you will not be Muslim until you are out from under my roof," Mom's words were harsh.

"Why can't I just convert? What do you care? I'm fourteen. I'm going to. You can't stop me."

"Yes Michaela, I can."

Dear Diary,
Wed., Oct. 5,98.

There is something seriously wrong with Nicholas. My parents are still not talking to me about it. I'm still too young.

This evening at dinner Mom and Dad told me they have some plans. I'm too young to have a say in anything. They're sending me to Cape

Forchu, near Yarmouth, to stay with my Aunt Lauren and Uncle Jacob. They have a son a year younger than me. His name is Nathaniel.

When I told *Aisha* she cried, and so did I. She wrote me a letter, and *Aisha's* mother made me two loaves of banana bread. When Mom found out, we had a good laugh about that. *Aisha* told me not to read my letter until I was on the bus.

The bus will leave from the drugstore at 10:00 tomorrow morning. I'll be in Yarmouth at 3:00 tomorrow afternoon. Aunt Lauren will pick me up.

Dear Diary,
Thurs., Oct. 6, 98.

The bus ride to Yarmouth was slow and boring, except I listened to music on my walkman. I read *Aisha's* letter.

Dear Michaela Crouse, (do you remember when we first met?)

You have been the most wonderful and caring friend. I hope that when you are truly ready, you will convert to Islam. But don't do anything too soon. You are in no hurry. I have faith in you. Stay strong.

Al salamu 'alaykum,
Aisha

Dear Diary,
Mon., Oct. 2, 99.

I can't believe that almost a year ago I packed my diary into a box. The diary that no one knew I wrote in (other than maybe Grandma), because it was something I always did when I was alone. Now here it is, with the same red cover, and red back, bound by wool, and I remember now that Grandma Swinamer bought it at a craft fair. I remember too that she inscribed something in the very front cover. I wonder if I wrote about that so long ago. All I have to do is flip the pages back through time to see, but a part of me just doesn't want to.

There is so much *Aisha* would be pleased to hear. I am now Muslim. I must pack this diary, once again, into a box, and send it to her. To my dear friend, *Aisha*.

Al salamu' alaykum

References

- *The Holy Qur'an,* "English translation of the meanings and Commentary on *Qur'an*"; The presidency of Islamic Research, Ifta, call and Guidance, King Fahd Holy *Qur'an* Printing Complex.
- *Sahih Muslim,* Dar Ihiaa' Alkutob Alarabia, first edition, 1955
- *Sahih Al-Bukhari,* Dar Al Shaa'b
- Other books of *Hadith, Ahmad, Abu Dawoud, Tabarany, At-Termithy,...*
- Dr. Ekram and Mohamed Beshir, *Meeting the Challenge of Parenting in the West, an Islamic Perspective,* 2nd ed., Amana publications, Maryland, 2000.
- *Readers Digest*, July 1999, "Parenting is prevention".
- *Readers Digest*, August 1999, "What matters most", a report from the ad council.
- Stephen R. Covey, *The 7 habits of highly effective families.*
- *Sound Vision* home page
- Stephen M. Wolf, "Countering violence", *US Airways Attache magazine,* July 1999.
- *Monitoring the future study*, Institute of social research, University of Michigan, 18/12/1998.
- Dr. Bettie B. Youngs, *Safeguarding your Teenager from the DRAGONS of Life*, Health Communications, Inc. Deerfield Beach, Florida

– Dr. Kathy Nathan, "Parenting Adolescents" Ottawa, Canada; unpublished work, 1996.
– *Ahmad Shawqi, Ahmad Shawqi's Poetry Collection.*
– Dr Hisham Altalib, *Training Guide for Islamic Workers*, International Islamic Publishing House and the International Institute of the Islamic Thought, Herndon, Virginia, USA, 1993.
– *SoundVision.com Newsletter*, Wednesday January 24, 2001, Shawwal 29, 1421.
– *SoundVision.com Newsletter*, Monday December 11, 2000, Ramadan 15th 1421.
– *SoundVision.com Newsletter*, Monday October 30th, 2000.
– R. Vance Hall and Marilyn L. Hall, "How to negotiate a behavioral contract" Pro.ed Inc, An international publisher, 1998.